A HISTORY OF
CRICKET

BENNY GREEN

A HISTORY OF CRICKET

BENNY GREEN

BARRIE & JENKINS

LONDON

To Michael Parkinson

First published in Great Britain in 1988 by
Barrie & Jenkins Ltd
289 Westbourne Grove, London W11 2QA

British Library Cataloguing in Publication Data
Green, Benny
A history of cricket
1. Cricket to 1988
I. Title
796.35′8′09
ISBN 0-7126-2080-X

Typeset by DP Photosetting, Aylesbury, Buckinghamshire
Printed in England by Butler and Tanner Ltd, Frome, Somerset

CONTENTS

PREFACE

Why another history of Cricket? The shelves are already well-stocked with perfectly adequate, and in a few cases more than adequate, histories, ranging from the classic solidity of Altham and Swanton to the heretical devices of Roland Bowen, the brilliant impressionism of Cardus' "Cricket" and the admirable concision of Roy Webber. A man would have to be a ranting egomaniac to think that anything he wrote could remotely be conceived as a replacement for any of the above books and dozens of others indispensable to me in compiling this history, which I offer as nothing more than the most modest of adjuncts to the vast body of cricket literature.

Every student of the game has his pet characters, and it dawned on me a long time ago that some of mine have suffered comparative neglect at the hands of historians struggling to contain so vast a theme between manageable covers. But it is their very devotion to duty in putting into their books all the facts and leaving out some of the characters which gives me license to leave out some of the facts and put in a few of the characters. I assure readers that my neglect of averages and analyses, great men and famous games, however reprehensible, is at any rate deliberate, and sanctioned, I like to think, by the precedent of W.S. Gilbert, who once wrote a play about Faust and left out the Devil. In any case those who must have mathematics will find them easily enough elsewhere, a simple fact which has encouraged me to say something about the likes of Billy Midwinter, Walter Raleigh Gilbert and Joseph Wells which I felt needed saying.

The writing of cricket books is one of those bad habits which becomes addictive to those weak enough to succumb. Because cricket was for many years my chief escape from what are sometimes laughingly called serious affairs, I promised myself I would never write about it. This is the seventh book I promised myself never to write.

Benny Green

CHAPTER I

A FALSE
AND LOVELY DAWN

—•—

T he vale of Hambledon dozes peacefully in the Hampshire hills, somnolent under the weight of history. Glowing in the vivid light of a summer morning, it has the aspect less of reality than of an English idyll plucked from the pages of some illustrated guide-book. Even the most insensitive clod playing cricket there today can hardly fail to notice, as he whiles away his time in the outfield, that the ground, like James Hilton's happy valley in *Lost Horizon*, seems to be protected by providence from most of the curses of modern life. The configurations of the landscape have placed him in a field ringed by gentle hills, like a figure at the centre of a saucer whose rising sides shelter him from the outside world. Standing on the boundary edge within this enchanted crucible, he finds it impossible to believe that only twelve miles away lies the maritime bluster of Portsmouth. Those twelve miles represent time as well as distance, for long-on, idly watching the bowler trundling up to the far-off crease, has stumbled into a time warp where the Prince Regent, having fattened himself up to the prescribed poundage, is about to transmute himself into George IV. No wonder that for two hundred years commentators, overwhelmed by the paradisal aspect of the vista before them, have tended to lose their heads. One idolater, striving for dithyrambic effect, described Hambledon as a "valley within a valley".

We can, perhaps, excuse this lapse, for a great miracle was once wrought on this grass, under the patronage of these benign hills. The most complex, the most beautiful, the most profound of all ball games was born here, was nursed and nurtured until it was strong enough to stride out into the great world beyond. Under the skies of Hambledon, to the accompaniment of bird-song and the humming of bees, the plick-plock of the bat against the ball first echoed on the English air. Hambledon is the acknowledged birthplace of cricket, for which reason it will retain for ever a privileged niche in the pavilion of English history.

The modern student, gazing about him at the rustic remoteness of Hambledon, cannot help drawing analogies with one of those ancient ports,

Winchelsea perhaps, whose once-teeming harbour has long since been silted up by the tides of history. There was a time when, for the famous sporting gentlemen of the nation, Hambledon was the centre of things, a symbol and a stronghold, the place where a man might make his reputation in a single afternoon. The Hambledon side could take on and defeat All England, and so All England aspired to come to Hambledon and best the local champions. The disproportion of this renown has beguiled dozens of later chroniclers, who have seen in the lineaments of the legend elements of the headiest romance. For the dream of Hambledon is the most pervasive of all sporting myths, the team-game analogue to Camelot and Valhalla. One of its most idolatrous boosters was the prolific critic, editor and poetaster Edward Verrall Lucas, whose essays on the Hambledon men are meat and drink to the anthologist, and whose awe in the face of the original score sheets of the club could not have been more ecstatic had he been a talmudic scholar and the score sheets the Dead Sea Scrolls. The extent to which this religiosity of approach is a purely English thing, utterly mystifying to foreigners, was brought home to Lucas when he rashly attempted one day to impress the ecclesiastical significance of the old score sheets on a certain visiting Canadian. That gentle humorous genius Stephen Leacock, child of a mother who had been raised in a home overlooking Hambledon and himself born in the village of Swanmore nearby, returned to England in 1921 to perform a lecture tour. During his visit he was commandeered by Lucas and taken on the pilgrimage.

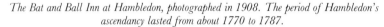

The Bat and Ball Inn at Hambledon, photographed in 1908. The period of Hambledon's ascendancy lasted from about 1770 to 1787.

Hambledon is, to all people who play cricket and love the game, as Mecca is to a Mohammedan. Here, more than anywhere else, began the sacred game, for there is no other adjective that can convey what cricket means to Englishmen than the word "sacred". Here, on the windswept open space of Broadhalfpenny Down was bowled the first ball, the first rushing underhand where bowling began. Here men in top hats planned and named the game, designated by a flight of daring fancy the strip of ground between the wickets as the "pitch", indicated the right side of the batter as the "off" side, and the left as the "on" side – names taken from [the] English carriage driving, christened the brave man fielding thirty feet behind the batter's bat as "squareleg" (he needed to be), invented the "over" and the "wide" and the "no ball" and l.b.w – to be carried round the world later as the abiding bond of the British Empire.

Leacock is doing his best. For all his dubious terminology and his inability to resist a joke at the expense of the mysterious "squareleg", he is doing what he can to take the effusions of the Lucas lobby with the required degree of reverence. Leacock knew that his mother's family, the Butlers, were still at Bury Lodge, where they were the custodians of the revered score sheets. It was this piece of information, imparted with casual innocence by Leacock to Lucas, which brought about the visit to the site:

> I mentioned to Lucas this family connection with the old score sheets at Bury Lodge. I found that he at once regarded me with a sort of reverence. Nothing would do him but we must drive down to Hampshire to look at them. This we did, Lucas supplying the car while I felt that my presence with him was compensation enough. The house was shut up, as the Butlers were in London, but a housekeeper showed us the scores, and then we drove up to Broadhalfpenny Down and stood there in the wind, well, just as people stand on the ruins of Carthage. After that we went down into Hambledon village to the pub, where I had all that peculiar gratification that goes with the return of the native. There were several old men round and it was astonishing what they could remember over a pint of beer, and still more over a quart. I had been away from Hambledon for nearly fifty years, so it enabled one to play the part of Rip Van Winkle. I didn't mention that I had only been there once before, for ten minutes, as a child of six.

And so Leacock's good-natured attempt to humour his friend collapses in a mild burst of facetiousness. Poor Leacock, a mere colonial found wanting when faced with the sternest test known to Englishmen, adherence to and respect for the glory of Hambledon.

Of course he need not have bothered. The entire Hambledon industry is bogus, a trumpery effect sanctioned only by its own longevity. Hambledon is no more the birthplace of cricket than Runnymede was of King John, or Mayfair of Noel Coward. Generations before the village became known to the outside world, cricket flourished all over the south of England, and was indeed so popular that there were intermittent attempts by local magistrates, prompted by their landowning masters, to put the game down.

There is of course no better proof of the popularity of any social activity than that the powerful should wish to see it made illegal, which seems to suggest that

Cricket on the Artillery Ground, Finsbury, 1743. Note the twin-stump wicket, white ball and curved bat. The shape of the bat was necessary as a counter to the art of underhand bowling, fast and along the ground. The scorer follows the game with his notches.

A match played at the Montpelier Gardens, Walworth, in 1796 between Greenwich pensioners with one arm and one leg for a purse of £1,000. The match generated such excitement there was nearly a riot.

when the golden age of Hambledon dawned the game was at least two centuries old, threatening to grow into a national institution. Against this background where lies Hambledon? The first printed evidence of the existence of its village side is dated 1776. But there is printed evidence of organised matches being staged in Essex more than thirty years before: of a match at Islington in 1719 between representative sides from Kent and London; of matches on Clapham Common in 1700. The first reference to Englishmen playing cricket abroad is dated 1676, when sailors on shore leave were seen performing the rites at Aleppo. In 1654 seven parishioners of Eltham in Kent were fined for playing cricket on the sabbath. Perhaps their impious athleticism had been inspired by the events in Sussex thirty-two years earlier, when six men were prosecuted for playing the game in a churchyard. At about the same time in the same county one Jasper Vinall was accidentally killed through the batsman's attempt to hit the ball twice in order to avoid being caught out. Records exist of a match played in 1550 at a Guildford school. Further back and still further stretches the trail until, with a reference to "Creag" in a Kentish parish in 1300, the investigator is finally drawn deep into the mists of pure speculation and left to find his own way home.

In this context the club which flourished on Broadhalfpenny Down is seen to be little more than a johnny-come-lately, an institution much closer in time if not in spirit to our own age than to the age of the Plantaganets. No credible published account of the genesis of cricket exists, and none ever will, for the excellent reason that nobody has ever been able to discover credible evidence of the event. As Roland Bowen has remarked, "History begins, and can only begin, with some kind of written record". The prehistory of cricket is concealed from the modern eye simply because for centuries it occurred neither to the players nor to the followers of the game that it might be interesting or instructive to commit the details to paper. All we can be sure of is that a team game with rather more than vestigial resemblances to the game we know had begun to appear certainly by 1300, that this manifestation took place in southern England, that it was at various junctures in its evolution considered to be a threat to the community, and that by the beginning of the eighteenth century the landowning aristocracy, having found its allurements irresistible, were guaranteeing its survival as a feature of English life. When Stephen Leacock examined those yellowing Hambledon score sheets, he was gazing, not as he and Lucas and many others believed, at the book of Genesis, but at obscure apocrypha of a much later age.

And yet there is a sense in which the fame of that village is justified after all, a sense in which authentic beginnings really did take place there. The moment we examine the circumstances, we stumble on one of the most extraordinary of all truths about cricket, a truth which applies to no other leisure activity to quite the same degree. Hambledon remains illustrious for a very specific reason. If it was not the first club to play cricket, it was certainly the first to inspire literary eloquence. It was the cricketers of Hambledon whose techniques and personalities first drew the attention of someone with pretensions to literary style, a man so moved to love and affection by what he had witnessed in Broadhalfpenny Down that, deliberately or not, he preserved the lineaments of his heroes for ever. The conclusion to be drawn from this sublime accident is that there is a curious symbiotic relationship between cricket and the writing of good

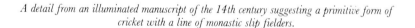

A detail from an illuminated manuscript of the 14th century suggesting a primitive form of cricket with a line of monastic slip fielders.

English. Not only does cricket, more than any other game, inspire the urge to literary expression; it is almost as though the game itself would not exist at all until written about. This is perhaps to make more of Bowen's observation regarding the vital necessity for written evidence than the major had in mind, but there is not the slightest doubt of its truth.

And yet even here, with the written record suddenly bursting into factual certitude, there remain areas of doubt and confusion no matter how meticulously the historian retraces the steps of the past. The destiny of Hambledon appears to have been settled in the middle of the eighteenth century by one Richard Newland, of Slindon in West Sussex. It was here, in the fields fringed by woods which remain to this day among the loveliest in southern England, that Newland instructed a pupil in the principles of cricket. Nothing else is known of Newland, and yet this one frail fact has been enough to ensure his place in the history of the game. The pupil was Richard Nyren, who soon after moved down to Hambledon. There, fortified by the technique which Newland had taught him, he became captain of the local club, gathering together a playing strength so neatly divided between plebs and patricians as to be a genuine representation of English rural society. This village side, its standing guaranteed by a blend of "aristocratic patronage and local enthusiasm", grew so rapidly in reputation that by 1780 as many as twenty thousand people might throng to its matches. The club's star players became celebrated far beyond the limits of the village. They succeeded in establishing cricket as an indispensable feature of the English summer. But posterity might have remained unaware of these facts had it not been for the club captain's son, who retained until the end of his life a deep regard for the heroes of his boyhood. Led by that bitter-sweet sense of loss which is so often the midwife to literary inspiration, Nyren took on the task of preserving the memory of his father's great eleven during the fleeting period of its memorable heyday.

By the end of the century that greatness had dwindled, and the entire chapter of Hambledon's glory might have gone unchronicled had it not been for a friend who suggested to John that he might care to record his reflections of the club in its heyday while the impressions were still fresh in his mind. John Nyren (1764-1837) had been a dedicated but not a remarkably talented cricketer whose association with his father's club dated from boyhood. His intermittent appearances for Hambledon, and his subsequent membership of the Homerton club, suggest that his love for the game never faded. He was a large-boned, prematurely-balding man six feet tall, whose gentle demeanour was matched by a physical strength spectacularly demonstrated on one famous occasion when, attending a prize-fight, he felt someone's hand in his pocket, grabbed the culprit and held him aloft as a warning to the rest of the crowd. A temperate man, once a choirmaster, a lover of animals and especially dogs, a wolfer of Kentish cherries, and a knowledgeable musical amateur, he married in 1791 the bizarrely named Cleopha Copp, a teenager of such resolution that three days after the birth of her first child she tripped downstairs to act as interpreter for

14

some French priests who had fled the wrath of the Revolution. An indifferent businessman who suffered calamity when his calico printing business was burned down, he still managed to win a reputation for helping others in distress. For a while after his marriage he lived at Portsea, later moving to Bromley in Middlesex, then to Battersea, then Cheyne Walk and finally back to Bromley, where he died in the summer of 1837, when the Victorian age was just eight days old. There is no question that he would have been forgotten long ago but for his publication in 1833 of a manual called *The Young Cricketer's Tutor*. This beginner's guide to the game, whose precepts were outflanked generations ago by evolving techniques, would hold little but antiquarian interest today were it not for the afterthought which Nyren tacked on to it, thereby ensuring its and his own immortality. This postscript, an extended essay entitled "The Cricketers of My Time", is the first example of authentic literature about cricket as distinct from cricket literature. Nyren recalls in it the great men of his father's all-conquering eleven, adopting for his purpose a style so utterly unlike his earlier pedagogic drone in imparting the principles of the game as to cast doubts in one's mind whether "The Cricketers of My Time" really was his work or someone else's. The doubt is compounded by the full title of the work as it is printed on the original frontispiece: "The Cricketers of My Time, or, Recollections of the Most Famous Old Players, the Whole Collected and Edited by Charles Cowden Clarke."

Suddenly for the first time the explorer into cricket's past, who has been floundering to find a foothold in the mire of the game's pre-history, finds himself on solid ground. If Richard Newland is no more than a name in a parish register, Richard Nyren no more than the left-handed landlord of Hambledon's "Bat and Ball" inn, John Nyren a mere literary tyro introducing his first and last published work, Charles Cowden Clarke is a prime sample of that exotic genus, the minor literary figure. Clarke's life, although it has shrunk to the proportions of a footnote in the lives of more distinguished men, is at least well documented. Clarke (1787-1877) was the youthful mentor of John Keats, who, being eight years his junior, looked up to him as a fount of wisdom as well as a source of faithful friendship. Both boys attended Clarke's School, whose headmaster was Charles's father, and no finer tribute was ever paid to any friend of any creative artist than that which Keats paid to Clarke: "I learned from him all the sweets of song." It was Clarke also who introduced the younger boy to the heady delights of Radicalism, which he had picked up inevitably through environment as well as heredity. His father, the school's headmaster, was a committed radical who had been a subscriber to Leigh Hunt's *The Examiner* from its first issue. When in 1813 Hunt went to prison for having published a few amusing truisms about the Prince Regent, the Clarke family kept up the renegade's spirits by sending regular supplies of fruit, flowers and vegetables from the school gardens, young Charles being deputed to deliver the consignments. Instinctively Hunt returned the compliment. In exchange for the bounty of Clarke's School garden, the beleaguered editor offered his opinions,

15

which were eagerly accepted by a young man at just the right stage of intellectual development to receive them. Clarke soon passed them on to his young friend Keats, who remained influenced by them for the rest of his tragically short life.

Soon Clarke grew from a young schoolmaster into a literary professional with a strong affection for cricket, and on becoming friendly with John Nyren it seemed natural to him to make a suggestion more radical by far than Radicalism. Why not codify memories of Richard Nyren's great side while there was still time? Up to this point the sequence of events is clear enough. It is what happened next which has remained in contention ever since. Did Nyren then begin to write? Or did he begin to speak his thoughts to Clarke, who then transcribed them? Did Nyren write first and then allow Clarke to rewrite? Did Clarke contribute nothing to the partnership but the prestige of his name? Or did the two men compose a joint chronicle? What does Nyren mean precisely when he says that Clarke "collected and edited" the text of his essay? Probably that he spoke his thoughts and Clarke transmuted them into a text. But whatever the process, it is a curious truth of "The Cricketers of My Time" that it is typical of neither of the two men to whom its authorship is attributed. Neither Nyren in his manual nor Clarke in his published lectures on Shakespeare, nor even in his reminiscences of Dickens, Keats, Lamb and Hunt, comes remotely close to the intimate anecdotage of "The Cricketers of My Time". The difference between Clarke's formal approach and the directness of Nyren's classic is well illustrated by Clarke's description of Nyren which may be found in the second edition of the work:

> A more single and gentle hearted, and yet thoroughly manly, man I have never known, one more forbearing towards the failings of others, more unobtrusively steady in his own principles, more cheerfully pious, more free from cant and humbug of every description. He possessed an instinctive admiration of everything good and tasteful, both in Nature and art. He was fond of flowers, and music, and pictures; and he rarely came to visit us without bringing with him a choice specimen of a blossom, or a manuscript copy of an air which had given him pleasure. And so, hand in hand with these simple delights, he went on to the last, walking round his garden on the morning of his death.

Only when Nyren eventually arrives on Clarke's doorstep waving a flower does the sketch come to life. The earlier effusions read less like the work of a professional writer than of some suburban employer composing a testimonial for a clerk aspiring to better things. Compare this with Nyren's recollections of John Small, the first English cricketer to win a reputation as a judge of a short run:

> He was a good fiddler, and taught himself the double bass. The Duke of Dorset having been informed of his musical talent, sent him as a present a handsome violin, and paid the carriage. Small, like a true and simple-hearted Englishman, returned the compliment by sending his Grace two bats and balls, also paying the carriage. We may be sure that on both hands the presents were choice of their kind. Upon one occasion he turned his Orphean accomplishments to good

account. Having to cross two or three fields on his way to a musical party, a vicious bull made at him; when our hero, with the characteristic coolness and presence of mind of a good cricketer, began playing upon his bass to the admiration and perfect satisfaction of the mischievous beast.

Towards the end of his chronicle Nyren describes the character for whom clearly he feels the warmest affection of all, and whom he has been saving as a climax to his little history. This is John Small, son of that Small who had been a leading member of the club in earlier days:

> Jack Small! my old club fellow! when the fresh and lusty may-tide of life sent the blood gamboling through our veins like a Spring runlet, we have had many a go-about together:
>
> > But now my head is bald, John,
> > And locks as white as snow –
>
> and yours have, doubtless, bleached under the cold hand of mayhap three score winters and more; but the churl has not yet touched the citadel. My heart is as sound as ever, and beats regular and true to the tune of old and grateful thoughts for long friendships. You, I am sure, can echo this sentiment. You are a musician as well as a friend, and know the value of steadiness in both characters.

In this effusion about an old cricketing comrade, as in the note on Small's father who charmed a bull with his music, Nyren is illustrating a vital precept about cricket writing which very few of his successors have digested, or apparently even noticed. It is that statistics, score sheets, averages and analyses can never be sufficient in themselves to convey the nature and spirit of the game. Cricketers, whatever the modesty of their arena, do not spring full-grown on to the grass like Venus from her cockleshell, nor do they cease to be the men they are the moment they leave the field. For all the thousands of books and billions of words which have been written about cricket, we know precious little about any of its masters except that they scored so many runs and took so many wickets. It is as though our knowledge of Disraeli were to consist in its entirety of parliamentary speeches, or Astaire of details of his dancing pumps. Too much writing about cricket has been merely mathematical. John Nyren understood from the first that either he must attempt a quintessential portrait across a wider range of sensibilities than may be perceived on the field of play, or not bother with the attempt at all. It is this exercise, not in reportage but in rounded portraiture, which lends to "The Cricketers of My Time" that warmth and penetrative insight which has proved so durable a preservative for two hundred years. So rare was this style of writing to become that generations later Lucas was to bemoan his own certitude that after Nyren there would be no great cricket literature. This was in 1907, with Neville Cardus already into his teens and looking back to the lost age of his childhood with the Trump and Maclaren of 1902.

But how did Nyren, this modest village cricketer and dedicated musical amateur, ever encounter Charles Cowden Clarke, familiar of the literary

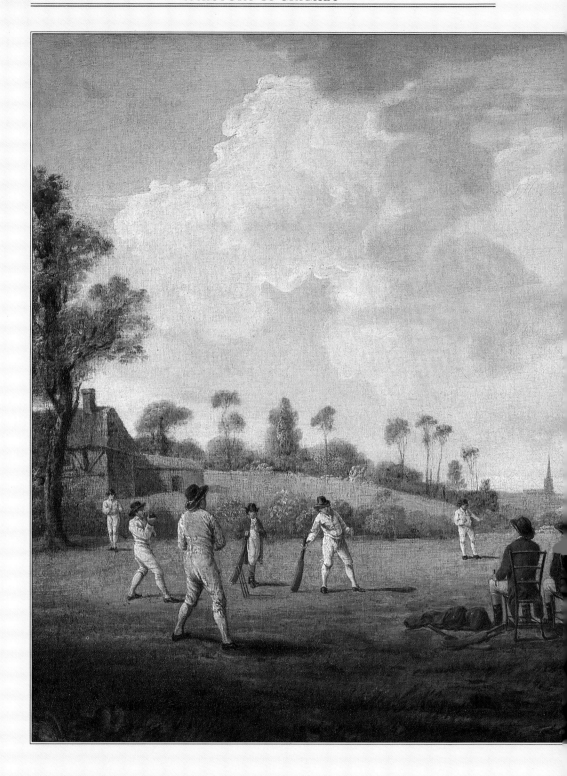

A game of cricket, c. 1790. Well illustrated here are the three-stump wicket and the change from curved bat to a blade with a backward arch.

celebrities of the day? It was Nyren's music which swung him into Clarke's orbit. For thirteen years he served as the choirmaster of St Mary's, Moorfields, whose organist was the publisher and composer Vincent Novello. In a famous essay Charles Lamb has described Novello's Sunday Evenings, and it was at these gatherings, at Novello's house in Oxford Street, that Nyren came to make the acquaintance of Clarke in an atmosphere conducive to good fellowship and mutual enthusiasms. Lamb says of these occasions that Novello,

> by the aid of a capital organ, himself the most finished of players, converts his drawing-room into a chapel, his weekdays into Sundays, and these latter into minor heavens.

Clarke seems to have taken to Nyren from the first, but much of his attention at these soireés was directed elsewhere, to Novello's daughter Mary Victoria, who became in time Mrs Cowden Clarke, published *A Complete Concordance to Shakespeare*, and, more to the point wrote down the only surviving account of the collaboration between her husband and his friend the gentle choirmaster:

> Nyren was a vigorous old friend who had been a famous cricketer in his youth and early manhood, and who, in his advanced age, used to come and communicate his cricketing expressions to Charles with chuckling pride and complacent reminiscence.

On such flimsy foundations was cricket's first descriptive classic composed. Had Nyren not been so expert in drilling a choir, had he not happened to come to Moorfields, had Charles Cowden Clarke not had eyes for the daughter of a distinguished musician, had Nyren not been in the habit of rambling on about the good old days, then "The Cricketers of My Time" would have remained unwritten, the feats of the men of Hambledon would have remained unsung, and the formal birth of English cricket flung forward to the year of some later fortuitous confluence of events.

In view of his enormous contribution to cricket, it is fitting that we should be able to see John Nyren a little more clearly than the vague images which float up from the testimonials of the Cowden Clarkes. Most pictorial representations of the cricketers of the emergent days are flawed by the inability of the artist to convey movement without implying a terminal case of arthritis. Like the paintings of racehorses in action in the days before the camera revealed what running limbs actually do, early cricketing art suffers from the limitation that its graceful heroes are reduced to gawky grotesques. To find an image of Nyren graced by the sophistications of real portraiture, we have to come forward to our own century, to an artist called Frank Reynolds, whose sporting interests drew him to the idea of building up from contemporary sketches and descriptions a full portrait. Destiny's choice of Reynolds as the ultimate preserver of Nyren's quiddity is a curious one. For most of his professional life Reynolds was associated with *Punch*. He served as Art Editor from 1920 to 1930, although his work had begun to appear in the magazine as early as 1906. From the outbreak of the Great War to the end of his life Reynolds was criticised for his persistent depiction of ugliness, and yet his portrait of Nyren is suffused with benignity.

There he stands, lolling gracefully against a tree, gazing at the artist with genial composure and evidently unaware of the melodrama unfolding behind him. Long-on is hardly twenty yards away, and the group of enthusing spectators, dogs and tethered horses is just to the right of the tree. But Nyren dreams on, left hand in trouser pocket, right hand holding to his side the topper which will soon be concealing his balding dome. The artist has caught cricket's first considerable chronicler at a moment of repose. Here in the Hampshire hills the world basks in a russet glow, a series of symphonic variations on the theme of autumn. The spaniel standing guard alongside his master is brown-and-white, the shade of its pendulous ears exactly matching Nyren's casual jacket. His waistcoat is golden, his trousers a paler yellow, his cheeks ruddy, the brown trunk and foliage of the tree casting a golden shadow on the grass. The light is beginning to fade, perhaps symbolically, and the sails of the windmill beyond the far boundary are still in the hush of early evening. The sentimental country gentleman against the tree dreams on, thinking of the days when his father led the greatest eleven in England. It is a face full of humour, the face of a modest connoisseur whose sensibilities are certainly refined enough to attract the company of folk like the Clarkes and the Novellos. In a sense John Nyren is cricket's first ambassador at large, his impeccable credentials the small volume of recollection which will establish the myth of Hambledon as the cradle of the game.

One of the most striking features of Hambledon was the extent to which cricket in the valley drew together all the classes. In Richard Nyren's time, the local blacksmith Richard Purchase played alongside the 4th Earl of Tanker-ville. In 1778 the club president was the Earl of Northington. Most significant of all, John Nyren writes of his father:

> He could differ with a superior, without trenching upon his dignity or losing his own. I have known him maintain an opinion with great firmness against the Duke of Dorset and Sir Horace Mann; when, in consequence of his being proved to be in the right, the latter has afterwards crossed the ground and shaken him heartily by the hand.

It was this commingling of the classes which led G.M.Trevelyan to make one of the most astounding of all claims on behalf of cricket. After noting that the game had begun to take a hold in the Hampshire and Kentish villages of Stuart England, and quoting a report from 1743 that "noblemen, gentlemen and clergy are making butchers, cobblers or tinkers their companions", Trevelyan proceeds with evident delight to record the fact that in 1746, when Kent defeated All England by one run, Lord John Sackville appeared in the winning side under the captaincy of the gardener at Knole. He then draws his dazzling conclusion:

> Village cricket spread fast through the land. In those days, before it became scientific, cricket was the best game in the world to watch, with its rapid sequence

Belanger's painting of a game between Kent and Hampshire, at Bishopsbourne, in 1774.
Standing as umpire at the bowler's end is the legendary 'Lumpy' Stevens (1735–1819),
bowler of fearsomely fast 'shooters' on the rough and ready pitches of the day.

of amusing incidents, each ball a potential crisis. Squire, farmer, blacksmith and labourer, with their women and children come to see the fun, were more at ease together and happy all the summer afternoon. If the French noblesse had been capable of playing cricket with their peasants, their chateaux would never have been burnt.

But the Sackvilles of Knole were just too late to present the French aristocracy with the safety valve of cricket. The third Duke retired from the field on his appointment as Ambassador and Plenipotentiary at the court of Louis XVI, and in time the idea occurred to him that the English ought to begin exporting their game. He arranged for the first ever overseas tour, to Paris, but the pioneer tourists, on arrival at Dover, were met by the patron himself, who had left France in a considerable hurry. It was 1789 and the fall of wickets had been pre-empted by the fall of the Bastille. The Duke remained dedicated to the game, which was now about to enter on the second great phase of its development.

Yet some years before an event had occurred, completely overlooked by the cricketing brotherhood, which was to have the most profound effects on its future. On the morning of 19 April 1770, just as the new season was about to start in England, the Yorkshire sea captain James Cook took the frigate *Endeavour* on to the Great Barrier Reef and sighted the south-eastern coast of Australia.

CHAPTER II

CITY GENTS

———•———

If ever proof were needed of the sympathy of cricket with cricketers, of its reflection of its period, of its capacity for changing with the men who play it, this proof is to be found in the men who followed Hambledon. As the game moved, like the population, from the farmlands to the new-growing cities of the beginning of the nineteenth century, so its great players were no longer the villagers but the Regency bucks.

John Arlott, Cricket

W hether or not the heroes of Hambledon ever realised it, the tides of history were flowing fast against their retention of the cricketing lead. By the time Nyren's memoirs were published, the outline of contemporary London was already beginning to form at a headlong rate. The sprawling estates of the Harleys, the Cavendishes, the Portmans, the Burlingtons, the Bedfords, the great offices of state, the vast mercantile palaces, were vaulting across open country burying mile after mile of green fields under the weight of speculative development. By the time the Prince Regent became king, London had established itself as the first city in history to support more than a million lives. In 1821 William Cobbett published *Rural Rides*, recording the contours of an England which would soon be unrecognisable. His Great Wen was an irresistible magnet, attracting wealth, ambition, talent, power, pulling the whole of England out of balance, gathering up the best and the worst, the finest and the foulest, the most accomplished, the most outrageous, the most original. It was inevitable that it should, as a mere incidental, become the centre of the burgeoning, new national game of cricket. In 1787 it flung its huge shadow out over the Hampshire hills, dwarfing the homely cobblers and farmers, and relegating their Hambledon cricket side to a mere outpost of the sporting world it had once dominated.

Most of the more influential men in this shift of power were well enough known on Broadhalfpenny Down, either as players or as patrons. The Earl of Tankerville, the Duke of Dorset, the Duke of Richmond, the Earl of Sandwich

Rowlandson's caustic view of a match between the women of Hampshire and Surrey at Ball's Pond, Newington, in October 1811.

and others, were devoted to cricket, not just at Hambledon but anywhere. Cricket could be said almost to have constituted their entire existence. The Duke of Hamilton actually married a young lady soon after being smitten by the elegance of her stroke-making in a ladies' match. But much as they enjoyed their rustic interludes, these grandees were essentially men of affairs, men at the heart of events, men who belonged to London, where they might fill in the time with such pleasantries as the occasional duel or the pursuit of some new fashionable mistress, and where they took good care to arrange for themselves the most comfortable and the most comforting facilities available to a gentleman of means.

They all became members of an establishment in Pall Mall called the Star and Garter Inn, a more spectacular institution than its name suggests, in whose numberless rooms were housed the members of assorted dining clubs. In Georgian London any pretext was enough to justify the formation of a dining club or society, the attraction for a man grown temporarily disenchanted with the company of ladies being obvious enough. Some of the sporting frequenters of the Star and Garter, tiring of conventional pastimes like bird-slaughtering and the mindless persecution of foxes, took to driving out along the mud-spattered lanes of St Marylebone to White Conduit Fields, a public space long since buried under the weight of change, its only headstone the lowering walls of King's Cross Station. Here, on the bumpy grass, dressed in their ordinary clothes, which included frilly shirt, waistcoat, hat, breeches, and buckled shoes,

The Gentlemen's Club at play on the Cricket Field near White Conduit House, Islington.
This was one of six engravings of 'Manly Recreations' published in 1784.

the cricketers played their private games under the public gaze, an indignity against which their patrician souls rose in revulsion. The White Conduit Club was nothing like the world of Hambledon, being exclusive to the sons of gentlemen. As the rules stated: "None but gentlemen ever to play". And when gentlemen play, it is not seemly that the rabble should be allowed to watch them. Trevelyan's picture of an idyllic integration of classes may have been true for a little while, but the moment the players and the patrons returned to the sophistications of metropolitan life, the English genius for class snobbery reasserted itself on the field of play.

The solution was simple enough. One day it occurred to the Earl of Winchilsea that he and his friends might purchase a tract of their own land and there disport to their hearts' content, away from the prying eyes of the hoi polloi. The Earl, whose responsibilities at this time appear to have consisted in their entirety of being Lord of the Bedchamber, and finding that his duties were not so arduous as to preclude all other activities, agreed with his friend Colonel Charles Lennox (soon to metamorphose into the fourth Duke of Richmond) that the most practical way of proceeding was to find a hireling to do the work. They did not have to look far. Among the hired hands at White Conduit Fields was a bowler to the gentry who also served as ground attendant. His name was Thomas Lord. He seemed a quietly capable and discreet sort of chap, so Winchilsea commissioned him to look around for a stretch of greenery closer to the heart of town, somewhere suitable for private cricket which would avoid the burden of toiling through the rutted, muddy lanes to Islington. Neither Winchilsea nor his fellows had any idea of the nature of the man they were dealing with, but if it was a swift outcome and a satisfactory conclusion they desired, then they could not have hit upon a more formidable agent.

Thomas Lord (1755-1832) was the son of a Yorkshire Catholic yeoman farmer who had made the mistake of backing the wrong horse in the Jacobite Rebellion of 1745, after which he found himself reduced to the indignity of labouring on what had formerly been his own land. But old William Lord, having ruined the family fortunes, had also unwittingly guaranteed their revival by siring Thomas, one of the shrewdest and most acquisitive men in the history of cricket. In spite of his vital role in the evolution of the game, Thomas Lord is a much vaguer figure than most historians have seemed willing to admit. Neither his dates nor his antecedents, nor the dates of birth of his several children, are anything like as precise as we have been led to believe, and even the famous portrait by Morland, with its alert eyes and complacent mouth, is recognised as a likeness only because his patrons said it was. Attempts at precise biographical summary have appeared in recent years, but the apparent exactitude of the facts may be a shade misleading. His dates have never been confirmed beyond dispute. Did he die in 1829 or in 1832? Even the corroboration of his existence implied by his playing record is fogged by contradiction, so that we will never know if, as some witnesses insisted, he was a very fast bowler or, as others have maintained, a very slow one.

Thomas Lord, the property speculator who gave his name to the headquarters of cricket.

He seems to have been a batsman of moderate competence; and to judge from the evidence he was also a handsome man with an imposing presence and considerable charm. It was this ability to please which proved more useful to him by far than any technique he may have acquired as a cricketer. Lord was not so much an athlete as a businessman of acumen. When the Earl and his friends came along with their offer, it was the chance that young Lord had been waiting for, and he seized it with such resolution that two hundred years later the fruits of his labour have outlasted almost all the monuments of the epoch. Ironically it is doubtful if he cared one way or the other about cricket. Liberated from that sentimental commitment to the game which animated the moods of his masters, Lord began playing the greater game of property speculation like a true virtuoso, the acquisition of a home for the White Conduit Club being only one among dozens of such deals, and perhaps not the first.

Indeed, Thomas Lord was one of nature's landlords, a man with the aspect of a games player and the soul of a manipulator, and once Winchilsea and his friends gave him his opportunity he flowered in the most spectacular way. Contemporary records show him to be a dealer in property all over central London, and he soon became so prosperous that he was able to settle down as one of the burghers of St John's Wood, and work up a successful business supplying wines and spirits to the gentry. Looking back, it is easy to see how he won his place in society. He was one of those rare men who can draw the line precisely between servility and the assumption of an affable parity with his betters. He became accustomed to the company of princes, was well known to George IV, and for a time supplied wines for the royal table. His secret was deference masking shrewd instincts of commercial aggrandisement. And nothing he did in his profitable life ever remotely approached the grand adventure of the White Conduit Club.

Soon after Winchilsea had a few words with him, he leased a tract of land from the Portman family, on the site where Dorset Square stands today. By May 1787 Winchilsea and his friends had baptised the turf with a match played between members of the club, having first taken the precaution of erecting around the perimeter a ring of high wooden fencing to frustrate the idle curiosity of ordinary folk. Within weeks matches were being played there for sums of

A 1,000-guinea contest at Lord's between the Earl of Darnley's team and the Earl of Winchilsea's. The latter carried away the prize.

money varying from a hundred guineas to a thousand. Soon the name White Conduit Club became pointless, and the gentlemen inside the palisades began to think of themselves as members of the Marylebone Club, assuming in the process a responsibility for administering the laws of the game, and taking on the mantle of the premier club in England.

The problem was to know which laws to administer. There were so many regional variations in the way the game was played at any one time in the emergent years that what might pass muster in Kent would be frowned upon in Hampshire, and what was perfectly acceptable in a Wiltshire village might be regarded as a gross breach of manners in the purlieus of St John's Wood. During the seventeenth century, for example, it was within the rules for a batsman to avoid being caught out by charging at the fielder attempting to take the catch and bundling him over. In 1744 this terrifying weapon in the batman's armoury was limited in a specific way which sheds a lurid light on the original spirit in which the game was played: from that date any action taken by the batsman to avoid being caught out was limited to bodily contact, the clear implication being that up to now the conventional tactic had been to wallop the fielders with the bat.

In the Duke of Richmond's Articles of Agreement dated 1727, the length of

Overleaf: A match at Kenfield Hall, near Canterbury, c. 1780, with horses about to interrupt play. Coincidentally, the period saw a brief vogue for novelty games of cricket on horseback

the pitch is specified as twenty-three yards. The Laws of 1744 amend this to twenty-two. Leg-before-wicket dismissal is first mentioned in 1774. The redness of the ball is confirmed in a poem published in 1753, the efficacy of this choice being suggested by the fact that green and red are at opposite ends of the spectrum, it therefore being impossible for the human eye to focus on both simultaneously. The picture which begins to form is hopelessly confused, except that it confirms once again that by the time of the emergence of the all-conquering Hambledon eleven, cricket had already reached a fairly sophisticated stage in the formal development of its rules and conventions. The game as played by Nyren's heroes not only differed in several aspects from the patrician game at Lord's, but featured at least four procedures which would have rendered the play quite unacceptable to the modern sensibility. The wicket consisted of two sticks instead of three; all bowling was underarm; prepared pitches were unknown except for cutting the grass with a scythe or cropping it by releasing a herd of sheep; and all bats were curved chunks of wood weighing up to four pounds and unsprung, so that on contact with the ball the striker might suffer a jarring shock from fingertips to shoulderblade. Such elements of primitivism did not disappear or evolve by nature's whim alone. Every one of the traditions of the modern game was once a heresy insisted upon by some brave spirit who refused to accept existing conventions, or who, by being the victim of pure fluke, became the central figure in some epoch-making amendment to the rules.

It was John Small of Hambledon who revolutionised defensive play by abandoning the curved bat in favour of the straight blade. This bold experiment not only introduced into the language that most potent symbol of probity, the Straight Bat, but even emended the nature of its patron's livelihood. Small, who was a shoemaker-turned-gamekeeper when he joined the Hampshire heroes, ended his days as a maker of cricket bats and balls. As to the size of the bat, the comic improvisor here was a Mr White of Reigate who, recognising that the batsman who was successful in keeping the ball out of his stumps might bat on indefinitely, had the bright and perfectly legal idea of using a bat measuring exactly the same width as the wicket. Howls of anguish from frustrated bowlers rose up in the Hampshire hills, and by the time their echo had faded the laws decreed that no bat measure more than $4\frac{1}{2}$ inches in width. It was the same John Small who was at the heart of the great debate on the desirable number of stumps. Early cricket featured only two stumps, with a third spanning them like a bail. One day in the summer of 1775 Small won a game single-handed, because on several occasions the opposing bowlers penetrated his defences only to see the ball fly between the sticks without disturbing them. After that, cricket became famous as the game of the three straight sticks. But the most revolutionary change of all, from underarm bowling to roundarm, was a more gradual and very much more disputatious affair. Around the year 1790 the Hambledon star Tom Walker one day raised his arm, and was received with such a torrent of abuse that he hastily lowered it again and resumed more conventional ways. But Walker had released the genie from the bottle, and soon other experimenters were trying it too. In 1806 a Kentish cricketer called John Willes became a consistent roundarm bowler, even though the aristocrats of St John's Wood fulminated against the blasphemy. It is said that Willes first realised the potential of the new style of bowling while watching some of the ladies of his family playing a cricket match of their own. The voluminous skirts of the players made a legitimate underarm delivery impossible, causing the bowling arm involuntarily to rise to what was virtually the roundarm position. Willes won considerable fame in country matches as a roundarm bowler, and proved to be a profound influence on later, greater bowlers like William Lambert, James Broadbridge and the greatest of all, William Lillywhite. When Willes came to Lord's in 1823 and bowled his new-fangled deliveries, he was resolutely no-balled by the umpires, becoming so enraged by this treatment that he flung the ball down in disgust, leapt astride his horse vowing never to play again, and galloped irascibly out of the ground and out of our story for ever.

Comparable in significance to the evolution and eventual significance of roundarm bowling was the amendment to batting technique pioneered by yet another Hambledonian, William Fennex, who breached the unwritten code that a batsman must stay in his crease and await the arrival of the ball. This convention meant that batsmen usually found themselves facing a rising ball. Fennex decided to step out and clump the ball as it pitched on the turf, a solecism so horrifying that the first time his father witnessed it he shouted, "Hey, boy, what's this? D'you call that play?" But at least Fennex's breach was one of mere etiquette; what Willes had done was to flout the law. It is revealing that as early as the affair of John Willes, the grandees of Marylebone were already taking up their conventional position as defenders of the last ditch. While the world of cricket generally was demonstrating its preference for the roundarm method of delivery, the lawmakers of Lord's continued to deny progress by instructing umpires to no-ball the new style. But if attitudes at St John's Wood were already congealing into the unbending conservatism with which the club was to be associated in later years, the members were also becoming expert in one of their most renowned instruments of policy, the absorption into the canons of Holy Writ of the very blasphemies they had always denied. In 1827 some experimental matches were played at Lord's in which roundarm was closely scrutinised. The result was that roundarm became legalised and underarm began rapidly to disappear from the playing fields of England.

The evolution of the club at Lord's from an exclusive set of pioneers to a social centre for the gentry happened at lightning speed for a variety of reasons. The rising class of mercantile entrepreneurs, straining to ape their betters, embraced the game with all the passion of arrivistes anxious not to be identified. The true aristocrats, having come into the game through induction into its ways on their own country estates, were keen to enjoy their new rustic pursuit in the metropolitan heartland. Large sums of money were there to be won through the great gentlemanly obsession of the age, gambling. The swelling population of

London comprised a huge audience waiting to be invited to join the feast. But what of Trevelyan's theory regarding the democratisation of English society through cricket? As we saw, Trevelyan's speculation was true enough but not for long. By the time Lord's club was established, English society on the cricket field was once again reflecting the divisions of English society at large. By 1800 as many as 5,000 spectators might pay sixpence each to come to watch their masters playing the game. Yet the profits accruing were not nearly enough to satisfy the acquisitive Thomas Lord. The premises were effectively under his control, and he could use them for whichever fringe purposes might suggest themselves as a source of useful additional revenue. In the emergent years of the ground Lord staged foot races, hopping contests, balloon ascents, pigeon-shooting orgies, exhibitions of velocipede riding, anything which might pull in the paying customers. At one stage he even had the Marylebone Volunteers performing obscure military convolutions at the ground, and yet neither this departure nor any of the others seems to have struck his masters as undesirable or incongruous.

What manner of men were these true owners of the club, these pioneer underwriters for the expenses of cricket? They represented a type of Englishman who long ago faded into history. The nation no longer produces them because the social conditions necessary for their nurturing have either evolved or been legislated away. Lord's grandees were men of independent means, much self-esteem and little culture, dominant personalities with that resolve to have their own way in all things no matter how outlandish which a later age calls eccentric. Although they saw themselves as staunch patriots and men of honour, they were not above breaking the laws of the land when it suited them, particularly with regard to duelling. Nor did they regard the wagering of large sums of money on the outcome of a match as being in any way a contradiction of the spirit in which they insisted the game ought to be played. Between them they must have slaughtered half the wildlife in Britain, yet they looked upon themselves as true gentlemen, which is to say that they never went to work. They represented that sub-species which made its last stand in the voting lobbies of the House of Lords on the occasion of Mr Asquith's Finance Bill of 1910, engendering the gravest constitutional crisis in modern parliamentary history for no better reason than that they failed to see why they should connive at their own extinction. Among their saving graces was a genuine love of cricket, and very often that very English sense of humour which expresses itself through a pretence of irascibility. But it is sometimes difficult to know whether this gift for the absurd was a calculated effect or an unconscious aberration, whether these men were comedians or absurdities, satirists or buffoons, whether they confront us with the spirit of Stephen Leacock or of W.S. Gilbert, whether posterity is inclined to laugh at them or with them. As individual types they remain scintillating specimens, Regency bucks whose morality was far better suited to the rumbustious world of Fielding than to the sobrieties of Trollope waiting just around the corner. They ate and drank too much, they were arrogant, insensitive, obstinate and reactionary. And we forgive them all this and more in acknowledging that without them cricket might never have survived.

Of this group of self-appointed leaders, none is more typical than George "Squire" Osbaldeston, one of Thomas Lord's most vociferous supporters and counsellers. A man who regarded Lord's very much as his private club, which in a sense it was, Osbaldeston was accepted at his own evaluation as a "sportsman", a term which did not quite mean what a later age assumes. It meant, for instance, that a man was a virtuoso in the art of blowing defenceless creatures into small pieces, that he would think nothing of challenging a fellow-

George Osbaldeston, ferocious fast underhand bowler and all-round egomaniac who gained the nickname "Squire of all England".

sportsman to a duel, that among his dearest pleasures was the persecution of foxes and that he would embark on the wildest, most witless challenges simply to prove his nerve. In 1831, long after he had reached what is supposed to be the age of discretion – Osbaldeston was born in 1777 – he fought a duel with Disraeli's friend Lord George Bentinck, later the Duke of Portland. As usual the duellists, having expended their courage in the issuing and acceptance of the challenge, and their energies in arriving at Wormwood Scrubs, resorted to what one chronicler has described as "life-saving antics". The Duke's son fired first and missed, at which Osbaldeston fired into the air shouting, "The bet's off", thus ensuring that although the age of chivalry was dead Lord George and he survived the farrago at Wormwood Scrubs.

In that same year the Squire embarked on one of the more pointless exercises known to the age, the equestrian spectacular. He wagered one thousand guineas that he would ride two hundred miles in ten consecutive hours. The wager was won, thanks to the stratagem of changing horses every four miles, Osbaldeston's winning time being less than nine hours. That a grown man could take the trouble to ride fifty different horses in a day simply for the purpose of arriving at a place where he had no particular desire to be, says much for that spirit of cracked perversity which so perfectly characterises Osbaldeston and his type. Indeed, so spectacular were his feats that they were transmuted at last into pure fiction; if the student of cricketing arcana cares to look into Sir Walter Scott's *Rob Roy*, there he will find Sir Hildebrand Osbaldistone, whose name and lineaments are much too close to those of Osbaldeston to be merely coincidental. Among the Squire's best-known exploits were his summary execution of ninety innocent pheasants in a hundred shots, his refereeing of the Caunt-Bendigo Heavyweight Championship match in 1845, his interrupting of his own hunting indulgences to rescue a boy from drowning, and his renunciation of parliamentary life on the pricelessly understated grounds that it "was not exactly in accordance with his tastes". The editors of the Dictionary of National Biography, winking at the ninety pheasants, the fifty horses and the slapstick at Wormwood Scrubs, suggest most fulsomely that "nobody who knew him would imagine for a moment that he was capable of doing anything approaching an ungentlemanly action". Perhaps they had in mind that escapade at a ball where the Squire, desirous of protecting a certain lady's honour by providing her with the armour of a choice bloom, rode fifty miles to deliver it to her.

But the most passionate love of his life was for cricket, and when finally he settled down he could hardly have chosen a spot much closer to his beloved club without actually bivouacking on the pitch. He took up residence at Number 2 Grove Road, where he died in his 80th year in 1866. The shocking irony was that although he could relax in his drawing-room and hear the plick-plock of the bat striking the ball, he was denied access to the councils of the club, through a dispute with the most remarkable cricketer of his generation.

As a bowler Osbaldeston was one of the fastest the game had ever seen, and he was also a dangerous hard-hitting batsman. His partnership with the professional all-rounder William Lambert was regarded as virtually unbeatable, and when in 1810 the Squire issued a challenge to another formidable duo of Lord Frederick Beauclerk and one other, the cricketing world was highly diverted. The match was for fifty guineas, and when, just before the proceedings were due to start Osbaldeston was taken ill, and asked for a postponement, Lord Frederick, displaying that instinct for sporting generosity which so strikingly characterises the history of English games, replied, "Play or forfeit". Osbaldeston responded with the insistence that the match should proceed, with Lambert taking on the opposing pair singlehanded. Beauclerk rejected the idea as absurd, to which Osbaldeston responded with a perfectly straight face, "Play or forfeit". The challenge match at last began, and Lambert, showing considerable cunning, resorted to a stratagem which reminds us of the still primitive state of the rules at that time. Lambert scored 56 and 22, and dismissed Beauclerk and T.C. Howard for 24 and 44, running out an easy winner by 14 runs. Knowing of Beauclerk's notorious temper, Lambert bowled a long succession of wides, until at last the batsman's rage became so violent as to destroy his concentration. Lambert then bowled a straight ball to dismiss the apoplectic Beauclerk, victim of that loophole in the law which did not punish the wide delivery. But though forced to pay up the fifty guineas, Beauclerk took revenge by waiting for a chance to destroy Osbaldeston. His opportunity came one day when Osbaldeston, in a fit of pique, resigned from the club. Later in life, now living under the very walls of the ground, at the house in Grove Road, he applied for re-election, only to be blackballed unto death by the vengeful Beauclerk. Revenge was ever a dish best eaten cold.

Cricket history has known no more unmitigated scoundrel than the Reverend Lord Frederick Beauclerk. Neither has it known many more colourful all-rounders. Outstanding with bat and ball, feared for his sharp tongue and his violent temper, Beauclerk was a greedy man who thought nothing of cheating if a match happened to go against him. Although officially a gentleman cricketer, he budgeted his affairs on the assumption that his income from cricket would not be less than £600 a year. His ascendancy in an age rendered arthritic with servility was due largely to his exalted lineage: he was a son of the Duke of St Alban's and a direct if illegitimate descendant of Nell Gwynne. From his first appearance at Lord's at the age of eighteen to his retirement thirty-five years later he dominated the English cricket world generally and Lord's club in particular, being instantly recognisable on the field of play in his dress of white stockings, nankeen breeches, scarlet sash and white beaver hat which, in moments of frustration he would dash to the ground and practise the choreography of splenetic rage. He has been defined by one historian as a figure as giantesque in his own age as W.G. Grace was in his, and although there is no comparative judgment on Grace which makes much sense it is certainly true that it was Beauclerk, rather than any of his gentlemen friends, who became the embodiment of the Marylebone Cricket Club, a ruler of autocratic whim and unredeemed selfishness.

There remains the curious question of his assumed religious allegiances. Beauclerk is one of those irreligious rogues with which the history of the Church of England is so liberally endowed. In that context of pietism in which the mores of reverend gentlemen tend to be reviewed, Lord Frederick's misdemeanours, his sharp practice, his oafish contempt for any sort of compassion, his utter lack of charity, his persistent bullying and belittling of rivals, may all appear outrageous. However, in the real world of fleshly sacerdotal licence he was by no means a freakish or even a very unusual figure. The history of English Christianity in Beauclerk's time makes a diverting comedy of rapine, abduction, seduction, sedition and bacchanalian excess compared to which the modern church is as a cloistered retreat to a beargarden. Beauclerk's ecclesiastical contemporaries were not above running their horses up the sides of church buildings in order to shoot a fox, nor to populating diocesan residences with bevies of blowsy mistresses, so perhaps the manipulation of the outcome of a cricket match by extra-cricketing means was hardly a heinous crime. Beauclerk (1773-1850) was amoral, belligerent and unprincipled. On one occasion he took such violent exception to the conventional view that a gentleman would rather lose a game honestly than win it by foul means that when an intrepid Hambledonian batsman called Tom Walker proved invulnerable to his bowling, he raged and swore, blasphemed against the faith he represented, dashed his hat to the ground, all in an attempt to intimidate the enemy into submission, a reaction which drew from the phlegmatic country bumpkin Walker the remark, "I doan care what ee zays".

As a man, and more specifically as a man of the cloth, Lord Frederick was an even worse joke. He was Vicar of St Alban's from 1828 until his death, during which time none of his parishioners ever discerned in him any faint twitch of piety. His relationship to Christianity was that of an absentee landlord. As Roland Bowen wrote:

> He often seems a kind of equivalent to the former bishop of Autun, the eventual Duc de Talleyrand-Perigord, a cleric without, it would seem, the faintest interest in being a clergyman, or any kind of Christian, and one can well imagine a man like Beauclerk, once he had survived the initial terror of a revolution, becoming in the end one of its most distinguished servants.

More eloquent even than Bowen's vituperation are two other factors, his face and his subsequent freakish apotheosis. In the portrait showing him in fancy dress, the podgy cheeks compress the lips into a line of petulant obduracy. A quiff-curl of vanity peeps down over the broad forehead, suggesting a touch of cherubic benignity rudely contradicted by the bold sceptical eyes glaring coldly at a position somewhere in the vicinity of silly mid-on. It is the minatory face of a vain, powerful, handsome man determined to have his own way – a nasty piece of work, as the saying goes. Had any of his flock dared to question his occasional practice of delivering a sermon from the pulpit while sitting astride his horse, the very least they could have hoped for from such a man was a verbal mugging. No doubt in his own defence Beauclerk would have invoked the Cornish vicar who took an axe to the family pews in order to settle some small doctrinal dispute, the reverend country parson who issued regular bulletins of hunting news from the pulpit, the Bishop of Derry, whose pleasure it was to settle questions of preferment by holding curate's races, and dozens of others whose view of the Gospels would greatly divert posterity if only those views were known.

But the most revealing feature of all concerning Beauclerk, and in a sense his finest hour, was his remarkable enshrinement a century after his own death in the annals of English fiction. Just as "The Cricketers of My Time" underwrites the immortality of the Hambledon myth, so will a minor novel

The young Lord Frederick Beauclerk, descendant of Charles II and the most accomplished, and arrogant, amateur all-rounder of his day.

of the 1940s preserve the impenitent spirit of Beauclerk. In its own eccentric way, *The Devil at Woodford Wells* is a memorable piece of work designed to preserve Beauclerk from oblivion. Its author, the dramatic critic Harold Hobson, describes it as "a fantastic novel", by which he means a macabre comedy of diabolonian ethics in which Beauclerk, long dead and sitting at the right hand of Lucifer, returns to haunt his old stalking grounds in the early years of the Second World War, disturbing still further a London already disrupted by the Blitz by disclosing several scandalous facts about his contemporaries. He insists, for example, that the long hiatus in the playing record of John Nyren was due to his parallel career as a Napoleonic spy, and that the eventual fate of that other demonic dupe, Max Beerbohm's Enoch Soames, was to become an associate of Beauclerk's. Hobson appends to his text at least one other sensational speculation concerning the history of cricket and its effect on the social destinies of England. The first member of the royal family to show devotion to and skill at the game was Frederick Louis, Prince of Wales, patron and captain of the Surrey club. In 1751 the Prince was struck by a ball and died of his injuries a few days later. Hobson's narrator reflects that had the Prince not participated in the fatal match, he would not have been struck by the ball, and would not have died while still a young man. Within a few years he would have become King, relegating the monarch we know as George III to the sidelines, and thereby rendering the retention by Britain of its American estates a distinct possibility. Beauclerk's opinion on this remains unspoken, but there is little doubt that he would have been inclined to be more loyal to the Prince than to the King.

Although in time Beauclerk became too old to lord it any longer on the field of play, his temperament remained misanthropic to the very end. Friends at Lord's noticed the years gradually reducing the scope of his operations but not the vehemence with which he executed them:

Lord Frederick might be seen at the entrance-gate of the old pavilion, generally smoking a cigar, and attended by a little snapping white cur, which never bit anyone but examined the calves of everyone who went in and out and growled. (His lordship was the only man allowed to take a dog on the grounds.) Sir Spencer Ponsonby-Fane recalls Lord Frederick sitting by the scorers, on the field of play, and peremptorily ordering off the ground any spectator who was unfortunate enough to incur his displeasure. As to the gradual change time wrought in him, Mr Pycroft has said: "At first I used to see his Lordship taking a bat to show some young tyro 'how fields were won'; then, after a few seasons in which he sat in the pavilion as the Nestor of the M.C.C., he was fond of leaning on some friend's arm, or seeking a sheltered corner and shrinking from every breeze; and last of all he used to appear in his brougham, his health and strength fast failing, with a lady nurse at his side."

CHAPTER III

IF WISDEN COMES, CAN SPRING...

———•———

While the fashionable world busied itself with the gambling and gossip of the metropolitan game, cricket was spreading across the nation, flourishing in the most unlikely places, and establishing itself beyond challenge as the national game. When in 1803 the headmaster of Eton, Dr Heath, forbade his boys to play a match against Westminster School, the cricketers defied him and went on with the fixture, at which the gentle doctor flogged the entire eleven, the elegance of his stroke-play being the admiration of all who experienced it. By the middle of the eighteenth century cricket was being played in Scotland and Wales, by which time the Irish had been familiar with it for a century. By the early 1800s the colonists were playing cricket in America. Before the end of the century it had reached Canada. Cities like Sheffield and Nottingham and Leicester began playing series of representative matches, which suggests a fairly sophisticated structure of local cricket in the north. The conventions of Gentlemen v Players and Oxford v Cambridge were firmly established long before the accession of Queen Victoria. Most significant of all, cricket was beginning to attract the attention of those not directly concerned with its techniques. William Pitt had made a cricketing reference when introducing one of his Defence Bills during the Napoleonic Wars; and, most bizarre of all, at one of the last committee meetings of the Hambledon Club, in 1796, among those present was ''Mr Thos Paine, Author of the Rights of Man''. As Paine was officially resident in Paris at this time, under sentence of death *in absentia* for treasonable acts against the Crown, he must have been very fond of cricket to have chanced arrest and execution in this way. The truth was that by the opening of the Victorian age cricket had so entrenched itself in English life that its decline and disappearance would have been unthinkable. The final accolade came in 1841, when Lord Hill, Commander-in-Chief of the Army, issued a directive ordering the preparation of a cricket ground close to every army barracks in the country.

But there had already been a far more profound indication of the advance of

Forerunner of the modern county game. A Nottinghamshire XI play a visiting Leicestershire side, c. 1830, with an improvised beer tent doing brisk business. The first recorded 'county' match took place at Dartford in 1709 between Kent and Surrey. The County Championship as we know it began to take root in the 1860s.

the game in English life, something of such immense significance that it is included in every cricket anthology and yet omitted from every cricket history. In 1836 the young journalist Charles Dickens began publishing instalments of *The Pickwick Papers*. The upshot was unparalleled in the annals of literature. Within weeks Dickens was a world celebrity and his book an accepted comic masterpiece. The nation went Pickwick-crazy, naming its children and its pets after the eponymous hero of this sprawling saga. Pickwick clubs sprang up, attended by people wearing Pickwick coats and Pickwick hats. And Dickens, shrewd enough to realise what had happened, was careful to include in succeeding episodes all those set pieces of life with which the common man, and the common reader, was familiar, from Saturday night balls and country Christmases to army parades, altercations in the law courts, by-elections, dancing, eating, drinking, laughing – and cricket. The match between Dingley Dell and All-Muggleton is described in terms which make it perfectly obvious that the fixture has long been a regular feature in the local calendar. As the two villages are located in Kent, we can assume that by 1836 a cricket match within the county was a familiar sight, and that the English had already become acquainted with one of the richest of their jokes, the spectacle of otherwise sober and solemn gentlemen making genial fools of themselves in a ball game. The date can in fact be put further back, because Dickens, as usual, is locating the events of his tale in some indeterminate corner of the recent past, in this case his own early boyhood. The fixture between Dingley Dell and the All-Muggletonians must have taken place around 1820, which places Kent among the first cricketing counties.

Indeed it was Kent which produced the third wave of virtuoso players, building up a county side so strong that it was considered a suitable opponent for the Rest of England. At the heart of the brilliant Kent eleven were three famous men, the first of whom, in size as well as in reputation, was Alfred Mynn, known as the Lion of Kent for his physical prowess and as Alfred the Great for his huge bulk. He stood over six feet, and as a fast bowler was considered fearsome by his contemporaries. Yet it is difficult to picture a man weighing more than twenty stone flinging down whirlwind deliveries. Mynn (1807–61) was an amateur, and of what the reference books define as yeoman stock, which probably means he was obliged to work for his living. He is said to have learned the rudiments of roundarm bowling from Willes, but it was evidently some time before he acquired the control to combine great pace with consistency of line and pitch. Mynn strikes us in several respects as being a sort of trial run, or preliminary sketch, for the colossus of the Victorian age, W.G. Grace. Like Grace, Mynn was a huge man whose bulk impeded neither his skill with bat and ball nor his powers of endurance. When fielding at slip his vast hands, described by one witness as being like legs of mutton, caught everything which came within reach. As a batsman he was a dangerous hitter who could turn the fortunes of a game. A gentle creature, full of good humour, generosity and sportsmanship, Mynn was one of the best-loved cricketers of his time. His tombstone at Thornham, where he was buried in 1861, reads, "Alfred Mynn, Champion of English Cricketers", a reference to his victories in single-wicket matches over the years.

Among his team mates there flourished one of the greatest batsmen of the nineteenth century, Fuller Pilch, a Norfolk man who had been tempted south in response to the blandishments of Kentish enthusiasts who paid him £100 per annum to reside within the boundaries of their county. Pilch's great contribution to the evolution of batting was his perfecting of forward play, enabling him to place the ball through the off-side field and thereby thwart the pace of the roundarm bowlers. From descriptions of his style, it would seem that Pilch would go on to the front foot and stroke the ball away as it hit the ground, making virtually every fast delivery a half-volley. Through a long career which flourished into the 1850s, Pilch was a star of the Kent side, remaining so in love with his adopted home that after his retirement he settled down as landlord of a public house in Canterbury, where one day he was bearded by the interviewer Frederick Gale, who asked him to discuss the great days of the Kent side.

> Now I will tell you just what the Kent eleven was to my mind; it was an eleven of brothers who knew one another, and never knew what jealousy was. It is true that I was paid to come into the county, but bless my soul, as soon as any man had been twelve months among the cherry orchards and hop-gardens and the pretty Kentish girls, he couldn't help becoming Kent to the backbone. Why, look at the support we had, and look at the money in the county. All the land almost was held by rich noblemen and gentlemen; and the farmers many of them very high, and had leisure to enjoy themselves. Why, the cherries would go on a-growing, and the hop-bine keep on creeping, night and day, whilst they were looking at a cricket match.... When they wanted a match they would send for Ned Wenham and me and say, "We want a good match; can you do it?". Well, then we used to reckon what it would come to, and they were at our backs if there was any money wanted. But we never asked for it if we made a good thing. Now don't you see, here was the difference between those times and these; there were few railways and matches were scarce, and some of our eleven, put on different sides, would draw all the county round for a two-day match in a nobleman's park. For

Fuller Pilch, a Kent stalwart from 1836 to 1854 and the first batsman to secure a reputation for style, honing the art of forward play.

45

"Kind and manly" Alfred Mynn, yeoman of Kent and the first universally acknowledged of cricket's "champions". In his heyday he stood six feet one inch and weighed 20 stone, dominating the field with his stately and dignified presence.

instance, Mr Felix and Alfred Mynn were given one side, and Ned Wenham and me and Adams the other. Then, don't you see, we were out for a two day holiday, and the whole town enjoyed themselves, and the principal innkeepers used to arrange to have our company on different nights, and very often a lot of gentlemen would come too, and hear a song, for we had rare singing about in the county, and if Mr Felix had his fiddle with him – for he could make music on anything, from a church organ to a pair of tongs – it was a treat. I remember one night when there was a concert, or theatricals, or something. Mr Felix was playing in the band, and old Lillywhite was sitting behind him and saw the music and he said, "Muster Felix, you are bound to have an overthrow or two over all those crooked notes".

Pilch was unquestionably a great cricketer, but the modern reader may be forgiven for wondering if Pilch's skill with the bat outdid his natural talents as an extempore social historian whose casual exchanges with Gale reveal more of the structure of English rural life than a dozen textbooks on the subject. Pilch's Kent is the Kent of *The Pickwick Papers*, even down to Mr Tupman's corroborative dithyrambs regarding the fair Kentish ladies, and the regional autonomies of a Dickensian England yet to be partitioned by the railways. Like Dickens, Pilch also seems aware that the England he is describing, although only the day before yesterday, has gone far beyond recall. Even allowing for the excessive nostalgia which so often, and so understandably, afflicts the retired athlete, there is a striking sense of loss in Pilch's recollections. By the time of his chat with Gale, he was living in the first community in history whose urban masses outnumbered its rustics. For thousands of years the maximum speed attainable by any human, rich or poor, had been that of the horse. Now, suddenly, the railways were beginning to annihilate distance, smashing down the invisible barriers sealing off county from county. Probably none of this occurred to Gale, who was preoccupied with the problem of how conviviality and technical command could have raced along in such happy harness in the world evoked by Pilch's reminiscences. Here too Pilch had a simple answer, which he expands into a dazzling mirror image of Trevelyan's vision of an England democratised by the intimacies of a ball game.

Two glasses of gin-and-water were about my allowance; and when some of the company were asking me to drink, I told the landlord, "Let the gentlemen pay, and you leave the gin out of my glass"; and nobody knew it, but I was wetting my pipe with cold water half the evening. Ay, and haven't I seen some good company in many a butler's private room when we were playing a great match. Ay, and drank rare good stuff, too. The gamekeepers used to drop in by accident, and the ladies' maids and the housekeeper; and I have known some of the young gentlemen staying in the big house come down and smoke their cigars and talk cricket; for I say gentlemen were gentlemen, and players were players, much in the same position as a nobleman and his head gamekeeper might be, and we knew our place and they knew theirs; and if some gentleman had not so much money as some of the present day, they had a precious deal better manners than some whom I know, and weren't hand in glove with the players one moment and bullyragging the next. Many of the players were gamekeepers, carpenters and other trades, and, when the match was over, went back to their business and felt that they had had a good holiday. Why, money couldn't get a gentleman into the Kent eleven. Someone might say to me, ''Pilch, Mr So-and-So, the rich brewer or banker's son, wants to play in the county eleven.'' ''Very well,'' I used to say, ''Let me see him make a good hand against good bowling and see what he is worth in the field, and if he is good enough he shall play.'' I didn't much like gentlemen in the eleven unless they were heart and soul cricketers; they might be up late dining or playing billiards or cards or what not overnight, and lose a match, but I knew a good one when I saw him.

Pilch's fine independence of spirit, which flowered out of his eminence as a cricketer, did him little good once his playing days were over. When Gale interviewed him, he was host of a Canterbury public house, but at some time during his retirement he set up as a tailor and went bankrupt; and by the time of his death in 1870 he was a forgotten, impoverished old man. One wonders whatever happened to all those young men who had once gathered in the butler's pantry, lit their cigars and talked cricket with him.

Pilch's reference to Felix introduces the third of the great stars of the Kent

The cut, demonstrated by the charming cricketer-intellectual Felix, whose manual Felix on the Bat *was the first thorough analysis of batsmanship.*

eleven, and one of the most incongruous figures in the pageant of English cricket. Nicholas Wanostrocht was the nephew of a Flemish immigrant who had arrived in Camberwell to start a boys' school. On the death of the school's founder, the headmastership had been taken over by his brother, Nicholas's father, but when Wanostrocht senior died soon after, his son found himself left to run the enterprise at the age of nineteen. A natural left-handed bat of great style, Wanostrocht played under an alias for reasons which tell us a great deal about the social standing of the game during the Georgian period. At the time young Wanostrocht became the unlikely proprietor of a school, cricket was still associated in the public mind with gambling, cheating and drinking. The surface probity of the Victorian age, just around the corner, could have been foreseen by nobody, and so Nicholas, having been exposed too many times to the priggishness of the platoons of future gentlemen under his command, resorted to the innocent subterfuge of a double life, an imposture so guileless that long before the end of his playing days the schoolmastering episode had faded to a dim memory. It is almost as though W.G. Grace, fearful that his patients might prefer not to be treated by a cricketer, were to have changed his name to Smith in the expectation of masking his eminence. Felix matured into one of those players whose universal popularity is founded on what might be defined as extra-mural virtues. Just as, a century later, Cecil Parkin was to endear himself to the Old Trafford crowds by his mischievous tomfoolery, and Patsy Hendren was to win the hearts of the congregation at Lord's with his boyish fun, so Felix became one of the best-loved players in the game because of his infectious high spirits and lack of malice. One of his contemporaries wrote: "Felix, the facetious, active, jostling, merry, notch-getting Felix, who makes cricket what it really should be, a lively and amusing as well as a scientific game, and who loves a jest as well as a fourer."

In fact, Felix loved cricket far too well for his imposture to have any chance of success, and as his cricketing fame quickly spread so did the school registers at Camberwell get shorter. In an attempt to recover his fortunes Felix closed the school down and started a new one at Blackheath, but once again education took second place to cricket, and for the second and last time Felix was obliged to close down. None of this seemed to depress him in the slightest, and towards the end of the Blackheath debacle he was heard to remark: "Anyhow, I have eleven boys left – who shall beat any eleven boys in England." The boast was almost certainly justified, because Felix, for all his levity, was the first theorist of the art of batsmanship, no doubt giving all his boys a thorough grounding in the principles of at least one item in the curriculum.

Indeed, seen in the context of the cricket of his age, Felix represented a new genus, the cricketer-intellectual. Pilch has described to us how his teammate could induce music from almost any instrument, and we know that he was also an accomplished painter, a good classical scholar and an entertaining amateur writer. Yet he threw in his lot with cricket, giving up schoolmastering for the pleasure of the company of the likes of Mynn and Pilch. Some of the horseplay indulged in by the Kent side of those days might strike the modern sensibility, wearied with the decline of etiquette, as naive, but the crowds revelled in it:

> A. Mynn delivered a ball off which a catch was given to N. Felix, who was fielding point. Now Felix was a jocose, amusing fellow who even during the process of the match would play antics. On missing the catch he immediately fell to the ground, held his head down, tucked up his knees and folded his arms round his knees, in fact made himself as much into a ball as possible. Mynn walked up to him, took hold of him by the collar of the flannel jacket, and in a jocose manner also, held him up with one arm extended at full length for a second or two. Felix, though rather short, weighed about eleven stone. This anecdote proves Mynn's great strength.

It also shows the remoteness of the cricketers of Mynn's time, who wore flannel jackets in the field. Among those who came to admire either the flannel or the cricket was the Prince Consort, who galloped into Lord's one day in June 1846 to examine the contents of the pavilion, glanced at the game, which happened to be between Felix's eleven and Pilch's eleven, and then galloped out again, no doubt asking himself why his countrymen were congenitally incapable of being serious about anything for more than two or three overs at a time. In a match at Horsham in July 1854, Felix had a bad day with the bat but took several wickets. After the game he suffered a stroke which ended his playing career. Some years later, coming across an account of the match in his copy of *Scores and Biographies*, he pencilled in the margin alongside the scores this curious comment:

> After this match I was most kindly admonished by Almighty God, being struck down by paralysis when in the enjoyment of good health.

But cricket loved Felix too well to allow him to drift away from the game, and was quick to utilise those other aspects of his talents which expressed themselves in two ingenious inventions. It was Felix who designed the first tubular batting gloves, and Felix again who was responsible for one of the most bizarre mechanical contrivances in the history of sport. His skill in batting against fast bowling owed much to this invention of his, which he christened the Catapulta:

> The history of this machine in its original form is traced back to the Romans; when with its gigantic energies it could propel, to a much greater distance than could the human arm, weighty javelins, large beams of wood headed with iron, and heavy stones.

But Felix's most famous achievement was his manual on the art of batsmanship, *Felix on the Bat*, the first thorough work on the subject ever written. The illustrations were executed by an old pupil from Felix's Camberwell school, the Pre-Raphaelite painter George Frederick Watts (1817–1904), sometime husband of the child-bride Ellen Terry, and painter of fulsome allegories like "Time, Death and Judgment", which had such an awestriking effect on that dedicated village cricketer Siegfried Sassoon. Watts did his work for Felix too

50

A commemorative silk handkerchief marking the Grand Jubilee Match played at Lord's in July 1837 between North and South to celebrate the M.C.C.'s fiftieth anniversary. The South won on the second day.

well, because the illustrations were so sought-after that collectors ripped them out and tossed aside Felix's text, making the book one of the very rarest in the bibliography of cricket. Once he retired from active play, Felix continued to travel up and down the country, becoming the speechmaker in residence for the United England XI, reporting their matches for *Baily's Magazine*, and keeping a diary of the club's tours illustrated with skilfully executed water-colours.

At this point, with Felix's transition to travelling spokesman for an itinerant eleven, we arrive at another watershed in the evolution of cricket, encountering in the process one of the canniest cricketers of the nineteenth century, someone whose amendment to the economic base of the professional game places him alongside Thomas Lord. Fuller Pilch's wistful recollection of an England unencumbered by the railways may mislead his readers into assuming that once the President of the Board of Trade became the first sacrificial offering on the altar of internal combustion, railways began sprouting like bindweed. In fact the rearguard action fought by the equestrian lobby was sustained for another hundred years. In the 1860s Lord Palmerston was still cantering to work down Piccadilly, the last Prime Minister ever to arrive at Westminster on horseback. A generation after Palmerston the hansom cab was clopping out the closing measures of the century, and when the 1902 Australian tourists travelled from their Birmingham hotel to play the first Test, they arrived at Edgbaston in a coach drawn by two white horses, with a liveried driver at the reins. The last London-to-Brighton Royal Mail coach set out from a yard near Guy's Hospital in 1905; the London Fire Brigade did not put its horses out to grass until 1911; and Londoners were still using horse-drawn buses up to 1916. These points have a vital relevance to the spread of cricket across England, obliging clubs to make long journeys down rutted roads, to outposts so far removed from the metropolitan sophistications of Lord's and the Oval that the arrival of a strange crew of cricketers whose fame had travelled before them was seen as an event of the deepest social magnitude.

Although the development of first-class cricket in England has been essentially a development of county clubs, with local landowning grandees as presidents, in the mid-nineteenth century star cricketers began taking to the highways, bringing their skills and virtuosity to distant country towns and remote villages, much as a travelling circus might dazzle the rustics by exhibiting a dancing bear, or a chimpanzee apparently intellectually more accomplished than the local schoolteacher. The history of the travelling elevens is no more than an interlude between the birth of the various county organisations and their eventual ability to sustain a national championship, but it is a very brilliant and highly significant interlude, which centres around two of the most enterprising cards of their day. Nor is it a coincidence that both of these innovative men were professionals, for the emergence of the travelling elevens was essentially an attempt by the paid players to liberate themselves from the patronage of the gentleman-cricketer. That it succeeded was largely due to a man with an instinctive grasp of business principles.

On Christmas Eve, 1798, a Nottingham bricklayer called Clarke became the father of a son who was christened William. At first this son followed in his father's footsteps, but while still a teenager he became a good enough bowler to take his place in the emergent Nottinghamshire county side. Soon after, he gave up bricklaying for good, becoming a husband, a father and host of a public house which, so long as he remained there, was the recognised headquarters of local cricket. The turning point in his career came in 1837 when, by this time a widower, he gave a virtuoso exhibition of the art of combining business with pleasure by marrying the widow who kept the Trent Bridge Inn. Although already at an age when most modern cricketers would be contemplating retirement, Clarke still had his great years before him. Apparently incommoded not at all by the loss of an eye while playing squash, Clarke, in the year of his second marriage, virtually established county cricket at Trent Bridge. Yet for all his progressive ideas about taking the game to the people, Clarke was in the technical sense an extraordinary anachronism. In an age when all bowlers delivered roundarm, Clarke reverted to the old underarm style, a method by now so archaic that it paid him huge dividends because of its unfamiliarity to the rising generation of batsmen. If we add to the strangeness of his delivery his acute judgment of character and his mastery of bowling tactics, we can begin to see why it was said of him that many of his wickets were already taken before the ball had left his hand. One contemporary wrote:

> It was perhaps fortunate for Clarke that his art was allowed to lie fallow till the old-fashioned batsmen had passed away, and thus it came out as a novelty to men used to the short-pitched and the inaccurate, of "no length in particular", which must ever be characteristic of the roundarm bowling. At first Clarke took all the best batsmen in. For the first time they had encountered a man with the head to see the weak point in their game, and with the hand to pitch at the very stump and with the very length that they did not wish to have.

Several of Clarke's observations have come down to us, showing the quality of his thought and the streak of analytical ruthlessness with which he went about his business. He once asked a batsman, "I beg your pardon, but aren't you Harrow?", and on it being confirmed, altered his field placing with the remark, "Then we shan't want a man down there". Being a bowler of slow lobs which looked innocuous enough, he was aware of the theoretical danger of annihilation he was running every time he put himself on to bowl. "Without head work, I should be hit out of the field. If I were to think every ball, the other side wouldn't make a run." While the rest of the eleven was preparing for a match by practising, Clarke would be found conducting a microscopic examination of the wicket; while they were enjoying the lunch, he would limit himself to a cigar and a bottle of soda-water, taking consolation for this self-denial each evening by devouring a whole goose.

But the greatest innovative stroke of Clarke's life came in 1846, when he organised a troupe of travelling professionals called the All England X1. Most of his recruitment was done in Nottingham, but to buttress the playing strength he brought in the Kentish stars, as well as two outstanding bowlers from Sussex, Lillywhite and Dean. Clarke was captain, manager and entrepreneur, travelling everywhere in search of a game which might prove profitable, spreading the gospel of cricket so zealously that it is said that to this day there remain outposts of rustic civilisation which have never seen a major match since Clarke's gladiators passed through nearly a century and a half ago:

> To budding cricketers the Grand Match of the season, played against the All England XI, was a landmark in their lives and, just as the sturdy village lad might try his luck and take his hammering from the hard-bitten professional boxer at the fair, so the local youths would try their best to bowl a batsman of the calibre of George Parr or stand up for an over or two to Jackson, whose pace was "very fearful".

There were those who despised Clarke for his professionalism, and who doubted the true worth of a match against the All England XI. How could it be possible, argued the opposition to Clarke, for hired hands to play day after day, wearied as they were with travel and quite unconcerned as to the outcome of the cricket? To the Reverend Pycroft, the man who collected the money at the gate for the All England XI was "a creature"; the players did "not care a button" for the game itself; they played "not for the score only for the till". Of course the reverend gentleman, practising quite a different profession himself, could afford to be superior. For his part, Clarke cared not one of Pycroft's buttons about what people might think of him. He was a hard-headed businessman running an arduous enterprise demanding patience, resilience, physical endurance and a sense of humour. In *Kings of Cricket*, Richard Daft describes a typical experience of Clarke's men, later evoked by H.S. Altham:

William Clarke, wily underarm bowler and founder in 1846 of a touring All England XI which brought cricket to the provinces.

> Here is a typical adventure of the eleven after a match at Redruth, in Cornwall. They were driving a coach-and-four in inky darkness along a moorland road, with a deep

ditch on either side of them; to make matters worse, a thunderstorm came on. Old George Parr, the then captain of the side, was thoroughly nervous, and his apprehensions were not exactly allayed by the ceaseless volley of matchless malediction poured out by his neighbour, an officer who had ridden in the charge at Balaclava, but found his present experience far more alarming. Parr, who was convinced that any moment might be their last, besought him to moderate the flow of his language, lest he might die with all his imperfections so manifestly upon his head. At last, however, they struck a lonely cottage, and rapped on the door for food and shelter. A window at length opened to the vision of an old man in a nightcap and with a blunderbuss at his shoulder, which he proceeded to level at George Parr's head. As he was as deaf as an adder, it was with the greatest difficulty that he was at last convinced of their peaceful intentions, and persuaded to let the travellers in. After a hearty meal, the party were assembling to continue their journey when one of their number, the great fast bowler John Jackson, was found to be missing. Repeated calls were unavailing, but at last he emerged from the dairy looking as if he had been disturbed in the middle of a shave, as the lower half of his face was completely coated in what looked like lather, but which subsequently transpired to be clotted cream.

Very often Clarke's teammates would be his opponents in other matches. Felix in particular was much exercised by the challenge of Clarke's bowling when he was obliged to face it. At last he wrote a pamphlet entitled ''How to Play Clarke, Being an Attempt to unravel the Mysteries of the Ball, and to show What Defence and Hitting are to be Employed Against This Celebrated Bowler''. The first time Felix faced Clarke after the publication of the pamphlet the scorebook read: ''Felix, bowled Clarke, 0''.

In 1852, predictably, rebellion burst out in the ranks. Clarke's underlings, maddened beyond endurance by their master's arrogance in the field and his parsimony off it, broke away and formed a rival attraction, the United England Xl, which before the end of the season was playing fixtures and proving as successful as the All England Xl. The leader in this daring enterprise was a man even more resourceful than Clarke, the one cricketer of his time whose name is today part of the English language, and whose stroke of inspiration created one of the durable freaks of world publishing. Among Clarke's battery of bowlers was a Sussex cricketer called John Wisden, whose career, which finally ended with the close of the 1863 season, had been a momentous one. At Lord's in 1850, playing for North v South, he took all ten wickets in an innings, every one clean bowled. (That Wisden, a native of Brighton, should have performed for North against South is explained by the fact that he and George Parr had recently acquired a new ground at Leamington and were therefore northerners, at least for the time being.) Although a competent enough batsman to have opened for the Players, and to have scored a century for Sussex against Kent, it was certainly his bowling on which his fame rested in his playing days. Sadly the details of many of his most spectacular performances are lost in the fogs of prehistory; even his great feat for North against South nods only curtly at statistical exactitude by being claimed ''for scarcely thirty runs''. Of that

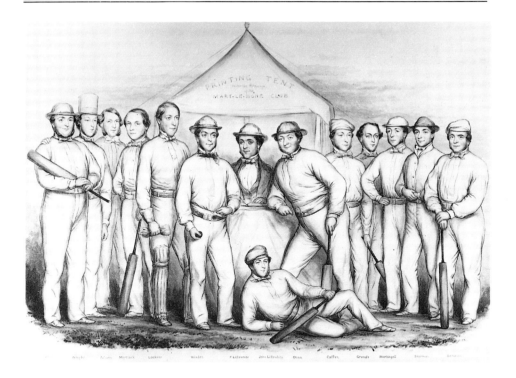

*The United England XI of 1852. John Wisden, holding the ball, and Jemmy Dean, with
the bat, were its moving spirits. Between them stands Frederick Lillywhite, publisher of the*
Guide to Cricketers *(1849–66).*

achievement W.G. Grace said: "A very good authority who witnessed the
performance told me that he kept up his break from the off from one to two feet
right through the innings". Wisden also bowled unchanged through both
innings twice at Lord's, once took six wickets in six balls in America, and in all
matches in the 1851 season took no fewer than 455 wickets.

Even more remarkable than his prowess as a bowler was the physique with
which he achieved it, for whatever else may happen in cricket there is no
question that John Wisden will remain the smallest, weakest, frailest successful
fast bowler in the annals. Born in Brighton on 5 September 1826, by the time
he made his debut for Sussex nineteen years later he was no more than five feet
four inches tall and weighed seven stone.... Although with maturity he found
a little more weight, he remained throughout his playing days a strikingly small
man who fully justified the soubriquet "the Little Wonder". By the time he
retired, having once taken over 1,300 wickets in four consecutive seasons, and
earned fame as an invincible single-wicket opponent, he must have guessed that
his place in cricket history was secure. Like Clarke, Wisden was very much more
than an outstanding athlete, and it must have seemed unlikely to his
contemporaries that his retirement would mark his disappearance from the
game, any more than it had for Felix. By temperament Wisden was an
entrepreneur and organiser of formidable resource who had given evidence of

his potential long before his retirement. Soon after his successful defiance of Clarke he began to cast a shrewd speculative eye on the commercial possibilities open to a man in his situation. There were occasions when his perspicuity flowered into authentic wit, and as a coiner of epigrams he could even rival Oscar Wilde. When in 1882 Wilde sailed for New York as a kind of animated sandwich-board on behalf of Gilbert and Sullivan, he is said to have responded to the spectacle of the Atlantic Ocean by confessing to disappointment. When the same experience befell Wisden on his American tour of 1859 with Parr's side, he glanced at the heaving waters with the appraising eye of the hardened bowler and observed, ''What this pitch needs is ten minutes of the heavy roller''. It was unlikely that so bright a man would agree to fall out of the public eye merely because he had arrived at the age of sporting discretion. As for the direction his schemes might take, he had already provided the broadest of hints.

In 1855 he had gone into business with Fred Lillywhite, and the pair of them had opened ''a cricketing and cigar business'' in New Coventry Street, Leicester Square. By this time the name of Lillywhite was already famous in sporting circles for one particular reason, and it seems likely that Wisden, taking note of his partner's success in another venture, decided to emulate it. The modern age tends to forget that Wisden's historic act of 1864 was by no means original. There had been cricket handbooks and annuals long before his retirement, the

The All England XI of 1859 which toured Canada and America, winning all five of their matches, including one against a Montreal XXII. Holding the ball on the right is the huge express bowler "Foghorn" Jackson.

most successful of which, *Lillywhite's Guide to Cricketers*, had been established as early as 1849. Nor was Wisden's first attempt at a yearbook particularly distinguished, on either a commercial or a strictly functional level. What is truly shocking about the first edition of Wisden's *Cricketers' Almanack* is not that its circulation was poor but that it deserved to be so. It is bad enough that the book should consist of a mere 112 pages, much worse that most of those pages are filled with material of the most wildly incongruous nature. Evidently Wisden was at a loss to know what to put into his book and, like most editors in that predicament, had decided to put in everything and anything. The sparse entries on current cricket were padded out with match-cards of games already more than fifty years old, including an exhaustive record of Gentlemen v Players matches. Even this had proved insufficient, and so Wisden had been pushed to the comically desperate extremity of appending a list of the winners of the Derby, Oaks and St Leger since 1779, the fact that China was first visited by a European in 1517, the rules of Bowls, Quoits and Knur and Spell, the date of foundation of the Antiquarian, Astronomical, Ethological, Geological, Horticultural, Microscopical, Pharmaceutical and Philological Societies, the results of the University Boat Race, the length of the chief British canals, the dates of the principal battles of the Wars of the Roses, and a brief disquisition on the constitutional implications of the trial of Charles I.

But slowly, patiently, Wisden began to play himself in. Soon dispensing with irrelevant material, by 1866 he was including full scores of the previous season's important matches. In 1867 he introduced "Births and Deaths of Cricketers", and in the same year included his first advertisement, for "John Wisden and Co's Patent Catapulta, the principle of working of which will be shown at 2, New Coventry Street, Leicester Square". In 1870 came the first match accounts; in 1872 an essay introducing the records of each county. But it was not until 1887, three years after Wisden's death, that there

LEFT: *John Wisden, smallest of the great speed merchants, shrewd entrepreneur and founder of the cricketer's Bible*
RIGHT: *The frontispiece of the first edition of Wisden's* Almanack, *revealing the editor's charmingly eclectic attempts to fill its pages.*

The Cricketer's Almanack,

FOR THE YEAR 1864,

BEING

**Bissextile or Leap Year, and the 28th of the Reign of
HER MAJESTY QUEEN VICTORIA,**

CONTAINING

The Laws of Cricket,

AS REVISED BY THE MARYLEBONE CLUB;

THE FIRST APPEARANCE AT LORD'S AND NUMBER OF RUNS OBTAINED BY

MANY CRICKETING CELEBRITIES;

SCORES OF 100 AND UPWARDS, FROM 1850 TO 1863;

EXTRAORDINARY MATCHES;

ALL THE MATCHES PLAYED BETWEEN

THE GENTLEMEN AND PLAYERS,

AND

The All England and United Elevens,

With full and accurate Scores taken from authentic sources;

TOGETHER WITH

The Dates of the University Rowing Matches,

THE WINNERS OF THE

DERBY, OAKS, AND ST. LEGER;

RULES OF

BOWLS, QUOITS, AND KNUR AND SPELL,

AND OTHER INTERESTING INFORMATION.

LONDON:

PUBLISHED AND SOLD BY JOHN WISDEN AND CO.,

AT THEIR

CRICKETING AND BRITISH SPORTS WAREHOUSE,

2, NEW COVENTRY STREET, HAYMARKET, W.

*May be had of all respectable Booksellers in the United Kingdom, or
forwarded free by the Publisher to any part of Great Britain for 13 Stamps.*

1864.

[One Shilling.

came the great watershed, a full list of batting and bowling averages for the past season and a full fixture-list for the next. In 1888 there appeared the first essay on a topical theme, and in the following year readers were beguiled by two further innovations, photographic illustration and a Cricket Records section. In 1892 came the first obituary notices, and from 1895 the practice was established of including amateurs and professionals together in the first-class averages. The final refinement for the Victorian period came in 1899, when the averages were computed in the modern style, to two decimal places. By 1900 the *Almanack* included for the first time more than 500 pages of editorial text. By 1950 it had doubled in size again, and a generation later each annual edition was more than ten times the thickness of the inaugural edition.

Wisden's great accidental monument to himself is yet another example of the way that cricket history, cricketing biographies, cricketing reputations, seem to require the sanction of the printed word to come fully alive. The codification of the feats of forgotten cricketers, the names and addresses of first-class umpires, details of Test matches played between ladies, the match-card for some obscure public school fixture whose participants are all forgotten even by their own descendants, the names of the presidents of each first-class county, details of matches in the Sheffield Shield, the Currie Cup, the Shell Shield, the Plunket Shield, the Ranji Trophy, the Quaid-e-Azam Trophy, the Lakspray Trophy, the Margaret Pedan Memorial Test Series, even the details of the Lords and Commons fixtures, all these arcane items and thousands more clamour to receive the tiny crumb of authenticity, mention in Wisden's *Almanack*, a status which imperceptibly, as the seasons slip by, evolves into a sort of immortality. The feats of heroes who have been dead for a century and who were celebrities only to each other, are faithfully preserved between the buff covers of John Wisden's tablets of the law. The almanack is only the most amazing example among many of the part played in the history and development of cricket by writers and publishers. If Wisden comes, can spring be far behind?

CHAPTER IV

COUNTRY GRACES

E nglish cricket came of age on 18 July 1848, when Dr Henry Mills Grace, a Somerset man living in the neighbouring county of Gloucestershire, celebrated the arrival of his fourth son. Already growing up in the house at Downend, a village four miles from Bristol, were Henry, born in 1833; Alfred, 1840; and Edward Mills, 1841. Two years after the fourth brother came the fifth and last, G. Frederick. Four girls made up a family which by Victorian standards was by no means immoderately large, although the clannishness of the Graces and the addiction of the males to the same two professions could sometimes create the illusion of whole regiments of them advancing across the Victorian landscape, stethoscope in one hand, cricket bag in the other. In the *Strand* magazine for July 1895 Dr Mills Grace's fourth son is the subject of an ''Illustrated Interview''. The illustrations include a full-page group portrait of the family, posed before a hillock, and looking less like a family than a Sunday School convention. The occasion is the annual Grace family picnic, to which none but relations were invited. There are 45 Graces in the photograph, ranging from matriarch to nephews and in-laws, giving us a priceless glimpse of one of the most remarkable dynasties of the nineteenth century. The men look distinctly more inviting than the women; and although the issues of consanguinity have proved too complex for the caption writer, who has been able to put names to no more than half of the picnickers, we know at any rate from his partial labelling that sister Fanny was a grim-faced character with a jaw like a steel trap, that few of the other ladies looked much better, and that the wife of Edward Mills Grace seems surprisingly devoid of any sense of humour considering she is married to one of the best straight-faced comedians of the epoch.

But of course our eyes are on the young giant with his back to the hillock, a friendly-looking soul whose long black beard conceals much of the youthful face. For these are the days before the legend of W.G. has spread across the Empire, before his marriage, before he has qualified to become a doctor like his

Forty-five members of the formidable Grace family on their annual picnic. W.G., bearded and genial, is standing in the centre of the back row. E.M. is surrounded by female relatives in the third row. To his left his sister Fanny fixes the camera with a basilisk glare.

father and his uncles and his brothers. Later the waistline will swell, until by the time the photograph is published in the *Strand* Grace will weigh more than twenty stone. The eyes will become hooded by the pouches and wrinkles of age, and wintry flecks will soften the contours of the beard. Neville Cardus has defined Grace as an Eminent Victorian, and again as ''a representative Victorian''. Eminent Grace undoubtedly was. Representative he most certainly was not, although at first glance that beard seems representative enough. The idea of Grace without whiskers is as unthinkable as Denis Compton with them, which is why the most wondrous of all the photographs of Grace shows him as a member of the 1863 All England XI. W.G. is fifteen years old and unbearded. It is hard for our imaginations to build a bridge connecting the bewhiskered genius of English cricket and this slim, smooth-cheeked youth in the white cap. Because of his beard, Grace lines up well with Carlyle, Tennyson, Trollope, Salisbury and the rest of the patriarchs of the period, although in terms of achievement, always acknowledging the limitations of his vocation, he ranks higher than any of them. Even Carlyle would never claim to have improvised the French Revolution, nor Salisbury the Conservative Party, but modern batting is more or less the invention of Grace.

When he played his first innings, three not out at the age of nine, the game was a rustic riot whose rules were still to be codified. There was no effective County Championship, declarations and boundaries were unheard of, umpires a disorganised rabble, Australia the far side of the moon. On unprepared pitches men in striped shirts and bowler hats sent down four roundarm deliveries per over. By the time Grace retired, after 44 seasons of first-class cricket, Hobbs was in the ascendant, Tate a promising apprentice, Hammond and Bradman just over the horizon. Most of the milestones by which the modern batsman marks his progress towards perfection were placed there by Grace. He was the first first-class cricketer to score a thousand runs in May, first to score a thousand runs and take a hundred wickets in a season, first to score a century on his debut against Australia, first to reach a century of centuries. In the hundred years since his entry, only eight men have passed his mark of 126 centuries, only five his total of 2,876 wickets, and only one his bag of 871 catches. When in August 1876 he scored cricket's first triple hundred, batting eight hours to make 334 against Kent, the world was suitably impressed. In his next match he made 177 before moving on to play Yorkshire, where he made 318 not out. Two miracles in one week, and prefaced the month before by a score of 400 not out against a Twenty-Two of Grimsby. But there are at least three other aspects of his career which justify Cardus's felicitous claim that ''he orchestrated the folk music of cricket''. It was Grace who put paid to the theory that the faster you bowled the more effective you were likely to be, Grace who widened the repertoire of stroke play, Grace who synthesised forward and back play into a comprehensive technique.

Because there is almost no tangible evidence to support the claim that Grace was the greatest cricketer of all time, we must deduce what we can, balancing playing conditions then and now, and the relative weakness of the opposition Grace faced. Yet we can only react in awe to the gulf between his achievements and those of his closest rivals. With the possible exception of Bradman, no cricketer in history has so dwarfed the feats of the next best men. Between 1868 and 1874, when he topped the English batting averages for seven consecutive seasons, the margin between his average and that of the runner-up was usually vast. In 1871 he averaged nearly seventy-nine runs per innings. The next man in the list averaged just under 40. That he was not so much a great cricketer as an athlete of genius can be deduced from the times he returned at the athletics meetings of his younger days. Running the 100 yards on grass he came in at just under

The beardless fifteen-year-old W.G. (second from left), in 1863, playing for a local XXII against William Clarke's All England XI.

11 seconds; in the 200 yards hurdles, 28 seconds; 440 yards, 52.2 seconds. All of this suggests that had the Olympic Games been revived a generation earlier than they were Grace might well have picked up some medals in Athens. Even after his retirement from cricket, he was not done with competitive sport, and became the first captain of the English Bowls team. He seems also to have been a formidable pugilist, a fact suggested by an entry in the diary he kept on board the S.S. *Mirzapore* when in October 1873 he set sail for Australia accompanied by eleven cricketers and his newly-wed wife:

> Nov 1: Malta, supped at the United Services Club. Made speech. On board again. Leapfrog and boxing; nearly killed one of the team.

He was, in fact, the exemplar of the Englishman of his time, a generation which was mad about sport and which, in the years between 1860 and 1885, would create the most lasting of all the monuments of Empire, the codification of team games. Indeed he was literally born into an atmosphere of sporting pioneering. In the 1840s the Graces, buoyant on the rising tide of Victorian expansion, went about their business, delivering babies and administering corn plasters, galloping around the country on errands either of mercy or sporting concern, sometimes both at once.

The moment his first son was born, Henry Mills Grace began converting the front lawn into a cricket pitch, and later, when the growing family moved across the road into a larger house, "The Chestnuts", he did the same, converting part of the orchard into a small ground, and setting the scene for one of the domestic set pieces of the Victorian age:

> The family practices were conducted under strict rules, a quarter of an hour's innings for the grown-ups and five minutes for the small ones, who had to take it out in fielding. As E.M. was now a big strong boy with a natural pull, and there was a wood and a quarry in the direction of long-on, the fielding was in the nature of salvage work. Mrs Grace and the girls looked on, and threw up a ball if it was hit near them, and occasionally bowled, but only to the very small. There were three fielders, however, whose names must never be forgotten, an immortal trinity in the history of cricket, Don, Ponto and Noble. They were particularly useful when the ball was hit into woods or water, but they did not only field out in the deep. All three were prepared to stop the hardest shot with their chests, and were not afraid of a catch. Ponto in particular had views on the game and the direction in which a ball should be hit. His place was by the bowler, and he strongly deprecated E.M.'s pull.

In this benign atmosphere, W.G. matured rapidly. His first cricketing recollection was of watching old Clarke's All England X1 playing against the local Twenty-Two led by Henry Mills Grace. A year later when Clarke's side returned, no fewer than five Graces were in the home side, including E.M., who was sent for from school to help repel the invader. The prime mover in this rapid advance of the younger Graces was their mother, the formidable Martha, a fine judge of technique and a matriarch resolved that her sons should distinguish

W.G.'s mother Martha, dominating figure in a unique cricketing family, the only woman to be accorded the honour of an obituary in Wisden's Almanack.

themselves. For many years she was the only woman allowed entry into the exclusive male preserve of Wisden's ''Births and Deaths of Cricketers'', which was only fitting, for few ladies can ever have known more than Martha about the births of cricketers; with their deaths too she was to become tragically acquainted when in 1880 Fred, the youngest of the Graces, only a few days after

The quintessence of unruffled Victorian self-confidence. M.C.C. members pose proudly in front of the pavilion at Lord's in 1874. Built in 1826, after a fire had destroyed its predecessor, it was replaced in 1890 by the present pavilion.

making his England debut, slept between damp sheets, contracted congestion of the lung and died. For the moment, all that concerned Martha was how to further the careers of her sons. She wrote to George Parr, recommending that he invite E.M. to join the All England X1, adding a postscript that she had another boy growing up who would be a better batsman than any of his brothers because his back play was sounder than theirs. The startling prescience of this remark tempts us to wonder what sort of picture Martha presented to the world. As she grew older, her corkscrew ringlets tended to hide under the mobcaps of the day, but one portrait of her remains unforgettable. She is found sitting on a bench in the garden. Behind stands her favourite medlar tree, and at her right hand is balanced the harp which she would strum sometimes on summer evenings, a sybil in silk skirts to whom her adoring sons deferred for as long as she lived. When they were away playing in a match, a message was sent to her each evening telling how they had got on. In 1874, when W.G. and G.F., were in Ireland with the United South side, the following information was despatched to ''The Chestnuts'':

> Handed in at Dublin, 7.49 pm. Received at 9.15 pm.
> From W.G. Grace, Dublin, to Mrs Grace, Downend.
> Self made one hundred and forty not out. Fred one hundred and three. Four out.

And who better than Martha to savour the joke made by the reporter W.E. Knight, after a match in which E.M. had opened the innings and carried his bat for 200, while his brother Alfred, going in last, made 28 not out? Knight must have been waiting for the chance half his life, as he described the situation: ''A doctor at the beginning and a doctor at the end. Such is life.'' The lions of English cricket acknowledged Martha's unique status among them, and when in July 1884 the news was brought to Old Trafford of her death, the match between Lancashire and Gloucestershire was stopped to allow W.G. and E.M. to hurry home to be with the family.

One of the truisms about W.G. is that he built half the cricket pavilions in England. Because of the irresistible magnetism of his personality, crowds thronged to see him wherever he played, which meant that prosperity followed in his wake like a golden stream. One of the most revealing items of apocrypha in cricket literature is the notice said to have been seen outside a cricket ground: ''Admission 6d. If Dr Grace plays, admission 1/-.'' Whatever the truth of that, it is certainly verifiable that between them W.G., captain of the county side, and E.M. secretary-treasurer, more than once conspired to raise the price of admission to a match, having decided that the fixture was ''a Grace benefit''. A century after the event, when all the dust had long since settled, the secretary of the Gloucestershire County club published a memoir in Wisden about this tendency of the Graces to treat the county side as a commercial enterprise which might at certain junctures be made to increase its yield.

> A collection was taken during Midwinter's innings and Mrs Grace presented him with £25. This happened to be another of those Grace testimonial games. With

brotherly solicitude E.M. raised the gate charge from 6d to 1/- without informing the committee.

We find ourselves confronted here by one of the central issues in Victorian society in general and in English cricket in particular, the definition of a man's standing among his fellows. The Graces enjoyed the status of gentlemen-cricketers, that is to say, amateur athletes comfortable enough not to accept money for playing. For any gentleman to do so was considered beyond the pale, even though there were instances of this breach of the unwritten code which were common knowledge inside the game yet unsuspected by the general public. Where Grace and his brothers appear to have differed from their fellow-gentlemen in this exercise in the art of genteel chicanery is that they made no real attempt to keep their affairs a secret. When in 1893 Grace undertook the second of his two tours to Australia he received £3,000 as his fee, a huge sum of money for those days, and an altogether astonishing one for a man assumed not to accept money for playing cricket. This instance, and several others of acceptance of payment by W.G. as a casual item of public knowledge, has perplexed all his biographers, who have striven to exonerate their hero from charges of intention to deceive. Their conventional defence has been that as Grace was the biggest attraction in the game, a man whose mere presence on the ground could add thousands to the gate, and that as he was an undisputed genius, and as, in order to play at all, he had to pay a locum to nurse his medical practice, then the payment of fees was perfectly within the accepted code. That Grace justified his payments, that he earned every penny of them, that he was often out of pocket after paying a locum, all this is true. But it is beside the point. An authentic gentleman was understood to be a man so placed that, whenever he felt the inclination to indulge in his favourite pastime, he could afford to follow that inclination without bothering to practise his profession at all – or, as in some cases, even bother with the pretence that he had one. The history of cricket in those days is crammed with examples of outstanding amateurs who were obliged to cut short their careers and waste away their talent fooling about in the City, instead of doing what Grace did – bending the rules to suit himself. What is puzzling is that Grace, for reasons best known to Victorian society, should have felt the need to brazen out the anomaly of his predicament.

To what extent he believed in all this nonsense it is impossible to guess, but because away from the cricket field he does not seem to have been a very subtle man, it is doubtful if he ever bothered to think his position through. Had he done so, he might have added at least two more memorable achievements to his long list of battle honours. Had he taken the giant step of renouncing his amateur status and disclosing the details of his income by way of explanation, he might have put paid once and for all to the hypocrisy of a two-tiered social structure in the game which was to endure for a hundred years. He might even have stumbled upon the truth about the great gentlemen-players divide, which is that it had less than nothing to do with money and everything to do with social pretensions and style of education.

The Gentleman v. Players game at Lord's in 1895. W.G. is coming in to join A.E. Stoddart at the crease. The trio in the centre are (left to right) J.T. Hearne, G.A. Lohmann and Arthur Shrewsbury. That summer Grace, then 47, became the first batsman to score 1,000 runs in May, along the way notching up his 100th first-class century, 238 against Somerset in front of a huge crowd at Bristol. He celebrated his double century with a jeroboam of champagne in the middle.

Let us take the extreme examples of Albert Knight and Gilbert Jessop, two cricketers with whom Grace was well acquainted in the latter part of his life. Knight was an opening batsman of such unwaveringly fundamentalist tendencies that before receiving the first ball of an innings he would pray for assistance from the Creator of the Universe. He later published a book whose style is so inscrutable that to this day there remain passages whose precise meaning is unknown. And yet Knight, for all his erudition in the realms of philosophy and metaphysics, was indubitably a professional. Jessop, a cricketing genius who, after an expensive education at Cambridge University, was still capable of writing "I am still to infernally busy to ... ", for all his illiteracy was unmistakably a gentleman. Had Knight never received a farthing from Leicestershire in return for his honourable labours for the county, the indelible stamp of his professionalism would still have been there. And had Jessop become a millionaire from the exercise of his stunning heresies at the batting crease, he would have been recognised instantly in the library of any gentlemen's club as an amateur born and bred. Curiously, W.G. was a product of neither half of the equation. Neither a public schoolboy nor a university graduate in the conventional sense, he was a typical product of the professional classes of England, although the word "professional" held a meaning very different in the doctor's surgery or in the solicitor's office from in the cricket pavilion. Just as in Turgenev's novels the family doctor and the family tutor are permitted to dine at the family table while the gardener and the groom are not, so the doctors and teachers of Victorian England were deemed to be gentlemen rather than hired hands.

The desperate urgency of the distinction might strike us as slightly crazed, but whether or not it was a symptom of some sort of social dementia, its talismanic importance in the society through which Grace and succeeding generations of cricketers moved should never be underrated. To make a breach with tradition would have been considered an act of treason to one's class, a crime for which the only punishment was ostracism.

There is an entertaining exposition of the complexities of class in an early novel by P.G. Wodehouse. *Psmith in the City* tells of young Mike Jackson, a clerk in a Lombard Street bank whose one gift is to make centuries. Having been educated at a public school, and being the youngest of several cricketing brothers, all of whom play as amateurs, Mike elects one day to play in a match at Lord's instead of attending to his duties at the bank. He makes a brilliant hundred but loses his clerical post. What to do? So far as the reader is concerned there is no dilemma at all. It is perfectly clear that Mike could become a professional cricketer, earning a wage and winning glory concurrently. But in Edwardian England, as in the England of Grace's day, life was not so simple. It is instructive to follow Wodehouse as he first defines Mike's predicament and then resolves it for him. After the brief euphoria of his triumph, and reminding himself that he now has no job, no money and little prospect of acquiring either, Mike suffers an abrupt deflation of spirits, at which his friend Psmith announces that pater will subsidise Mike's university education and then employ him as an agent for the Psmith estates, on the understanding, naturally, that he will be given as much free time as he wishes in which to follow his cricketing fortunes.

Mike's rescue by the Psmiths was the standard dream of every impecunious amateur of the period, a fairytale ending to a frankly fairytale problem. As it happened, there was a more likely, far less lurid resolution which might have occurred to Mike, a way in which a gentleman might earn his living from the game and yet still appear not to. The institution of the paid secretary of the county club constituted a bolthole through which many a needy gentleman scuttled to salvation. Mike, being the product of a goodish public school, might conceivably have managed as a penpusher, but during the action of the story the idea eludes him. Instead, he considers the alternative, of becoming a professional cricketer, and soon rejects it for a succession of reasons. He would be obliged to address his own brothers as "Mister" on the field, which would be dreadful, while they would have to call him "Jackson", which would be even worse. He would have to stay at boarding houses while they lorded it at the best hotels, and would be expected to enter the field of play by what Cardus has described as "a side entrance, a sort of exit from the servants' quarters". At one point Mike wrestles with the problem of how to minimize the degree of shame he will visit on the family were he to dwindle from a Gentleman to a Player:

> It was impossible that he should play for his own county on his residential qualification. He could not appear as a professional in the same team in which his brothers were playing as amateurs. He must stake all on his birth qualification for Surrey.

And so Mike elects not to embrace the serpent of professionalism, and is rescued from the consequences of his own quixotry only by the last-minute arrival of the marines in the form of Psmith's father. W.G. would have understood perfectly, and applauded when sympathetic social forces galloped to the rescue.

What of Grace's "published works"? There were four of these, *Cricket* (1891); *The History of a Hundred Centuries* (1895); *W.G.* (1899); and *W.G's Little Book* (1909). We know that Grace was a cheerful philistine, a man who once advised a younger cricketer to give up book-reading because the small print harmed the eyes and reduced one's effectiveness on the field. And when his young friend J.M. Barrie published a book about his old university tutors entitled *An Edinburgh Eleven*, he tells us that Dr Grace showed some interest until it was explained to him that its contents had nothing to do with cricket. But before dismissing any of Grace's four published works as rubbish, it is as well to keep in mind the advice of Neville Cardus never to be rude about the autobiographies of cricketers "because you never knew who wrote them". For all his rejection of the literary life, W.G. enjoyed the casual friendship of several professional writers, some of whom lent a hand when there was a book to be written. These ghosts included his friend W. Methven Brownlee; E.D.H.

Sewell, an unjustly neglected virtuoso in the practice of eccentricity; and William Yardley, the brilliant batsman who became the author of Gaiety farces and burlesques, and, intermittently, a dramatic critic. But the only ghost who has left any record of the process by which a book of Grace's came to be written is the religious journalist Arthur Porritt, who was responsible for *W.G.*, with the sub-title *Cricketing Reminiscences and Personal Recollections*. According to Porritt, the Doctor had agreed with the publisher James Bowden of Covent Garden to produce a volume of reminiscence for the year of the Jubilee. As the months slipped by and no word on the subject was forthcoming, Bowden had the bright idea of suggesting a collaborator. According to Porritt, "Grace accepted me with the utmost heartiness, and although the task of getting material from him was almost heart-breaking, I enjoyed the job immensely". Each week Porritt would spend three half-days at Grace's home at Sydenham, discussing the contents of the book. Sometimes he would draw a blank and come away with nothing. At other times he would succeed in tickling the Doctor into a stream of reminiscence rich enough to provide the raw material for a whole chapter.

> Grace's mind functioned oddly. He never stuck to any train of recollection, but would jump from an event in the '60s to something that happened in the last Test match. Often I left his house in absolute despair. Once at least I asked leave to abandon the enterprise but was urged to persist. I remember distinctly one age-long afternoon when I was trying to get out of W.G. something of the psychology of a batsman making a big score in a great match. All he wanted to say in recording some dazzling feat of his own was: "Then I went in and made 284." "Yes," I replied, "but that is not good enough. People want to know what W.G. Grace felt like when he was doing it. What thoughts he had, and what the whole mental experience of a big innings means to a batsman." "I did not feel anything. I had too much to do to watch the bowling and see how the fieldsmen were moved about to think anything."

Porritt had to contend with another, deeper problem. Grace was not only not a bookish man; he had a genuine terror of being mistaken for one by his comrades in the pavilion. At one point in the composition of the reminiscences, Porritt had used the word "inimicable". Grace reacted instantly with "No, that word can't go in. Why, if that went into the book I should have the fellows at Lord's coming to me and saying, 'Look here, W.G.; where did you get that word from?'"

The crowning irony of Porritt's collaboration with Grace is that, although he failed in his finished volume to learn from Nyren's example and breathe life into a sackload of statistics through the regenerative power of anecdote, when he came to write his own reminiscences he was able to bring the Doctor to life more vividly than any other writer has ever managed to do.

> About him there was something indefinable – like the simple faith of a child – which arrested and fascinated me. He was a big grown-up boy, just what a man who only lived when he was in the open air might be expected to be. A wonderful kindliness ran through his nature, mingling strangely with the arbitrary temper

of a man who had been accustomed to be dominant over other men.

His temper was very fiery – perhaps gusty is a better word – and his prejudices ran away with him. He detested Radicals in politics and disliked umpires who had ever given him out LBW. He would have made an excellent subject for a modern psychoanalyst who might, from W.G.'s stores of forgotten cricket lore, have extracted for us a classic of cricket literature. Reverting to his choleric temperament, I think I once did make him really cross. It was when I flatly refused to believe his statement that he had only one lung, and had, in fact, had only one lung since his childhood. ''Who,'' I asked him incredulously, ''is going to believe that?'' I simply could not credit it. Grace was, for the moment, nettled, and then he said rather testily, ''I'm not going to have you doubting what I say. I'll call my wife and she'll confirm what I have told you''. He called Mrs Grace, who corroborated W.G.'s story. Then I apologised and we made peace.

This description of Grace, one of the very few in which it is the citizen rather than the cricketer who comes to life, raises several interesting points. Porritt's claim that Grace hardly ever seriously lost his temper contradicts so many stories of his outbursts of irascibility on the field that one wonders if Porritt is not being strictly truthful. Almost certainly he is; the apparent discrepancy is explained by the near certainty that a great many of Grace's exhibitions of ill temper were informed by that underlying sense of humour, or perhaps of comic absurdity, which was a key to his temperament. How much authentic spleen, for instance, was behind his action in the match played at Sheffield Park in 1884 between an England X1 and the Australians. According to F. Ashley-Cooper:

> W.G. called for a gauge to test the bats of P.S. Macdonnell and A.C. Bannerman. The former's was found to be a trifle too wide. It was then suggested that one of W.G.'s bats should be tested, and much amusement was caused when the very first one would not pass muster.

The same straightfaced larkiness characterises the anecdote concerning W.G. bowling deceptively innocent-looking donkey drops to a young batsman in the hope of inducing a rash swipe and an easy catch. The batsman refused to play Grace's game, patting each ball decorously back along the turf to the bowler, who, after a few overs, was heard to remark, ''If you go on doing that, I shall take myself off''. That he was a skylarker and a buffoon there has never been any question, and of all his biographers it is Bernard Darwin who does most to bring out this vital aspect of Grace's character. Darwin was befriended by W.G. the patriarch, and remembered him afterwards as a typical West Country farmer, ''in a square felt farmer's hat, a black tailcoat and waistcoat, watchchain, dark trousers, boots made for muddy lanes, a solid blackthorn stick with a silver band''. And, being a typical West Country farmer, Grace was not altogether an abstemious man:

> His regular habit while cricketing was to drink one large whisky and soda with a touch of angostura bitters at lunch, and another when the day's play ended. He never dieted, ate sparingly, and was a non-smoker.

But not, apparently, a non-snuff-taker. More than half a century after his death, a Mrs Margaret Doyle wrote to a national newspaper concerning the friendship of Grace with her father, the Somerset cricketer Robert Ford: "As a little girl I often sat on the Doctor's knee and saw him take snuff, sometimes even having a sniff from his silver box myself. Many's the time I pulled his whiskers. He was a dear man, with such a hearty laugh, and often he would press a half-sovereign into our hands." Darwin, who offers no explanation for the fact that although Grace ate sparingly he grew to over twenty stone, had the opportunity to study not only Grace's alcoholic consumption but also its effects:

> A whole bottle of champagne was a mere nothing to him; having consumed it he would go down on all fours and balance the bottle on the top of his head and rise to his feet again.

Darwin goes on to describe the performing of convolutions which seem uncharacteristic and yet in some vague way redolent of the age:

> A.J. Webbe remembers, at his mother's house in Eaton Square, W.G. marching round the drawing room after dinner bearing the coal scuttle on his head as a helmet, with the poker carried as sword

With which recollection we arrive at one of those disconcerting moments when the confluence of fact and fiction, of myth and reality, tempts us to abandon our frame of reference altogether and seek the truth elsewhere. Like the famous photograph of Douglas Jardine, predatory and aquiline in his Harlequin cap, peering through the rapidly dispersing fog of his own misgiving as he sets out for a short run, the vision of Grace playing the fool with a coal scuttle on his head suggests a plane of existence worlds removed from the pavilion at Lord's. For if with a sudden rush of comprehension we see that what is nudging our subconscious about the Jardine photograph is its unmistakable evocation of the spirit of Sherlock Holmes, then just as surely Grace among the fire-irons becomes one of George Grossmith's Holloway Comedians, that crew of genial suburban rowdies whose harmless indiscretions so delighted the soul of Lupin Pooter – none more than the aspiring thespian Burwin-Fossleton who, in his obsessive impersonation of Henry Irving, "more than once knocked over the fire-irons, making a hideous row - poor Carrie already having a bad headache".

Darwin also confirms Porritt's implication that Grace, so far from being a thinker who intellectualised his own batting technique, achieved his technical orthodoxy through pure intuition. He quotes the Doctor's son, Admiral Edgar Grace, who recalled that the only attempts W.G. ever made to teach his own children to play the game consisted of "taking a bat and saying 'This is the way to do it'". Perhaps, adds Darwin, it was because according to Canon Edward Lyttelton, "no one ever had a more unanalytical brain". We learn also that by 1865, the year when Grace began shaving, he stood over six feet tall and weighed eleven stone, that C.G. Lyttelton, later Lord Cobham, recalled his physical presence at the time as "having some appearance of delicacy", and that within a year or two the flirtation with the razor was over for ever, Grace

'The faster they bowl, the better I like them'. W.G. at the crease, equally at home off the front or back foot, playing with a bat which seemed 'all middle'.

W.G. in his M.C.C. cap, a painting in oils by Archibald Stuart Wortley, 1890. Fifty-five years later Neville Cardus wrote of the Doctor: 'Grace was the Representative Man of his epoch; the crowds flocked to look upon him – and thus he changed cricket to a national affair, a spectacle as well as a game ...'

having decided to consign his features to what Darwin defines as "the jungle tide of nature". Darwin's last word on his hero takes the form of an enchanting anecdote:

> When my eldest daughter was two years old, W.G. kissed his hand to her in the prettiest way, as she gazed at him through the window. I have always impressed on her that if she lives to be a hundred she can never have paid to her a pleasanter honour.

Thus Darwin closes the record on this spectacular Englishman. We know little of what he ate, virtually nothing of what he thought, what kind of domestic creature he was, what he did on winter evenings apart from bridge sessions with the medical men of Clifton, what entertainments he preferred, which politicians he abhorred, what memories he cherished, honours he coveted, kindnesses he performed, sicknesses he cured, holidays he took. Oddly vivid glimpses like the one with which Darwin takes his leave, of an old man performing an affectionate gesture to a tiny child, are therefore doubly revelatory, suggesting more of Grace's temperament than all the statistics in all the almanacks. In strolling leisurely through the water meadows of Edwardian memoirs, diaries and biographies, the reader sometimes finds himself confronted by one of these unexpected glimpses of Grace, seen from an unaccustomed angle in an unfamiliar context, and the very fact that these delightful encounters strike us as utterly uncharacteristic of the Grace we think we know, only proves how incomplete a portrait we possess. There is for instance the surprising experience of a prominent Liberal journalist of the period, H.W. Nevinson, who recalls sitting on various committees for Working Men's Playing Fields, and that "Grace was often among them, always silent", to which intriguing fragment of information we react by wondering what manner of meetings these were that they could have induced W.G. Grace, incessant chatterer and chuckler across the cricket fields of an epoch, to remain mute.

A view of a very different kind comes down from that gentle poet and sometime tailender for the Sussex Martlets, Siegfried Sassoon, who recalled that:

> ... as for W.G. Grace, the last time I beheld him he was trotting doggedly along behind a pack of foot-beagles; and while he pushed his way through a gap in the fence, I reverently computed that he must turn the scale at somewhere near fifteen stone.

As a country doctor W.G. made no claims to distinction. A local historian called A. Braine published a book of recollections in 1891, *A History of Kingswood Forest*, which incorporated a unique glimpse of Henry Grace sharing a patient with his famous son:

> Some years ago we remember a man dying of typhoid fever; the father and the son both attended the lad. The son, then a young man, had prescribed, and the morning following the father was to call and see the patient. He did so and found the lad worse. He quickly examined the medicine bottle and, turning red with

Trent Bridge, June 1899, and W.G. captains England in his last Test. Back row: R.G. Barlow (umpire) T.W. Hayward, G.H. Hirst, W. Gunn, J.T. Hearne (12th man), W. Storer, W. Brockwell. V.A. Titchmarsh (umpire); seated: C.B. Fry, K.S. Ranjitsinhji, W.G. Grace, F.S. Jackson; front: W. Rhodes (making his Test debut), J.T. Tyldesley.

rage, he stamped his foot, saying, "Damn the stupid fool!", and sent the bottle spinning from the window.

The same witness recalled a sick man arriving at W.G.'s Clifton surgery to be told, "You are like an old broken-down cab horse, and want whipping up". The patient took the advice badly until it was explained to him that what W.G. meant was that the comsumption of a bottle or two of beer would do the trick. His bedside manner was generally brusque, but he had a reputation for being gentle with his female patients. Whatever his skills as a doctor, Grace is the first medical practitioner in history who can claim to have saved a man's life on the cricket field. This remarkable reconciliation of his two callings took place at Old Trafford in 1887. Lancashire were hosts to Gloucestershire, whose eleven included A.C. Crome. He later recalled the match.

It is, in all human probability, due to W.G. Grace that I survive to write my reminiscences of him, for he saved my life at Manchester in 1887. I ran into the railings in front of the Old Trafford pavilion while trying to save a boundary hit, and fell on the spikes, one of which made a deep wound in my throat. They had to send out for a needle and thread to sew it up and for nearly half an hour W.G. held the edges of the wound together. It was of vital importance that the injured part should be kept absolutely still, and his hand never shook all that time. I should have known it if there had been any twitching of finger and thumb, for I was conscious most of the time and the nerves of my neck and face were severely bruised. It would have been a remarkable feat of endurance under any circumstances, but the Old Man had been fielding out for over four hundred runs and had done his full share of bowling. I have two reasons for mentioning this incident. One is obvious; the other is that it affords evidence of W.G.'s amazing stamina.

Croome was only one of hundreds of his contemporaries who regarded Grace with a blend of love, awe and idolatry. When the Memorial Biography was compiled in 1919, nearly fifty cricketers, from the crustiest Tory gentlemen to the most phlegmatic northern professionals, paid generous tribute to the man who had dominated their age. Each one of these witnesses had his own favourite Grace story. Perhaps the most memorable of all the recollections is that of H.D.G. Leveson-Gower, who recalled the morning in the early days of the Great War when he took W.G. on a visit to the Cattle Market at Deptford. ''When he appeared, all the girls proceeded to sing 'You Made Me Love You', at which the Old Man stroked his beard and said, 'It strikes me I could be quite comfortable here'.'' By then his course was almost run, even though for a man

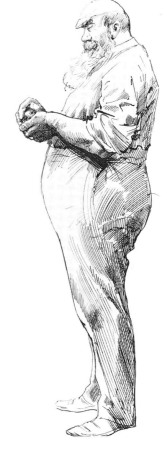

of such legendary physical powers and apparently iron constitution he was by no means an ancient. He died on 23 October 1915, at his home at Eltham, a mere sixty-seven years old but prematurely aged, it was said, by the prodigious strains he put upon himself throughout a lifetime of strenuous sporting endeavour. His fellow-doctor-cricketer Sir Arthur Conan Doyle later testified that the cause of death was a broken heart in the face of the appalling slaughter of a war whose methods he could not comprehend, and whose mindless brutality destroyed his faith in his own species.

The most telling measure of a man's stature is that he should become a frame of reference for greatness in his own lifetime. Judged by this criterion, the giant figure of Grace begins to bulk larger than ever, even in areas of which he could have had no knowledge, and whose awareness of his eminence would no doubt have staggered him. One of his protégés, Gilbert Jessop, nominated as the three most easily recognisable public men between 1894 and 1904 W.G. Grace, Mr Gladstone and General Booth of the Salvation Army,

The benign face of the Colossus. As a bowler, Grace was a wily exploiter of a 'high, home and easy' roundarm action.

81

then adding that of the three it was Grace who had to take precedence because "the man in the street would have distinguished him just as easily even if the Old Man had changed apparel with either of the other two, and I really don't think the same could be said were the situation reversed". It was not the first time that the name of Mr Gladstone had been linked with Grace's. As early as 1869, when W.G. was clean bowled for a duck in the match at Canterbury between South and North, the representative from the *Daily Telegraph*, straining to convey to his readers his sense of outraged stupefaction, wrote:

> Imagine Patti singing outrageously out of tune; imagine Mr Gladstone violating all the rules of grammar – and you have a faint idea of the surprise created by this incident.

That prince of poor taste Andrew Lang, searching for a worthy simile for Grace's style, finally settled for the prose of Henry Fielding. Walter Sickert, attempting to convey the depth of isolation experienced by James McNeill Whistler in London after having savoured the artistic life of Paris, likens it to "W.G. Grace settling at Arles or Tours at the age of twenty-five and getting, for the rest of his life, such practice in cricket only as Arles or Tours could afford him". And Sickert adds, "His cricket would certainly not be what it is now". Barrie described his great literary hero George Meredith as "the W.G. of letters", a metaphor which some would consider more flattering to the novelist than to the cricketer. Even Bernard Shaw, who once suggested that Englishmen can never play cricket, they can only work at it, wrote of the baritone singer Charles Santley: "To the Briton with a turn for music, he is just what Dr Grace is to the Briton with a turn for cricket." In the best of all novels about life in Fleet Street, *The Day Before*, H.M. Tomlinson, attempting an impressionistic passage to convey the headlong rush of Europe towards the great smash of the war, mentions the assassination of President McKinley, was between Russia and Japan, Votes for Women, and then:

> Dr Grace omitted from Test team. Well, he recalled a long-gone cricket season when that item read as if Rome were at last desolate.

And when one of those contemporary beards, the one belonging to Anthony Trollope, came back into its own in the mid-twentieth century, causing the republication of the Palliser novels, Sir Shane Leslie, in his introduction to *Phineas Finn*, conveyed his approval with:

> It has been one of the literary surprises of our time to witness Trollope's recall to favour. Seeing his novels open on the table is like suddenly finding Dr Grace batting at Lord's or an equally heavily swathed Mrs Langtry walking in Hyde Park.

Only one occasion is recorded on which Dr Grace had direct contact with this larger world, one on which he was certainly outmanoeuvred by the opposition. The great cartoonist Phil May one day published a drawing of a cricket match in which one of the fielders was represented wearing wicketkeeping gloves. The solecism intrigued Grace, who wired May: "Why does short leg wear wicketkeeping gloves?" May wired back from Fleet Street at midnight; at 2.30 in the morning Grace was awakened to receive a telegram reading: "To keep his hands warm."

In his introduction to *Phineas Finn*, Shane Leslie defines figures like Trollope and Grace as "part of the national baggage", in which claim he is certainly justified in the case of Grace, who represents the unconscious response of the game of cricket to the unspoken demand that in order to establish itself once and for all as an indispensable aspect of the English experience, it must create one towering representative personality who would incorporate technical perfection, richness of temperament, and an abundance of the indefinable quality of Englishness. It was not really to do with cricket at all, any more than the love for Dickens was to do with prose, or for Miss Nightingale with the wards at Scutari. In February 1892, at Toole's bandbox of a theatre at Charing Cross, a comedy called *Walker, London*, written by a dramatist then unknown to London audiences called James Barrie, opened to gales of laughter. The play included in its cast-list a character simply described as "W.G.", a young boy who spends three acts declaiming on behalf of cricket. Nobody who attended any of the 511 performances of the play needed to have the joke explained to them. There is no evidence that William Gilbert Grace ever saw the play, but had he done so, and had he, on taking a hansom afterwards to Paddington Station to catch the Bristol express, indulged the impulse to discuss what he had just witnessed with a friend, we can be confident that the train would never have left without him. Darwin tells us that whenever the Doctor happened to be chatting to a friend on the platform, they would "wait respectfully for him to take his seat before starting westward".

CHAPTER V

THE CORONER

———————•———————

I t was inconceivable that so idiosyncratic a man as W.G. Grace would
have been content to surround himself at the Gloucestershire club with
ordinary men. In fact that county side, which in the mid-1870s was
generally regarded as invincible, and was perfectly capable of taking on and
defeating the rest of England, comprised a fascinating compendium of
individuality, quirkiness, laughter and impudence. At the very heart of the side
was a personality in some ways more remarkable even than W.G. His elder
brother Edward Mills Grace was born in 1841, seven years before W.G.; and
these mutually devoted brothers represented violently opposing poles of style
and temperament. While W.G. in his young days was inclined to shyness and
self-effacement, E.M. blew like a hurricane through the halls of orthodoxy. Self-
assertive, utterly indifferent to every opinion but his own, inclined to autocracy
and likely at any moment to improvise some outrageous eccentricity or
blatantly to outface the canons of cricketing law, E.M. was perhaps the most
widely-loved and admired cricketer of his day, a true original who could always
be relied upon for a few good stories. But the most remarkable thing of all about
him was his batting method, which flew so aggressively in the face of the
conventions that his influence on the psychology of batsmanship remains
undimmed to this day. Later generations who saw Bradman or Vivian Richards
pulling a ball round to leg from outside the off-stump may be able to picture
dimly what kind of figure E.M. cut at the crease. His recipe was to hit the ball
hard and often, and although his blatant cross-batted solecisms ought to have
brought catastrophe, his magnificent coordination between hand and eye made
it possible for him to maintain his leading position in the English game for many
years.

No more striking contrast with W.G. can be imagined. The two brothers are
almost like representatives of different epochs in English history, E.M. a
reminder of Georgian rumbustiousness and empirical daring, W.G. the true
embodiment of solid Victorian orthodoxy and respect for traditional principles.

*The Gloucestershire XI in 1888, dominated by W.G. and E.M. Grace. In the 1870s
Gloucestershire's all-amateur side was almost invincible.*

Yet the pair of them opening an innings together was one of the great spectacles
of English cricket, each man an impassioned admirer of the other, and both
likely to erupt into laughter at any moment. Photographs hint at the contrasting
temperaments of the two men. W.G. seems benign, with a kindly smile, homely
features with just a glint about the crinkly eyes of benevolent despotism. But
E.M., caught in a pose of studied indolence on the front porch, flannelled and
buckskin-booted, bat held across his stomach, peaked cap perched over the
black mutton-chop whiskers, has about him a faintly menacing air at odds with
the domestic quietude of the knickknackery glimpsed inside the door. It is the
face of a man who can not only see a joke but likes to go looking for one, yet not
a man to engage lightly in argument. E.M. looks brisk, even brusque, in
contrast to his younger brother, who will always do things in his own good time.
It is the difference between fatherly solicitude and avuncular michief. Yet the
two men had much in common. Both retained until the end of their days an
abiding love of family and of cricket. Both possessed qualities of leadership and
a sense of responsibility. And both were medical men. W.G. is still referred to
today as the Doctor, E.M. as the Coroner, although there were occasions when
cricket took precedence. When the choice confronted E.M., he would announce
that a post-mortem was required and then go off to fulfil his more pressing

sporting commitments. His younger brother, under no illusions about E.M.'s cavalier attitudes to rules and regulations, told one of his biographers: "E.M. was a coroner, but I shouldn't like anyone to hold an inquest on his cricket."

This is the most revealing observation ever recorded on the subject of Edward Mills Grace the cricketer. It seems likely that the broad streak of obduracy which was a feature of Edward Mills Grace's behaviour on the field, as well as of W.G.'s, owed something to heredity. One of the maternal uncles of the Grace brothers was Alfred Pocock, a natural player of ball games and an enthusiastic teacher. It was through his patient tutelage that E.M. and W.G. in particular became accomplished players, although E.M.'s heretical batsmanship, said to have been born of his use as a small boy of a bat several sizes too large for him, could hardly have been the result of coaching. The Pococks were authentic English eccentrics, and it is their strain rather than that of the more conventional Graces which informs the antics of the cricketing brothers. Alfred, when in later years he graduated to the status of great-uncle, took to the teaching of chess and the brewing of his own champagne from imported grapes; but it was the figure of his father, George "Grandfather" Pocock, who shows that perverse determination to get the better of opponents at all costs which we have come to recognise in W.G. and E.M. Old George was animated by two passions, religion and box-kites, and expressed his enthusiasm for both of these obsessions with the sort of frenzied, slightly crazed cheeriness with which Dickens endowed Mr Dick. In villages where the natives seemed not to be regular churchgoers, he would erect what he called "an itinerant temple", which proved to be an ordinary tent, under whose sheltering canvas he would preach the gospels. As to his other preoccupations:

> Granfer Pocock's passion for kites was equally fervent. He invented a kite-drawn carriage in which he incredibly drove from Bristol to London, knocking off chimney pots as easily as though they were bails and terrifying the wives of toll-keepers who felt that only the devil could so swiftly propel carriages along the roads of England without horses.... There was one experiment of this innocently diabolical old gentleman the thought of which, even now, makes the blood run cold. So great a faith had he in his various kites that he allowed his daughter Martha to be suspended in her chair and carried across the terrifying chasm of the Avon Gorge. It is a shattering thought that the very existence of the greatest cricketing family the world has ever seen once literally hung by a string.

There was another act of obduracy performed by old George which not even his formidable powers of casuistry could ever have reconciled with the charitable principles of the religion he professed to love so deeply, and which has its exact parallel in E.M.'s boyhood:

> George Pocock was the organist of Portland Wesleyan Church at Kingsdown, near Bristol, and in addition to playing the instrument, owned it. Unfortunately for the church, there arose a sad disagreement between the organist and the deacons, each side wanting its own way over certain matters, and at last Mr Pocock, being unable either to force his point or obtain a compromise, not only

refused to play any more but, leaving the church, took with him the organ upon which he performed so important a part of the Sabbath service.

The writer happens to be describing matters ecclesiastic, but his choice of words has about it a prophetic ring when seen in the context of his grandson's temperament, particularly in the phrase "refused to play any more":

> At Kempe's School, Long Ashton, history repeated itself. This time, however, it was the wickets not the organ that were removed. It appears that the boys were playing cricket and E.M., who was batting, received a crack on the leg from a shooter. "How's that?" piped a small shrill voice. "OUT", came the chorus of other shrill voices; but E.M. wouldn't go. They argued and argued as small boys will and eventually, being over-borne by numbers, E.M. had to go. But he pulled up the stumps and took them with him.

This incident, apart from demonstrating the hereditary strain of Pocockian cussedness which passed down through the Grace children, shows the degree to which playing and winning at cricket always mattered to E.M. A few years later, when he first strode on to the adult cricket stage, his behaviour was recalled by his younger brother with affectionate attention to detail. When William Clarke brought his All England side down into Grace country, E.M., still a pupil at Long Ashton, performed so valiantly at long on that old Clarke, notwithstanding his legendary tightfistedness, presented the boy with a bat.

> E.M. put the bat in front of the pony carriage with great pride. I see from the scoresheet that E.M. was given out leg-before-wicket. I wonder if he was satisfied with the decision?

W.G.'s rhetorical question hints mischievously at the inability of either brother to acknowledge defeat on the cricket field. An adversary of E.M.'s called Frederick Leeston-Smith, who played for Somerset, liked to recall a match between his club, Weston-super-Mare and Thornbury, whose side E.M. led to so many glorious, boisterous and occasionally disputatious victories. This is how E.M. describes the incident:

> F.L. Cole made one off my first ball, Leeston-Smith made six off the second, six off third, six off fourth, six off fifth, when the umpire said, "I'm afraid it is over, Doctor". I said, "Shut up, I am going to have another", and off this one he was stumped. Weston-super-Mare had to follow their innings. Leeston-Smith came in first, and the first ball I bowled him he hit for six. The second also went for six, but off the third he was stumped again.

Note the truculence with which E.M. asserts his ascendancy over an opponent who has had the impertinence to hit his bowling about. Nor did E.M. restrict his field of bellicose operations to the game in progress, but would think nothing of carrying the fight to those not directly involved. On one occasion when E.M. was batting, and deliberately disrupting the game by pleading a succession of excuses, from a fly in his eye to the presence of a man moving behind the bowler, a bold spirit called Hathaway shouted out something abusive, at which E.M., his eye suddenly flyless, shouted back a threat to punch him the moment he was out. He was as good as his word, and it was only through the intervention of the other players that a free-for-all was averted. There was a similar, more famous occasion:

> After the match between Gloucestershire and the 1896 touring side had prematurely ended in the county's virtual annihilation, E.M. challenged the Australian, H. Donnan, to a single-wicket match. As E.M. ran up to bowl, some of the drunks began a chorus of jeers. E.M. turned on the ringleader like a charging rhinoceros and the unhappy toper, the fear of death heavily upon him, incontinently fled. Out of the ground and over the Downs the chase proceeded, and E.M. was absent for a long time. When he got back, even his most facetious friends felt diffident about asking him what he had done with the body. "He's still running," said E.M. grimly, and imagination toys with the fancy that somewhere on Ashley Down on moonlight nights the ghost of E.M.'s injudicious critic flees in eternal terror from a sturdy, and less ghostly pursuer.

At the end of the 1863 season, when George Parr took a side to tour Australia, E.M. was the only amateur to be invited. His situation in being surrounded by fairly unsympathetic professionals was invidious, but he later described what happened:

> My position with the Eleven has been somewhat difficult. It required no great perception to see that any little occurrence might raise bad feeling. At first one or two had almost looked for chances to try and quarrel but this had entirely passed. The Eleven had been attentive and kind to me, and now, when they were leaving me behind, two or three shook hands with me with tears glistening in their eyes.

E.M.'s decision to stay on after the tour was over was a surprising one considering his experience under Parr, which had been uncomfortable from the day the party set out from Liverpool. The magnitude of the enterprise can hardly be imagined by the modern reader, but in those days Australia represented gruesome unspoken dangers, although, not, curiously enough, from the generations of felons which the British courts had been exporting there. The real danger was said to be presented by the natives, and we read in the most thorough of all the accounts of emergent Australian cricket that at the docks, when Parr and his men were about to sail,

> several members of the England team had difficulty in getting away from relatives who believed they would be attacked and eaten by blacks in Australia.

The nine-week journey proved arduous and boring by turns, the only recorded interruption of E.M.'s shipboard routine being his extraction of a troublesome tooth from the upper jaw of a teammate. The shipboard diet had a disastrous effect on E.M.'s digestive system, and the moderate standard of his performances early on in the tour was thought to have come about through trouble in the galley rather than in the gully. As for travelling conditions, they were so spartan as to inspire the phlegmatic E.M. very nearly to poetic effusion:

E.M. Grace, popularly known as the Coroner, whose thrillingly unorthodox batting was matched by his endearingly eccentric behaviour off the field.

Driven by the coolest and ablest drivers that ever held the ribbons, the coaches dashed all night in and out of ruts and holes, over stones and mounds, round trees and logs, through creeks and gullies and waters that flow deep into the coach itself.

By the time he returned home to England, half the domestic season had passed, to very dramatic effect as far as the Grace family was concerned. E.M.'s younger brother had suddenly emerged as the leading cricketer in the family. In a match for the South Wales club against Gentlemen of Sussex, W.G., batting at number three, and praying the whole time that E.M.'s boat would dock in time for him to take part in the match "and give me heart", batted all day to score 170. In first-class matches for the season, his average was over sixty. Very nearly emulating the experience of Byron, E.M. had woken up to find his brother famous, and although thereafter he performed a great many prodigious feats, was never again quite the leading cricketer in the family. Not that he ever cared a fig for such eminence, nor was there ever the faintest trace of envy between the brothers. The rise of W.G. simply swelled the conspiracy, that was all. E.M. continued to play as he always had, striving to give the opposition no rest, and assisted now by a brotherly ally growing more formidable every day.

But it may be that E.M.'s most important contribution was off the field of play. For nearly forty years, from 1870, when the Gloucestershire County club was an infant child of the Graces, until 1909, by which time it was a world-famous organisation, E.M. served as club secretary, receiving £60 per annum in return for which he arranged fixtures, collected subscriptions, canvassed for new members and hunted down the old ones. As might have been expected, the style of his minutes of committee meetings sometimes approached the bizarre:

> Committee meeting held at the White Lion Hotel, Bristol, on Thursday, November 25th, at 3 o'clock. Present: E.M. Grace, and that's all.

Anyone who wonders why the secretary should have found himself so sadly isolated on the occasion of that meeting, and why, finding himself alone, he remained so cheerful about it, will find enlightenment in the minutes of the previous meeting. E.M., it seems, was enjoying one of his rows:

> After more conversation of not too polite a nature, as the Rev. J. Greene disputed the correctness of the notes taken by the secretary at the Committee meeting of the 20th, saying that his memory was superior to the black and white testimony of the secretary....

But to have dispensed with his services would have been tantamount to disbanding the club. The Graces *were* the Gloucestershire club, and in any case if E.M. was removed, or cared to resign, which five men could be found to fill his shoes? His performance as club secretary was positively heroic, and there was nobody at the club, not even the cantankerous Rev. J. Greene, who would have denied it.

E.M. had no office staff to do the vast amount of clerical work in his office as secretary, which, of course he carried on for some years after he had ceased playing; there was no shorthand writer or typist and he did all the work himself with an amount of care and attention to detail that was astonishing. Mr R. E. Bush, who knew him as well as anyone in the county, said that when a county game was in progress at Ashley Down early in the season, E.M. would be stopped a dozen times in walking through the enclosure by people wanting to pay their subscriptions, and he would take their money, put it in his capacious pockets, make a joking remark, and pass on. He never made a memorandum of the amounts he received, or a note to remind him of the numbers who paid, yet without fail the receipt and ticket would arrive the next morning.

On his retirement from office, E.M. received the proceeds of a subscription fund amounting to £600, and what one of his biographers describes as "a serviceable walking stick" presented to him by the Duke of Beaufort. Two years later he died, and it was somehow appropriate that the hymn sung over the grave of this notorious raconteur was "Tell me the old, old story". In its fulsome obituary tribute, Wisden's *Almanack* closed with this sad reflection on E.M.'s storytelling gifts:

> He was the cheeriest of cricketers – the life and soul of the game wherever he played. It was a great misfortune that he could never be induced to write his recollections of the cricket field. His good stories could be numbered by the hundred, and in conversation he told them with immense vivacity.

We have one more glimpse of the Grace brothers, which can stand as a symbol of the force of their impact on English cricket. In a match against Kent, E.M. hit a ball to point, where C.J.M. Fox was fielding. Falling awkwardly in his attempt to gather the ball, Fox rolled over in agony, at which E.M. dropped his bat, ran over to the stricken player and began to examine him. W.G., who was padded up in the pavilion, ran out to offer further medical assistance. Few invalids can claim to have had the attention of two doctors simultaneously, but Fox may have wished he was less fortunate. Both doctors realised that the trouble was a dislocated shoulder, and the spectators were greatly diverted to see E.M. sitting on the injured man's head while W.G. seized Fox's arm, placed one foot on his body, and jerked the shoulder back in place. A few seasons later, at Bristol, Fox was again playing against the Graces and again dislocated his shoulder. The same sequence of events took place, which establishes among E.M.'s many achievements his status as the only batsman ever to sit on a fielder's head. Twice.

CHAPTER VI

A GILBERTIAN TRAGEDY

T he Grace connection did not stop with the brotherhood but spilled over
into related areas of consanguinity. The obituary columns of Wisden list
twelve Graces besides several maternal cousins and nephews, including
one pioneer who emigrated to Australia, became a politician, and won fame of
a sort by filibustering one day in the state parliament for twenty hours without
stopping.

With one of these relatives in particular the mood suddenly modulates from
triumph and laughter to something much darker, something pathetic and even
tragic, ineffably Victorian in its faint odour of sanctimony and evasion. Walter
Raleigh Gilbert was the son of a sister of Martha Grace. He lived for a time in
his aunt's house at Downend, forging what should have been lifelong friendships
with his cricketing cousins. Having been born in London in 1853, Gilbert was
qualified to play for Middlesex, which he did on nine occasions in 1873 and
1874. He was an accomplished batsman, a canny slow bowler and an
outstanding deep fielder whose catches at long-on to the bowling of W.G.
became a feature of English cricket. He was also a typical Grace in his attitude
to the game. On one occasion he played a ball into his shirtfront. Both batsmen
started running, and for a moment the fielding side could see no ball. At last,
realising what had happened, the opposing captain appealed to the umpires,
who ordered Gilbert to stop running. He did so, unbuttoned his shirt and let the
ball drop to the ground. The umpires allowed six for the hit. It is not surprising
that when W.G. took twelve cricketers and his newly-wed bride to Australia in
1873 on a honeymoon tour, the resourceful and companionable Gilbert should
have been in the party, proving a useful team member and a congenial partner
for his captain on several kangaroo hunts. In 1876 he moved down to the West
Country and became one of the group surrounding W.G. In that year he
finished fifth in the first-class averages, with a highest score of 205 not out for an
England X1 against Cambridge University. He represented the Gentlemen
against the Players four times, and in 1880, after the premature death of young

Fred Grace, he took over the managership of the United South of England travelling eleven.

In the light of these facts, which seem to suggest a distinguished and interesting career, the reticence of cricket historians when it comes to W.R. Gilbert seems suspicious. Altham's monumental history of the game refers to him twice, as someone who "made a lot of runs" for the early Gloucestershire County sides, and again as a safe long-on to his more eminent cousin's flighted half-volleys. A.A. Thomson describes him as "one of the heroes of the early West Gloucestershire days", while Grace himself, in the appendices of *Cricket*, published in 1891, includes him in a list of "Leading Batsmen in First-Class Cricket"; and yet, in a text of more than 400 pages he makes no mention of Gilbert in the narrative at all. This is doubly odd, because a not-out double century in 1876 was still a rare occurrence. Indeed, next to W.G.'s own 344 at Canterbury, it was the highest innings by any batsman that summer. In the concluding section of the book, *Cricketers I Have Met*, Grace presents detailed biographies of no fewer than 121 of his contemporaries. Gilbert is not one of them, a curious omission to say the least. Was it fear of a charge of nepotism which caused Grace to omit his cousin's name? It is true that he also omits from the biographical summaries his own brothers, but then both of those gentlemen are referred to so fulsomely and so persistently throughout the text that by the time Grace arrives at his summaries, there is literally nothing left to say of them. How odd that a cricketer distinguished enough to be mentioned twice by Altham in approving terms, and for a biographer nearly a hundred years after the event to mention five times, should rate not a sentence, a phrase, a single word, from his own cousin who selected him as an Australian tourist.

The researcher's nostrils begin to twitch, as the pungent aroma of facts being cooked rises on the air. In such cases we always go first to the same oracle: the pages of Wisden. In attempting to locate Gilbert's obituary, the first task is to establish the date of death, and there, in the "Births and Deaths" section for 1938, appears the entry:

> Gilbert, Mr. W.R. (Middlesex and Gloucestershire) b Sept 16, 1853, d July 26, 1924.

This leads us to Wisden for 1925 where, sure enough, may be found the official obituary notice, which once again confirms our man's gentlemanly status by referring to him as "Mr". It opens with the splendid flourish of reminding us that Gilbert's initials stand for Walter Raleigh, causes a slight shock of surprise by listing the place of death as "Calgary, Alberta, Canada", lapses into euphemism, and then ends with these words:

> At the beginning of the 1886 season he became a professional, and the season was not very advanced before his career in first-class cricket ended abruptly.

But not half as abruptly as the obituary notice itself. Why the tight-lipped evasions? Was it because Gilbert had the cheek to turn professional at a time when all his cousins were proclaiming their amateur status? Perhaps, but if that was indeed the reason for Wisden's reticence, the punishment seems a little disproportionate to the crime, especially as late as 1925 when the obituary was published.

There are other, more baffling considerations. If Gilbert turned professional in 1886, as the obituary claims, why grant him his gentlemanly ''Mr'' in the notice itself? And why persist in listing him as ''Mr'' in the 1938 edition? Apparently he had forsaken his amateur status forever, so why was he not stripped of all typographical honours? The confusion is compounded when we refer to the ''Births and Deaths'' of that same edition of the almanack where in the obituary section he is buried with full gentlemanly honours. This is how the entry reads:

Gilbert, W.R. (Middlesex and Gloucestershire) b Sept 16, 1853, d July 26, 1924.

Wisden is contradicting itself hopelessly. In one and the same edition it has listed Gilbert as a professional in ''Births and Deaths'' and as an amateur in the very obituary which tells us that the man was a professional. What about that 1938 edition, where he is listed as an amateur once again? And what of the almanacks which were compiled closer to the date of his defection from his class? The 1902 edition lists him as:

Gilbert, W.R. (Middlesex and Gloucestershire) b Sept 16, 1853.

By now it is quite clear that there is something very peculiar about the case of this man Gilbert, something which so disconcerts his contemporaries that they have become literally incapable of knowing precisely who or what he was. The world of cricket had evidently become so confused as to be no longer capable of coherent thought on the subject, leaving a later age to extract what sense from the muddle as might be possible. So far as the bewildering changes of tack in Wisden are to be trusted, something like the following sequence of events appears to have taken place. In the early 1870s Gilbert begins playing first-class cricket and soon comes into the orbit of his brilliant cousins in Gloucestershire, enjoying considerable success. In 1886 he turns professional only weeks before a sudden mysterious loss of form ends his career. He is dismissed to the ranks of the hired hands by Wisden, and as for his famous cousin, he can hardly bear to mention Gilbert's name at all, except with reference to himself. Then in 1924, long after the brothers are dead and gone, news comes in from one of the outposts of Empire that Gilbert has at last joined his cousins, at which point Wisden is almost tempted to forgive him, as though in some vague way by finally removing himself he has expiated his sins. But then, Wisden, having weakened in the obituary, stiffens its resolve again in ''Births and Deaths'', and does not finally absolve the poor fellow from his breach of the proprieties until a moment in the late 1930s, more than half a century after he had committed it.

It could be claimed that by 1940, when Wisden was still listing him as Mr. Gilbert, W.R., his case no longer had the faintest relevance to the times. W.G.

had been dead for 25 years, E.M. for 29, Fred for sixty. And yet it seems to have mattered to somebody. There begins to form in the imagination an irresistibly comic picture of the annual editorial conference at the offices of Wisden, or perhaps in the committee room at Lord's, to decide who this year shall be forgiven his trespasses. And while this court convenes and the years slip by, Gilbert waits – in Calgary, Alberta – for the gesture of forgiveness. Mafeking is relieved, but he is not. The Great War is carried to its successful conclusion but Gilbert's case is not. Will reprieve ever come? So far as poor Gilbert is concerned, it never does, because he dies in 1924 still shorn of his honourable prefix, like a disgraced officer with his epaulettes snipped off. And then at last, at some time in the 1930s, he is forgiven and retrieves his title. Admittedly this is a wholly fantastical picture, but it is the only one to accommodate all the known facts.

But why Calgary? How does a Gloucestershire gentleman cricketer end up scoring centuries in Montreal? Why no word of explanation from Wisden, or indeed from anybody, about the vast hiatus in Gilbert's life between 1886 and his death forty years later? And why should any man's career suddenly disintegrate almost immediately after he turns to professionalism? Perhaps such questions represent no more than the idle curiosity of a sentimental antiquarian. The world with which they are concerned vanished so long ago that it is surely a vanity even to consider the finer points. Who remembers Gilbert now, and who cares? In reply we now reach the most farfetched of all the facts in the case, which is that in 1970, a full century after Gilbert had agreed to accept money in return for playing cricket, there were those who found the truth so unpalatable that they did everything they could to continue to conceal it. It says a great deal for the conspirators that it was not until 84 years after Walter Raleigh Gilbert's sudden defection from the family ranks, from the Gloucestershire side, from England itself, that anybody published any facts to explain the inconsistencies of the official record. The historian who broke ranks was Roland Bowen who, in a masterly work entitled *Cricket: A History of its Growth and Development Throughout the World*, provided at least the bare bones of the case, and then, as an afterword, added this extraordinary sentence:

> Another indication of the recurring instinct for suppression was a suggestion to me that if this story had not appeared in print before (it has not) it should not now.

It is at least conceivable that the Grace family at the time should have done everything in its power to hush up any disgrace attaching to members of the family. But who in 1970 would try to dissuade anyone from printing the truth? The descendants of the Graces? If so, they missed a priceless opportunity of seeming to be enlightened. We can afford to be candid about our grandfathers not only because all the issues involved are dead but also because being perfectly honest about our relations often fosters the useful illusion among the weak-minded that we are being perfectly honest about ourselves.

But perhaps it was not the Grace family who insisted on a continuing cover-up. Might it have been some misguided idealist among the councils of English cricket? Whoever it was who tried to silence a disinterested cricket historian, who or what were they defending? A lesser rogue who committed some absurdly insignificant crime in another age? Or a principle of gentlemanly gallantry which was finally legislated out of the laws of English cricket in the 1960s? There must be answers to these questions, and they could tell us a great deal about the manners and morals of Victorian England.

It becomes intriguing to locate the precise point at which poor Gilbert's virginity was returned to him, by whom and why. In 1934, for the ninth consecutive year after his death, the entry in Wisden reads: "Gilbert, W.R.", but in the following edition, dated 1935, we behold the "Mr" reinserted. Our first reaction to this act of charity is to wonder how it might remotely profit a man to lose his own soul and then get it back again ten years after his own death. And is it conceivable that there could have existed, as late as 1935, anyone feebleminded enough to bother about restoring a prefix to a corpse? The thought then occurs that perhaps this sudden gesture of forgiveness is explained by the unusually rapid changes of editorship at Wisden in the 1930s. But even this theory is frustrated by the facts. In 1934 there succeeded to the editorial chair of Wisden a Mr Southerton, who had been a contributor since 1894. Only a year after his accession Mr Southerton collapsed and died in circumstances which a great many of his journalistic contemporaries would gladly have welcomed, with a drink in his hand at a cricket dinner. He was succeeded by a Mr Brookes, who in subsequent editions allowed Southerton's belated action in the Gilbert case to stand. But what prompted Southerton to take that action? In the first of his two editions Gilbert is still unforgiven, in the second magically restored to innocence. Why? It is impossible even to make a wild guess at the motivation for this last link in a chain of circumstance which would be riotously comic were it not for the whiff of hypocritical outrage which wafts across poor Gilbert's far colonial grave.

However, once Roland Bowen had let Gilbert's cat out of the bag, it was only a matter of time before the zealots of cricket research, in which breed the English are richly endowed, unearthed the detailed explanation for the mess. Some years after Bowen, that most accomplished of all investigative historians of the game, Robert Brooke, published a paper called "The Tragedy of W.R. Gilbert", in which almost all our questions are answered. At the heart of the case was this vexed question of Gilbert's livelihood. Unlike his more famous cousins, he had no profession with which to augment his income, and when in 1880 he assumed the duties of secretary of the United South of England X1 he must have been greatly relieved to have found the means to remain a gentleman yet still contrive to feed and clothe himself. The first signs that Gilbert may not have been quite the ideal man for the job came in 1882, when a Sussex professional called Charles Howard, who during that season had appeared as a late replacement for someone else at Chichester in the match between the United South of England and the Australians, took Gilbert to court for his fees, which he claimed had not been paid. By the time of Howard's action, the day of the wandering elevens was nearly done. As the structure of first-class counties steadily developed, and as an embryonic county championship began to gain credence, the function of these nomadic clubs began to fade. Among those who felt the financial draught when William Clarke's old idea finally became passé, was the paid secretary of the United South of England X1, Walter Raleigh Gilbert, who at the start of the 1886 season featured in two disconnected events. As the season opened he was the subject of the weekly biographical portrait which was a popular feature in the weekly magazine *Cricket*. To be selected for this honour was not quite as coveted an accolade as, later on, to be chosen as one of Wisden's Five Cricketers of the Year, but it was still an impressive indication of how well respected and widely admired Gilbert was. A few days later Gilbert decided to grasp the nettle of professionalism and made a public announcement that from now on he would be appearing as a paid member of the Gloucestershire eleven (although not, as we have seen, as handsomely paid as his Gentleman-cousin W.G.). Gilbert's professional debut was at the Oval for his county against Surrey. In the interval between the Surrey fixture and Gloucestershire's next match, Gilbert simply disappeared. There was no word of explanation from the editors of *Cricket*, who had just published their extravagant tribute. Lillywhite's *Almanack* mentioned the loss without explaining it, while Wisden ended its match report of the Surrey game with its trusty formula in such cases: "... Gilbert, about whose subsequent disappearance from cricket there is no need to speak."

At the start of that fatal 1886 season, in addition to being hired as a professional by his old county, Gilbert acquired another engagement, as a professional with the East Gloucestershire club, whose home ground was at Cheltenham. On 4 and 5 June, the club acted as host to the Stroud eleven. On the opening day Gilbert bowled effectively but did not bat. On the second day he arrived at the ground at midday and entered the pavilion. Believing himself to be unobserved, he began rifling the pockets of the coats hung there and was caught in the act. Although the match proceeded,

> Gilbert's name was completely expunged from the scorecard as reproduced in the press. In one version his wickets are credited to "Smith" and only ten players listed in the side, while another report also has "Smith" bowling, but adds that "Mr E.L.Even did not bat".

On Monday, 7 June, the first day of the Sussex-Gloucestershire match at Hove, for which Gilbert had been selected, his place was taken by one C.H. Magretts, whose only first-class game this proved to be. Gilbert was otherwise engaged, at Cheltenham Police Court, charged with stealing a half-sovereign and a shilling. It was stated in court that several sums had been reported missing from the pockets of members' clothes in the committee room, and that on the day in question a detective had been set to keep watch. Giving evidence, the detective said that he had seen Gilbert take the money from the pocket of a

Captain Willes, the club secretary. On being challenged Gilbert had produced the half-sovereign, which had been marked. He then pleaded guilty to the charge and was sentenced to twenty-eight days' hard labour. Then came the second trial and sentence, at the hands of the family, who, no doubt recalling John Stuart Mill's observation that the Empire was a "vast system of outdoor relief for the upper classes", and perhaps taking a hint from the Cecils, who had wasted no time in despatching one of their younger sons, Cecil Balfour, to Australia after some fuss about a forged cheque, banished the unfortunate man to Canada on the understanding that he never came back. Nor did he. The only uplifting aspect of a sorry story is that once away from the scene of his microscopic misdemeanour Gilbert proceeded, in the phrase of his day, to make good, working for many years at the Land Titles Office in Calgary, and becoming one of Canada's outstanding cricketers. His son died while flying for the R.F.C. in the Great War, and his three daughters also served, in the Army Medical Corps. No breath of scandal or disgrace ever attached to Gilbert's thirty-eight years of exile, nor was there found to be even one square inch missing from the Land Titles Office when Gilbert finally retired from it. No wonder that those responsible for this act of appalling cruelty went to such fatuous lengths to keep its details a secret.

CHAPTER VII

BERTIE'S FATHER

The Graces, although by no means products of the fashionable public schools, were in the social sense natural amateurs. They were raised in warm, comfortable houses, born into respectable professions, and never failed to justify their status as leaders in county life by responding readily to cries for help from the needy over a wide area. Henry Grace would think nothing of being in the saddle all day, covering an area six miles in any direction from his home. The Graces were, as the saying goes, pillars of the community. But they did not represent the whole of the cricketing community, any more than did the grandees at Lord's or the landowning gentlemen who presided over and often subsidised the growing caucus of county clubs. There existed also a thriving population of two or three hundred professionals, hired hands whose elite played for the first-class counties, and whose skills matched and often surpassed those of their so-called betters. What of their lives? What of their living conditions, their financial standing, their prospects once they became too old for the rigours of the game? Wisden's obituary columns over the years are spattered with pietistic dying falls like: "Of the hardships that attended his last days there is no need to speak", or "sadly, his later years were blighted by misfortune". All over England young professionals who had been plucked from mine or factory, farm or smithy, by some discerning talent hunter, enjoyed their best years in the sun, and then returned to their former modest status. The more fortunate became publicans or small businessmen, but the slow slide into poverty became an all too frequent pattern. The picture which forms of the Victorian professional cricketer is necessarily speculative, for unlike their more formally educated colleagues they were unlikely either to write down their recollections or to attract the attention of some dedicated Boswell. On the rare occasions when we are able to muster a rounded portrait of one of these men, it is only because extraordinary circumstances apply. Considering the priceless value to the historian of any such rounded portrait, it seems surprising that closer attention has not been paid to the Victorian cricketer about whose private life more is known than of any other cricketer of the century, and certainly more than we could ever hope to know of Dr Grace.

Joseph Wells could claim the distinction of being among the oldest inhabitants of the Records section of Wisden. Like J. Grundy, Out, handled the ball in 1857; and E. Hinkly, V.E. Walker and John Wisden himself, all of whom took ten wickets in an innings, Joseph's one great moment of glory actually predates the almanack. He was born in 1827 in a tied cottage on the Penshurst Place estate where his father was employed as head gardener, a position which carried with it a certain prestige among the hundred or more servants attending the extensive needs of the Baron De Lisle. To be head gardener on a great estate was to have achieved as much worldly success as any countryman could hope for who had been born in the shadow of the great semi-feudal aristocracy of the day, and he was able to use what little influence he had to procure for his son a start in life similar to his own, as an under-gardener on the adjoining estate. But young Joe had neither his father's dedication, nor any of his passion for horticulture. Instead, every summer evening, the moment his duties were done, he would race the mile separating his employer's gardens from the Penshurst cricket field, snatching some brief practice before the gathering dusk began to obscure the outlines of the ball. As he grew to manhood, Joe moved on from job to job, always relegating his work to second place behind cricket. Between 1847 and 1855 he had six masters and appears to have walked out on all of them. It was the fifth of these posts, in the two years from 1851 to 1853, which forget the first link in the chain of events which was to endow him with a peculiar sort of immortality. The estate was Uppark in Sussex, tucked away behind a fold in the downs, and presided over by one of the oddest matriarchs in the kingdom, an ancient widow called Lady Fetherstonhaugh. As an eighteen-year-old dairymaid on the estate, she had accepted the hand in marriage of her employer, a septuagenarian rake who in younger days had introduced Emma Hamilton to a few of the minor pleasures of life. The whole countryside was scandalised by the alliance and stupefied by its success, which lasted for twenty years before the dairymaid buried her ninety-two-year-old swain and settled down to a life of seclusion, surrounded by a few faithful retainers and shunned by the county. Her unmarried sister lived with her as companion, and it was this sister who engaged a lady's maid called Sarah Neal, who had been at Uppark for a year when Joe arrived and soon began courting her.

By the end of 1852 Joe was addressing Sarah as "My own, my dearest", and after a series of crises culminating in the death of Sarah's mother and the departure of both the lovers from Uppark, they were married in November 1853. It was Joe's misfortune to have chosen as his life's companion the most uncongenial of partners, a born misery, a solemn godfearing pessimist whose grumbling piety was informed by the very best intentions and produced the most catastrophic results. Joe and Sarah represented opposing poles of the human condition. She trudged doggedly through a vale of tears, he did his best to follow his inclinations and eat, drink and be as merry as the fates allowed.

After a series of disasters and half-starts, the pair of them were misguided enough to invest their small capital in the proprietorship of a dingy chinaware shop in Bromley High Street. They lived on the premises in near-barbaric conditions and very soon came to see their pathetic enterprise as a prison from which there was no escape. By adding to the cheap cups and plates a selection of bats and balls, Joe contrived to bring the one great passion of his life a little closer to the daily drudgery, almost as though a well-oiled bat among the crockery might, by some unspecified process of spiritual osmosis, mitigate his predicament and bestow a state of grace on his wretched existence. Joe loved only cricket, which is hardly surprising. It was only on the cricket field that he could take his place as a man respected among men, and a virtuoso performer. Joe Wells the shopkeeper was a harassed, henpecked, disenchanted man beset by petty debt and bug-ridden squalor. Joe Wells the cricketer, on the other hand, was famous around the county and, once he had performed his record-breaking feat of 1862, even celebrated beyond its boundaries.

Sarah's reaction to all this was inexplicable. A resolute cricket-loather, her detestation of the game became positively paranoic once Joe had become widely renowned. Instead of grasping at the straw of a professional player's income, she execrated his time-wasting and bemoaned her fate at being tied to a wastrel who would not or could not take retail trade seriously. When Joe's reputation earned him the post of cricket coach at Norwich Grammar School and he absented himself from his own life for three months every summer, it seemed to him that perhaps the prison gates were inching open. Meanwhile Sarah, left behind in the shop to sell bats and balls to visiting cricketers, found the irony almost too painful to bear and began fretting at the additional debts piling up through the purchase of Joe's sporting goods. On 29 August 1863, she confided to her diary:

When her beloved small daughter died, Sarah repaired the breached sexual association with Joe in the hope that God would supply her with a replacement daughter. Instead Joe gave her another son, the Bertie who later recorded all the details of his father's life in such loving detail. In 1877 came the greatest disaster in Joe's life since his marriage to Sarah. One Sunday morning he began pruning the grape-vine, fell and suffered a compound fracture of the thigh-bone. The injury left him lame, which meant that he was cut off for ever from cricket and from the supplementary income it provided.

Soon the Atlas House enterprise collapsed, and with it the marriage. Sarah rushed for sanctuary back to Uppark, where she bumbled her way through her housekeeping duties until 1893, when she was dismissed for hopeless incompetence just in time for one of her sons to rescue her and provide her at last with what she had been yearning for all her life, a tiny crumb of material security which, with her obdurate faith, she mistook for the hand of God. Joe, meanwhile was pensioned off with a small weekly sum and went to live in a tiny cottage about three miles from Uppark. According to young Bertie, "He had relinquished the idea of earning anything, modestly but firmly". It was young Bertie who rescued him and reunited his parents by renting for them a small house at Liss. In 1905 Sarah slipped and fell downstairs, suffering internal injuries from which she died a few days later. Here is Bertie on Joseph's death.

> In 1910 my father woke up very briskly one morning, delivered a careful instruction on the proper way to make suet pudding to his housekeeper, Mrs Smith, insisted that it should be chopped small, protested against "lumps the size of my thumb", glanced over the *Daily Chronicle* she had brought him and prepared to get up. He put his legs out of bed and slid down by the side of the bed a dead man.

It is from young Bertie that we gather the information vital to the rounding out of the portrait of this cheerful professional cricketer. We learn that as he grew older he read a great deal, that he borrowed books from local libraries and picked up secondhand volumes at local sales, that he had a mind of "inappeaseable freshness", that as an old man he borrowed Bertie's old schoolbooks and set himself successfully to master algebra and the elements of Euclidean geometry, taking his studies as far as quadratic equations before retiring from the field, that he possessed "all the delicate and nervous muscular skill and the rapid conscious mental subtleties of a cricketer", that he had a countryman's deep insight into the nature of everything from a wagtail or a kingfisher to a trout or a crop of mushrooms. One bank holiday Joe felt the sudden urge to rediscover the scenes of his boyhood happiness, so he and Bertie set off back to Penshurst:

> We walked across the park from Tonbridge. He wanted me to see and feel the open life he had led before the shop and failure had caught him. He wanted to see and feel it again himself. "We used to play cricket here – well, it was just about here anyhow – until we lost sight of the ball in the twilight …". All his days my father was a happy and appreciative man with a singular distaste for contention or holding his own in the world. He liked to do clever things with his brain and hands and body, but he was bored beyond endurance by the idea of a continual struggle for existence.

There has survived a photographic portrait of Joseph in his later years, and it is quite clear from the easeful, relaxed pose that he has survived all the crises, weathered all the storms, laughed off mercantile failure and mockery of a marriage, and come safely home to harbour. Nature has played its hackneyed joke of transferring all his hair from his scalp to his chin, but the face is unlined, and in the eyes there is a friendly glow, as though looking in the general direction of leg slip he has seen there something to tickle his fancy. He wears a clean white collar and a dark cravat over a dark shirt, striped double-breasted waistcoat and wide-lapelled jacket to match. No doubt beyond the photographer's frame there lurks a pair of stout black boots. He looks comfortably spruce, a man well able to cope with any small problem which might appear, and buttressed, we suspect by the heartwarming fact that one of his sons, the wayward one, his favourite, has become one of the world's most famous men.

The photograph corroborates Bertie's impression of a healthy vigorous man who loves the outdoor life and the playing of games, an engaging sort whose tragedy was to fall in love with the wrong woman, to become ensnared by uncongenial domestic responsibilities, who was lamed in an accident, and who came at last to that comparatively happy ending in whose imminence he seems always to have believed. A very different picture emerges from the testimony of one of his grandchildren, who believed that the fall from the grape-vine was no accident, that it was an attempt at suicide brought on by unalloyed despair at the hopelessness of his situation, and that the failure to end it all obliged him to pick up the shattered pieces of his life and find a new kind of existence. As proof he nominates two famous novels which Bertie published, *The History of Mr Polly*, which

The improvident professional cricketer Joseph Wells, who fathered a prolific novelist.

first appeared in 1910, the year of Joe's death, and *The New Machiavelli*, in 1911. In *The New Machiavelli* the family return from church one Sunday morning to find the father of the house lying dead in the yard, having broken his neck while attending to the grape-vine. In *The History of Mr Polly*, our hero makes an unsuccessful attempt to kill himself while nonetheless convincing everyone that he is dead; in this way he flees from the drudgery of his shopkeeping life into a new free chapter as a wandering odd-job man. It seems likely that Polly is a composite portrait of old Joseph and one of his sons, who went with him to the cottage and determined to make a living as a watch and clock pedlar and repairer. Whatever the truth, there is no question that for the rest of his long life Bertie never lost his deep love for his sporting father, to say nothing of a schoolboyish pride in his feats as a cricketer. Here is that useful medium-pace right-arm bowler Pelham Grenville Wodehouse writing in 1932:

> I like Wells. An odd bird though. The first time I met him, we had barely finished the initial pip-pippings when he said, apropos of nothing: "My father was a professional cricketer". If there's a good answer to that, you tell me.

It is surprising that Wodehouse should have been so baffled. All that Bertie was doing was indulging in a little pardonable filial pride at the thought of what his father had been. It is not every famous novelist's father who achieves what Joseph Wells did at Brighton on a summer day in 1862, when, in a match between Sussex and Kent, he became the first cricketer in history to dismiss four batsmen with four consecutive balls.

CHAPTER VIII

MIDWINTER MADNESS

——•——

J oseph Wells represents a certain familiar ideal of the professional cricketer of his day, but it was not the only ideal. A humble gardener's boy with an inborn gift for the game but with no burning social ambition, Wells and his kind must have been a godsend to emergent county clubs looking for competence at cut-price rates. But there were other professionals, shrewder, more mercenary, altogether more worldly characters with the aim of rising through the ranks to some sort of modest independence. As the network of county clubs steadily eroded the territory available to the barnstorming elevens of Grace's boyhood, the balance of power, which had rested with hardened player-managers like Clarke, Lillywhite and Wisden, began to swing back to the gentleman-athlete, making the more acquisitive professional determined to strike the best bargain available in return for representing his county. At first the Gloucestershire club committee had no need to bother with such irksome problems. The sides it fielded were exclusively amateur, friendly groups of country gentlemen who loved to play and were well enough placed economically to indulge their tastes. Early histories of the county name a man called Hill as the first professional ever to play for Gloucestershire, but although in strict chronological terms he deserves his place, there is no question that the first professional to wield any influence at the club, and to establish the precedent of professionalism in the county, was a man so widely divergent in every way from the humble countryman Joseph Wells that, in examining the lives of the two men, it is hard to believe that they lived at the same time on the same planet. But before tracing the convoluted history of Gloucestershire's first famous professional, the need arises to pick up a neglected thread. It is time to return to that bright morning so full of promise in 1770 when Captain James Cook took the frigate *Endeavour* into Botany Bay.

Ever since that pregnant imperial moment, historians have differed as to exactly what the good captain was doing there. The swiftly waning utility of the American colonies as a rubbish dump for criminals meant that extensive new dumps would have to be found. But the British government was also aware of the trading advantages likely to accrue from a mercantile fortress in the eastern seas. Whether Captain Cook was given his sailing orders for both reasons or for neither is pure guesswork, but whatever the intention, events moved quickly once he had dropped anchor and claimed the continent for the British. By 1786 London had decided to send out settlers to what the modern mind thinks of as New South Wales. Two years later colonisation began. The export trade in felons was brisk, petty crime being one of the great growth industries of the Industrial Revolution. By 1830 more than fifty thousand convicted criminals had been dumped on the shores of the new land, including more than eight thousand women and girls. All these unfortunates were either employed by the government in the building of homes, roads and bridges, or assigned to private employers. As time passed, pardons became more frequent and the "ticket-of-leave man" blossomed into one of the stock characters of Empire, soon to be immortalised in the lowering bulk of Abel Magwitch in *Great Expectations*. The convict element provided useful cheap labour to the economy of a raw new colony which was also being settled by ordinary folk from Britain hoping to find a more lucrative market for their talents. As pardons were granted, and respectable immigrants began employing ex-convict footmen, butlers and workhands, so the lines of demarcation became blurred. By mid-century the export of convicts, which had swelled the local population by more than 150,000, was discontinued; long before then, the embryonic new society, moving with astonishing pace, had reached a modest plateau of sophistication whose diversions included the playing of cricket matches. The *Sydney Gazette*, on 8 January 1804, reported:

> The late intense weather has been very favourable to the amateurs of Cricket, who have scarcely lost a day for the last month. The frequent immoderate heats might have been considered inimical to the amusement, but were productive of very opposite consequences, as the state of the atmosphere might always regulate the portion of exercise necessary to the ends this elaborate diversion was originally intended to answer.

A generation later the same newspaper, still following its journalistic policy of impenetrable prolixity, went much further by taking the view propagated in England by Mary Russell Mitford, and later on by George Meredith, that expertise on the cricket field was an indispensable weapon in the lover's armoury:

> Cricket is now the prevailing amusement of the day. Let no man henceforth set up for sporting character whose name is not enrolled among the "gentlemen cricketers" of Sydney. Let no adoring swain hereafter think to "dangle at a lady's apron string" or "feast upon the smiles from partial beauty won", unless he can boast of excellence in handling a bat, or sending up a ball – the former will reject his company, the latter his addresses. Hyde Park is now almost daily graced by the aspiring youth of Sydney practising their favourite recreation, and respectable females looking on to enliven the scene. A new club has been formed

in addition to the one before existing, and we expect that New South Wales will soon be able to boast players that might bear away the palm of victory even at Lord's.

How had the colonists managed it? How had they contrived, within a single generation, to move from barren strands to so refined and delicately balanced a social organism as a game of cricket? Perhaps the most convenient way of explaining is to follow the progress of a family whose fluctuating fortunes qualify its members as archetypes of the emergent Australia.

In 1799, Edward Spencer Wills, younger son of an English county family, chafing at the constraints of the system of primogeniture which encouraged the eldest son alone to live a life of self-indulgence, decided to go to Australia to seek his fortune. Like many of his contemporaries he rapidly succeeded, by setting up as a merchant in Sydney. But the effort seems to have been too much for him, for in 1811 he died aged only 32, leaving a widow to cope as best she could with the raising of six small children. A year later the resourceful relict remarried, the lucky man being George Howe, editor of that same *Sydney Gazette* whose feature articles so ingeniously stretched the resources of the mother tongue to the very limits of verbosity. Further intimations of the younger-son syndrome became apparent when the fifteen-year-old Horatio, evidently driven half-mad by the journalistic excesses of his stepfather, began behaving like a conventional hero of popular fiction by running away to sea, experiencing adventures so excessively romantic that somebody among his descendants should have recited them to Robert Louis Stevenson, who would surely have incorporated them into *Island Night's Entertainment*. The ship carrying young Wills foundered off the Marquesas, and before long the survivors were in danger of losing their lives. According to the story Wills later told, he was saved only by the intercession of a local princess who, mistaking him for a gentleman, took him under her protection. Finally he managed to work his passage back to Sydney, where his sudden irruption into the bosom of the family greatly shocked its members, who had long since given him up for dead. His stepfather, still dispensing orotundities for a living, gave the prodigal a job at *The Gazette*. By the time he was twenty-one Horatio had married one Elizabeth Wyre and had set up house with her not far from Canberra. It was here, in August 1835, that they celebrated the birth of a son, Thomas.

Thomas's father, having had previous experience of the charms of travel, began to hunger for them once more, and when Thomas was four the whole family, which by now incorporated five thousand sheep and five hundred head of cattle, followed the current trend and moved south across the Murray River into what would, within a few years, become the state of Victoria. In 1840 the Wills family settled at a location which Horatio, who all his life laboured under the pathetic delusion that he was a man of religious sensibilities, called Ararat, in deference to his own superstitions rather than those of the local inhabitants, whose sad fate it was to be elbowed out of the way unheeded. This attitude of the Wills family, Horatio in particular, to the genuine Australians, was to have

Cricket at Melbourne in 1841. The Melbourne Cricket Ground was established in 1856, and the first Test between England and Australia was played there in 1877. The present ground is the largest in the world, with a capacity of 130,000.

profound effects, although there remains some conflict as to what Horatio's convictions really were. One respectable history of the emergent years of Australian cricket claims that Horatio "won the respect of local Aborigines". However, the admirably researched *Cricket Walkabout*, compiled by two zealous academics called Mulvaney and Harcourt, has this to say of the pietistic Mr Wills:

> Wills claimed to have established friendly relations with Aborigines near Mount William, where he settled around 1840. This certainly appears to have been the case. On the other hand, when it was proposed, in 1842, to establish an Aborigine Protectorate station on good land adjacent to his run, he protested to Lieutenant-Governor La Trobe in a manner which revealed stark self-interest and prejudice which was the norm even for benevolent settlers.

Although within the state of Victoria before 1850 dozens of settlers and hundreds of natives were killed in the intermittent war between them, Horatio proceeded on his way with all the aplomb of the perfect pioneer, confident and self-satisfied. As part of an idyllic childhood, young Tom took part in regular cricket matches, greatly encouraged by his father who, in 1852, took the course of action which goes far to explain how the new nation was to assimilate the intricacies of cricket in so short a time. Tom was sent to an English public school, Rugby naturally, where for four years he performed indifferently in the classroom and heroically on the playing field, ending his time there as captain of cricket and rugby football. He then moved on to Magdalene College, Cambridge. That is to say he enrolled without ever taking up residence, a contradiction which does not seem to have proved an impediment when it came to representing the university in the match against Oxford. At the end of 1856 Tom returned home to find that by the standards of physical fitness to which he had become accustomed on the playing fields of Rugby School, the local cricketers, having taken no real exercise in the winter, were in no condition to do their best. Tom now put his mind to the invention of a game which would keep the cricketers in condition through the winter without endangering their health in the process, as he had come to fear that Rugby Union might do. The result was a new game called Australian Rules Football, and it would have surprised Tom to be told that it was this invention of his, rather than his pioneering efforts on behalf of Australian cricket, which have caused him to be remembered. But even as Tom was pretending to study Livy at Rugby, the event was taking place which was to transform life in the colony and to bring about some violent adjustments to the family life of the Wills. In 1851 gold was discovered, first at a place called Clunes, then at Warrendyte, and finally at Ballarat, soon to become the focus of international interest as the world's richest surface goldfield.

The effect on Australian life, and particularly on the lives of those living in Victoria, was extraordinary. Virtually overnight, normal concourse was disrupted, business abandoned, families sundered, sobriety discarded, morality set aside, as what seemed like the entire population stampeded for the fleshpots of Ballarat.

> Within three weeks Melbourne, Geelong and Williamstown were emptied of most of their male population. Streets that had been crowded by drays were deserted. Farmers left their properties, professional men walked out of their rooms, and teachers abandoned their schools, which had to close. Ships in Port Philip Bay were left without crews, even their masters heading for the goldfield.

One of the incidental effects of this crazy flight was that Horatio Wills found himself without employees, and decided that it might be prudent to move on to Queensland. What followed has been described by a cricket reporter called Hammersley, although the heroic light in which he frames Tommy Wills has much to do with the close friendship between them. When Tommy sailed home from England in 1855, one of the other homecomers was Hammersley, and the two young men had quickly forged the foundations of a lasting friendship. It was Hammersley who was to hand over to Tommy the captaincy of the Victoria state side, Hammersley again who was to assist at the birth of Australian Rules Football. Here is his account of the fate awaiting Horatio in Queensland:

> A finer young man never donned the flannels than young Tom Wills. He was a very peculiar man, rather taciturn, but very good-natured and a very general favourite. I knew his father and mother well, the latter a most kind, affectionate mother to him, and I spent some pleasant days with Tommy on their estate at Point Henry, near Geelong, where we used to shoot ducks and quails. The old gentleman was a shrewd man of business, and looked well after Tommy, and it may be remembered how he and all his party, some 14 or 15 persons, were killed by the blacks on his station. Tom Wills has frequently told me that he never trusted the natives, but always carried two six-shooters and often warned "the governor" to do the same, but the old man prided himself on being able to manage the blacks from his experience of them in Victoria, and said they would never harm him. But one night they slaughtered the whole party at the camp, women and all. It may be remembered what a fearful slaughter of the blacks took place after this massacre, but the particulars as related are too sickening for recital.

Mulvaney and Harcourt refer to the massacre as "the greatest killing of white men by black men in Australian history", but then make the point that "white retaliations soon accounted for more than three times that number of lives". The account goes on to describe how Tommy escaped with his life only because he was away collecting stores two days travel down the track. After the tragedy, Tommy sought police protection but stayed on as station manager before returning to Victoria in 1864. In the light of this shocking story, it says much for Tommy's love of cricket that, when it dawned on the administrators of Australian cricket that there were other, less warlike games at which the Aborigine was adept, Tommy took over responsibility for the first Aborigine side, coaching them, playing alongside them, and espousing their sporting cause in a number of ways. Although by the time of the historic 1868 Aborigine tour of England Tommy's commitment had waned, there is no question of the quality of his pioneering work with the native cricketers. If he had survived for long enough to read Harry Altham's history of cricket, a work carrying an air of very nearly biblical authority, he would have been bewildered by the author's failure to make any reference to the tour, and his insistence on describing the white tourists of 1878 as the first ever to come to England.

Tommy became the first fluent all-rounder in Australian cricket, a bowler who could deliver slow, medium or fast, a magnificent thrower from the deep field, and a batsman whose style was ugly but effective. Like many of his contemporaries, Tommy drank heavily, and was essentially the outdoor type rather than a man capable of or interested in acquiring administrative talents. When he was appointed Secretary of Melbourne Cricket Club, he lasted for just one season.

> When he left office everything was in a muddle – club papers, books, cricket balls, cricket guides, Zingari flannels, cigars, spiked boots, everything one can conceive, stuffed together in the large tin box of the club. A most untidy mortal he was, and quite unfit for such work. His end was a sad one. He was attacked with softening of the brain, induced by his not taking care of himself which he should have done, and gradually became irresponsible for his actions, and in a fit of frenzy stabbed himself in the left side with a pair of scissors he snatched from the table. He sleeps quietly in the cemetery at Heidelberg, about 8 miles from Melbourne.

Tommy Wills played his last game in 1869 and died in the asylum eleven years later, which means that his life, if not his career, certainly overlaps that of one of Australia's great professionals, and a man whose fate, like Tommy's, was resolved by events beyond his control. The mad dash for Ballarat which had emptied the streets and shops of Melbourne by no means confined its influence to the colony. The sensational news that there was gold for the taking sent shock waves across the world, and among the distant backwaters to feel the reverberations was a hamlet inside the frontiers of the Graces' home county.

In the village of St Briavels, in the Forest of Dean, there lived a labourer called William John Midwinter, whose wife Rebecca presented him, on 19 July 1853, with a son christened William Evans Midwinter. Young Billy appears to have been a most unusual man, delightfully devious, the flower of a long line of dissimulators whose movements from county to county and from continent to continent form a bewildering but perhaps not altogether unusual Victorian mosaic. His father, finding himself unemployed, soon moved the family east to Cirencester in the vain hope of finding work, and by 1861 was reduced to the desperate gamble of emigrating to Australia with the intention of striking it rich at Ballarat. The pathos of the flight, preserved in all its sentimental appeal in Ford Madox Brown's "The Last of England", was underlined in the case of the Midwinters by their failure to find any gold. Before long, his hope of riches beyond the dreams of avarice having melted away, William Midwinter settled in the small town of Sandhurst, where he became the proprietor of the local butcher's shop. It was here that Billy formed his lifelong friendship with another

The Aboriginal touring side of 1868, the first team to visit England from overseas. Their star player was Johnny Mullagh.

famous hero of the early days of Australian cricket, Harry Boyle.

The two boys laid out a pitch, practised assiduously, and quickly blossomed into two of the likeliest young players in the Melbourne district. It was there that Billy's path must first have crossed that of W.G. Grace, on Boxing Day 1873, where the honeymoon tourists played their first match, against Eighteen of

Melbourne. Billy Midwinter did little in the match to attract Grace's attention, scoring only seven before being caught by Arthur Bush, W.G.'s best man, off the bowling of the bridegroom. It was not until the return match three months later that he made his presence felt. Amid scenes of wild excitement, he clean bowled W.G. and his brother Fred, playing a prominent part in an honourable draw. By this time Billy Midwinter had grown into an impressive figure, standing six feet two-and-a-half inches, weighing fourteen stone, and recognised as one of the best quarter-milers in the state, a good shot and a skilled billiards player. There was one other vital fact about Billy which Grace must have stumbled on in the course of his cricketing honeymoon, a fact which nobody then or for many years after seemed able to grasp. He had indeed been born in Gloucester-shire. In defiance of widespread confu-

The remarkable Billy Midwinter, the first intercontinental cricketer, who played for both England and Australia.

sion surrounding his place of birth, embracing theories about Yorkshire, Canada and Australia, Midwinter was as authentic a West-Countryman as the Graces themselves, notwithstanding the evident scepticism of the editors of Wisden who were soon to refer to him with magisterial stuffiness as someone "who is stated to be Gloucestershire born". For a century after the events of the 1873-74 tour there was a tendency to assume that, in accepting Midwinter's Gloucestershire credentials, Grace, understandably keen to recruit so talented a cricketer, had been guilty of disingenuousness. But Midwinter was the genuine article, and evidently some kind of arrangement was reached during the tour that if and when Midwinter should ever decide to play in his native land, it would be as a Gloucestershire cricketer. It evidently never entered Grace's head that in committing himself to such a pact he might be involving himself with a temperament more serpentine even than his own.

Midwinter duly arrived in England in time for the start of the 1877 season, bringing with him the prestige of having represented Australia against England in the previous year. Of the comic chaos which Midwinter's unheralded arrival was to bring about, much has since been written, none of which remotely does justice to the impudent brilliance and originality of the new recruit's improvisations. The 1877 season drew to a close and the cast now began to assemble for one of the great slapstick extravaganzas of cricket history.

Knowing, as he alone did, what ordeals the drama must hold in store for him, it would be interesting to know if, during that first season, Billy Midwinter ever had misgivings about his predicament, whether in the alien darkness of some county hotel bedroom he ever awoke suddenly with the beads of perspiration standing out on a troubled brow, whether in a contemplative moment in some quiet taproom corner, detached from the clanking tankards and brassy laughter of his team-mates, he ever had pangs of conscience, whether in gazing idly through the carriage windows of the Great Western Railway train watching the vivid light of the Cotswold summer falling away behind him he ever contemplated the practicality of jumping into a hansom at Paddington and finding blessed anonymity among the city's five million inhabitants. Probably not. Midwinter in his prime, before tragedy so casually brushed him aside, was a phlegmatic character whose calm confidence in his own indestructibility inclined him to let tomorrow take care of itself.

At the start of the 1878 season a party of Australian tourists arrived in England, comprising a cricket team and a great deal of that animosity which had been carefully stored away after the honeymoon tour. This success in preserving intact a hard core of malevolence had been due largely to the efforts of the manager of the tourists, John Conway, and his captain, the bearded David Gregory, whose appearance was so swarthy that he was taken for a kind of honorary Aborigine. The British at this time seem to have been wonderfully vague about the citizens of their Empire, and assumed that Conway's tourists comprised a collection of freaks:

> The team went straight from Liverpool by train to Nottingham, where a huge crowd, including the sheriff, local aldermen and noted cricketers, greeted them as they stepped on to the platform. Murdoch and Spofforth, who had been sleeping at the back of the train, slipped out unnoticed and mingled with the crowd. One burly bare-armed man wearing a blacksmith's leather apron exclaimed, "Well, I'm damned! They aren't black after all. If I'd knowed, I wunna come". Dave Gregory then alighted from the train and the man studied his black beard and skin browned by the Australian sun. 'Ah, 'ere's one's a 'arf-caste any 'ow," he commented.

In those days, when the sea voyage from Australia took six to eight weeks, it was considered an impressive feat to have survived the trip at all, let alone to be in a fit state to play cricket at the end of it. Only four years after Gregory's historic victory the *S.S. Peshawur* set sail for Australia with an England side on board, with the most hair-raising consequences. On the voyage out the ship collided with another, causing an injury to the fast bowler Fred Morley which smashed his ribs, eliminated him from most of the tour, and eventually led to his early death. And even if an Englishman did contrive to survive the rigours of such a journey, was there not a very real chance of his being eaten alive the moment he landed? It is certainly true that on the eve of the arrival of Conway's party, the President of the Cambridge University Cricket Club was under the impression that all the visitors would prove to have black skins. Others, unhampered by the advantages of a Victorian university education, were better informed, and knew perfectly well that Australia, so far from being short of white settlers, was positively bristling with them, drawn exclusively from the criminal classes, and whose Australian credentials were an unimpeachable testimonial to their prowess as homicidal lunatics. As late as 1849 the government of Lord John Russell had most generously sent, absolutely free of charge, a boatload of convicts to Melbourne. The town's inhabitants, insisting that a civilised township was no place to dump felons, and thereby implying that civilised townships can usually be relied upon to have plenty of felons of their own, had the whole consignment moved on to Brisbane, an action which unkindly hinted that Brisbane was clearly not a civilised township. No doubt in 1878 there remained people in the motherland convinced that all Australians were direct descendants of Bill Sikes, accustomed to whiling away the long pacific summers by slaughtering, dismembering and digesting each other. Dickens was still not long dead, and English perceptions of Australia may have had less to do with Gregory and his teammates than with Pip's of Magwitch, of whom he says "The abhorrence in which I held the man, the dread I had of him, the repugnance with which I shrank from him, could not have been exceeded if he had been some terrible beast". As the Reverend Arthur Ward said to the England cricketer A.G. Steel on hearing that Steel was soon to play against Gregory's men, "I hear you're going to play against the niggers on Monday", the joke being compounded by the presence at Steel's side when the remark was made of Gregory's ace bowler, Fred Spofforth. Certainly to the English batsman facing him for the first time, the demonic Spofforth may well have seemed like the very embodiment of Magwitch's malevolence on the Kentish marshes.

But the most succulent confusion of all was the one surrounding Midwinter's precise status as the 1878 season opened. He was by now a contracted Gloucestershire professional. But when later Conway and Gregory claimed that Midwinter had assigned his services to the tourists for that season, it seems likely that they were being perfectly truthful, and that Midwinter had pledged his services to two opposed masters. For a few weeks the crisis was averted, because in those days the Gloucestershire county programme did not begin until June. It so happened that on the day of the club's first fixture, 20 June, Australia was due to return to Lord's for the first time since the sensational victory over MCC. The whole of sporting London was eager to see whether that victory had been a fluke, or if the tourists could repeat it. Gregory picked his strongest side. Naturally it included Midwinter. But Grace, preparing for the match against Surrey at the Oval, also picked his strongest side. Naturally it included Midwinter. The championship campaign was about to open, the comic dance to begin, and Billy Midwinter's chickens to start coming home to roost.

With the sun beaming down on Lord's from a cloudless sky, Gregory's side prepared to bat, and before long their opening pair, Midwinter and Charles Bannerman, were sitting in the pavilion padded up and ready to start the innings. It has never been very clear exactly how far Midwinter hoped to carry his duplicity, but he could hardly have taken it much further than this. Grace had selected him for the side to play Surrey at the Oval. Gregory had selected him for the side to play Middlesex at Lord's. Midwinter had evidently decided on Lord's, and as he sat, padded up, bat in gloved hands, it must have seemed to him that his policy of bare-faced deception had succeeded after all. Of course there would be the wrath to come, but by then surely all the factions involved would be too inhibited by the consciousness of a fait accompli to make any serious attempts at retribution. The sun was shining, a game of cricket was about to begin, two sets of fees, one from Grace, the other from Conway, were in his pocket, life was indeed a pleasant affair. The susurrus of an expectant crowd wafted through the windows as Midwinter prepared to do battle. But had the seismograph of his conscience, never a very precise instrument at the best of times, been sensitive enough to register signs of the gathering storm, his contemplation of the serene St John's Wood skyline might not have been so composed.

Away to the south-east, at Kennington Oval, Grace was mustering his forces, only to discover that there were not quite enough forces to muster. The missing element was of course Midwinter, and it is one of the more revealing aspects of the affair that once having confirmed Midwinter's absence form the ranks Grace knew exactly where to find him. Instantly mustering a raiding party consisting of himself, his brother E.M., and his wicketkeeper Arthur Bush, Grace called a cab and set out for Lord's, where on arrrival he dashed into the Australian dressing-room and ''persuaded'' Midwinter, pads and all, to return with him to Kennington. No sooner had the Gloucestershire party turned for the race back to the Oval than Conway and Gregory were after them in a second cab.

In London that evening there were to be a fireworks display at the Crystal Palace, as well as the rather more demanding pyrotechnics in the centre of town where, at the Royal Opera House, just round the corner from the bedsitters of the Australian side, Madame Patti was singing *Aida*. Henry Irving would be holding the stage at the Lyceum in some melodrama too footling to distract any attention from him. For those disinclined to pass the day in contemplation of Grace's batting technique, there was the opportunity to see, and be seen at, the Grosvenor Gallery Summer Exhibition, while for those for whom exposure to the fine arts was too rigorous an exercise on a warm day, there was always the new painting by Mr Millais, ''The Bride of Lammermoor'', on show at the St James Gallery at a shilling a throw. Up in the far north the Queen was bravely preparing for the ordeal of transferring her black bombazine life from Balmoral to Windsor, and both she and Dr Grace, as they journeyed south and east respectively, the one from castle to castle, the other from pavilion to pavilion, would be sure to pass hoardings advising prospective customers that ''Bunter's Nervine gives instant relief for toothache'', unaware that they were gazing at the inspiration for the most famous fictitious schoolboy of the next century. It was

Ascot Week. In a few days Mr Disraeli would be packing his bags for the Congress of Berlin, and not long after his triumphal return Mr Hardy would publish his new novel, *The Return of the Native*.

Meanwhile a native of a different kind was being returned to the pastures of Kennington, although amid what recriminations we can never know. Sadly no hint of the conversational exchanges inside the Gloucestershire coach has come down to us. Did the impenitent Midwinter, hobbled by his pads, sit there stonewalling behind the defence of a stolid silence? Or did he shout genial colonial obscenities at his abductors? Was the Doctor laughing, or bellowing, or haranguing the driver and the horse in an anxious bid to retain his advantage of Conway and Gregory? The only possibility which seems wholly unlikely is that inside that swaying, racing carriage there was silence, for quite apart from what is known of the conversational gifts of W.G. when his enthusiasm was stimulated it is doubtful if there was ever silence in any enclosed space containing his older brother. Once the carriages unloaded their passengers outside the Oval ground, there were some heated exchanges until Grace, accusing his rivals of being "a damned lot of sneaks", swept self-righteously into the ground with Midwinter in tow. There followed a long epistolary campaign which finally sputtered out with a magisterial apology from Grace.

The confusions and contradictions of his allegiance having been resolved, at least for the moment, Midwinter continued to represent Gloucestershire. In 1880 he made his only century for the club and also took 73 wickets. His bowling form was equally good for the next two seasons. By now the Gloucestershire committee, realising how valuable an asset he was to the side, and all too mindful of his elusive nature, attempted to pin him down by offering him the sum of one hundred pounds, to be paid at the end of the 1893 season. The offer was made by letter signed by the secretary-treasurer, E.M. Grace, and Midwinter simply ignored it. A further letter was sent, and this time he replied in terms so fulsome that one might suspect him of sarcasm at the committee's expense. No doubt he thought he was in a position to be cavalier with the likes of the Graces. He had the liveliest of minds, and it was in 1880 at the very latest that he must have finally grasped the implications of the one great cricketing discovery of his life, the one which was to make so vast a contribution to the growth of international cricket and which, less than a hundred years later, was propping up the rickety facade of the County Championship.

The administrators of the game were no more able than the Graces to take Midwinter's measure. Although he had come to Bristol with the kudos of two Australian Test caps in his baggage, by 1881 the England selectors felt confident that he was English enough to represent the country of his birth. He did so four times in the 1881-82 tour of Australia, much to the chagrin of his old colleagues, whose reactions to his blatant disloyalty did not prevent them from welcoming him back into the Australian fold later in the decade. As this is by far the most blatant exhibition of the art of the turncoat in the entire history of cricket, and perhaps of all team games, and as one of its incidental effects was the notorious chase across London, it is hardly surprising that any other achievements which Midwinter might have claimed have been completely overlooked. To this day William Midwinter is remembered first as the man W.G. Grace abducted, and second as the artful dodger who danced rings round the administrators and law-makers of his time. Always on the look-out for the main chance, he seems to have cared nothing for such lofty sentiments as loyalty to club and country, remaining steadfast instead to that more pragmatic ideal, loyalty to oneself. Wisden records the awesome fact that his success in representing Australia against England twice in 1876 by no means inhibited him from then representing England against Australia four times in 1881, nor from then representing Australia against England on six further occasions between 1882 and 1886. Like the Graces and their cousin W.R.Gilbert, William Evans Midwinter was a card.

But neither the attempt to play in two different fixtures on the same day, nor the success in duping the selection committees of two bitterly opposed factions, can begin to compare with Midwinter's real stroke of genius, one so sublime as to transcend the merely sporting altogether and to soar up into the empyrean of metaphysical extravagance. For what this modest Victorian cricketer learned on his peregrinations across the sporting landscape of the nineteenth century was how to make time stand still.

Among his Victorian predecessors, Midwinter's only rival in the field had been the teenaged Charles Lutwidge Dodgson, who in 1847 had published a paper called "Where Does the Day Begin?". What was bothering Dodgson, just as it was one day to bother Joseph Wells' little boy Bertie, was the perception that time might after all be a moveable feast. Although young Dodgson was to grow into an implacable enemy of the game at which Midwinter excelled, his thoughts on the subject of time as it relates to place are nothing less than the reduction to textual absurdity of what Midwinter was soon to transform into stern practicalities. Here is Dodgson driving himself pleasurably mad:

> Half of the world, or nearly so, is always in the light of the sun; as the world turns round, this hemisphere of light shifts round too, and passes over each part of it in succession.
>
> Supposing on Tuesday it is morning in London; in another hour it would be Tuesday morning in the west of England. If the whole world were land we might go on tracing Tuesday morning, Tuesday morning all the way round till in twenty fours we got to London again. But we *KNOW* that at London twenty four hours after Tuesday morning it is Wednesday morning. Where, then, in its passage round the earth, does the day change its name? Where does it lose its identity?

Let us take Dodgson's second proposition, substituting for his hours and days the months and the seasons. The proportions are now transformed but the proposition remains intact:

> Supposing on Tuesday it is spring in London; in another day it would be spring

117

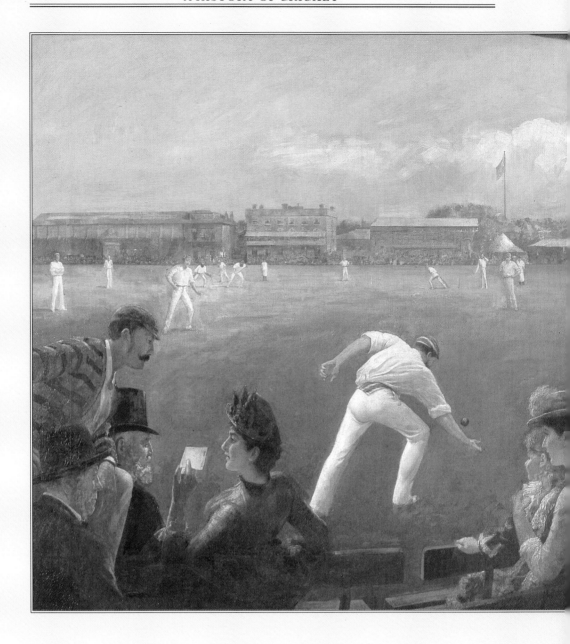

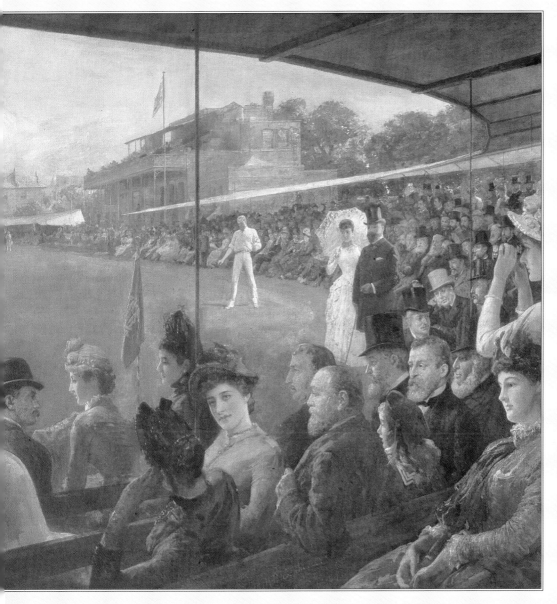

A cricketing fantasy, as imagined by the splendidly named artists H. Barrable and R. Ponsonby Staples. England and Australia at Lord's in 1886. On the right, approaching their seats in "A" Stand (later replaced by the Pelham Warner Stand) are the Prince and Princess of Wales. The Prince's close friend Lillie Langtry gazes boldly at us by the pillar. Inevitably, W.G. is at the crease, playing the 'Demon Bowler" F.R. Spofforth. The fielder on the boundary is T.W. Garrett.

119

in the west of England. If the whole world were land we might go on tracing spring, spring all the way round till in a year we got to London again.

Dodgson was to be haunted by this paradox for the rest of his life. In 1857 he was writing letters to the press about it. In 1860 he delivered a lecture on the subject to the Ashmolean Society. He was perpetually introducing it into his correspondence, forever bringing the subject up at the dinner table. It is one of two remarkable coincidences of the case that at around the time when the Midwinters were sailing for Australia, Dodgson, perceiving as well as they that here was a world where things tended to be upside down, wrote to an Australian cable office: "If I despatched a cable to you at 11.00 pm on Monday evening, at what time and on what day of the week would you receive it?" The reply was curt: "Consult our time-tables." The second, even more striking coincidence is that in 1878, the year in which William Midwinter was to find the twin time-spheres of his professional life, the Australian and the English, come into shattering collision in the pavilion at Lord's, a man called Sandford Fleming, realising that Dodgson's playful paradox represented a very real problem, invented the idea of the time-zone. Six years later the International Date-Line was established, leaving Dodgson, and millions of others, not altogether convinced that the problem had been solved.

But Dodgson, for all his whimsically precocious brilliance, was a theorist, an armchair traveller, and was to remain so for the rest of his life. In the person of William Midwinter, about whom Dodgson knew nothing even though they were contemporaries, the theorist finds his experimental traveller through time, an explorer who, if he could not arrest the advance of time, at least performed prodigies in withholding its progress for a few years. In order a savour the patient, childlike simplicity of the method, it is necessary only to retrace Midwinter's footsteps in the years between 1880 and 1882. In September 1880, having enjoyed a successful English season with Gloucestershire, Billy sailed for Australia in the *S.S. Lusitania*, and in April 1881 he sailed back again on the same boat from Melbourne to England, having in the meantime improved his social standing so considerably that the "W. Midwinter" included in the passenger list for the journey south had metamorphosed by the following spring into "W. Midwinter, Gent." Prudent mining investments were eventually to bestow on Billy the ultimate symbol of affluence, gentlemanly status as a cricketer. But for the moment he was still Gloucestershire's star professional. When he embarked once more for Australia at the end of the 1881 English season, he could luxuriate in the novel sensation of having all his expenses paid, for he was now returning to the colony as a member of the touring side led by Alfred Shaw and consisting in its entirety of professionals. At the end of that Test series he sailed back to England once more in time to join his county for the 1882 campaign, ending his spectacular association with the Graces in a match at Clifton against the Australian tourists. When those tourists sailed home he sailed with them, officiating as umpire in the matches they played in the United States on the way. But this time, when he finally arrived at what he persisted in calling home, a certain exasperation at his antics could be discerned among the locals. On his public pronouncement that he had now ceased to be a professional cricketer, considered himself to be "an Australian to the heart's core", and objected to being described as "an anglo-Australian", this most prodigious of all anglo-Australians had the questionable pleasure of reading about himself in *The Sydney Mail*:

> Are we to have another season of vagueness from this very slippery cricketer? One day he is an Australian, the next day an Englishman.

The Australian selectors, not being staff members of *The Sydney Mail*, then selected Midwinter to play against England, and he had the pleasure of scoring the winning hit in the fourth Test, and then, in the tourists' last match against Victoria, making 92 not out. When he returned to England yet again in 1884 it was as a legitimate and undisputed member of the Australian side at last, which meant that when he played against his old teammates at Cheltenham and at Clifton there was no question this time of any piratical tomfoolery. By now he was different in two quite profound ways from the young globetrotter picked up by the Graces. He was more inclined than before to live up to the self-

The mock obituary printed in The Sporting Times *after Australia had beaten England for the first time, and in the most dramatic fashion, at the Oval in 1882.*

In Affectionate Remembrance

OF

ENGLISH CRICKET,

WHICH DIED AT THE OVAL

ON

29th AUGUST, 1882,

Deeply lamented by a large circle of sorrowing friends and acquaintances.

R. I. P.

N.B.—The body will be cremated and the ashes taken to Australia.

bestowed soubriquet of "Gent", and he was, moreover, a Gent with a lady. At St Peter's Church, Melbourne, on 4 June 1883, on the day that W.G. was making a beggarly five runs for M.C.C. and Ground against Notts at Lord's, Midwinter was marrying Elizabeth Frances McLaughlan, daughter of a carrier from Paisley, Scotland.

Having by now become so consummate a master of the arts of duplicity and imposture, the amazing Billy understandably reached the conclusion that he was a born stockbroker. But this attempt to avoid going to work unaccountably failed, and he soon found more congenial duties as landlord of the Clyde Hotel in Melbourne, of which episode in his life Wisden was to write nearly a century later:

> Mr Christopher McGaffin, now 92, remembers as a boy being chased away from the horse-drinking trough by the tall, fair-haired Billy Midwinter. He continued to take an active part in the affairs of the Carlton Club, setting a fine example to the club's young cricketers. His keen perception and his humorous entertaining conversation were held in high esteem. He was invited to tour England with the 1888 team but declined on business grounds. He had moved to the Victoria, Bourke Street, but his eyesight was beginning to fail and he retired from active cricket.

In summarising his life, it is instructive to think again of the obsessional

The Australian touring side of 1884, led by W.L. Murdoch (seated centre). Murdoch was the first to score a double hundred in Tests (211 in 1884).

preoccupations of the Reverend Dodgson, who so very nearly anticipated what might be defined as Midwinter's Speculations on the Metaphysical Aspects of Time in Space when he wrote: "Half of the world, or nearly so, is always in the light of the sun." But it was neither Dodgson nor Joseph Wells' little boy Bertie, but Billy Midwinter who stumbled on the previously unperceived truth that as cricket can be played only in summer, and that as the earth moves forever round the sun, and that since it follows from this that somewhere on that earth it must always be summer, then there need never be any such lugubrious event as the last game of the season. Like some inspired flannelled pragmatist pursuing the dotty Carrollian riddle, "Where does the day begin?" to its eventual destination at the back of the beyond, Midwinter in 1880 finally flowered into what he had been threatening to become for some time – the first commuting intercontinental cricketer in history. By passing back and forth, back and forth, across the waters of the earth, Midwinter contrived to enjoy between the spring of 1880 and the winter of 1882, no fewer than six full cricket seasons, in the course of which stupendous feat he had outfaced the wrath of newspaper editors, the anger of county and state administrators, the disapproval of selection committees and the strictures of any moralists who may have been watching. As he settled down to the pleasures of marriage and fatherhood at the Victoria Hotel, basking in his local fame as a great celebrity, Billy Midwinter could look back on his life with some satisfaction. He had pulled it off. He had found that degree of independence which had always eluded his poor father, escaped the limitations of a working man's existence in the rural outposts of agricultural England, and could expect to sail on to a happy old age.

At this point the fates, which until now had indulged him so kindly, destroyed him utterly, with three hammerblows of frightful cruelty. In November 1888 his ten-month-old daughter Elsie contracted pneumonia and died. On 23 August 1889, while on the far side of the globe W.G. was carrying his bat for 123 in the match against Middlesex at Cheltenham, the beloved Elizabeth Frances died of apoplexy. Three months later his only surviving child, three-year-old Albert Ernest, followed his little sister and his mother, leaving poor Billy Midwinter bereft of his reason. In June 1890, while staying with his sister and her husband at Sandhurst, he become violent and had to be removed, first to the Bendigo Hospital and on 14 August to the Kew Asylum in Melbourne, where, paralysed from the waist down, he slowly declined:

> Happily one of his brief periods of consciousness on November 21st coincided with a visit from his old friend Harry Boyle, on his return from the Australian 1890 tour of England. He recognised him and spoke admiringly of W.G., Arthur Shrewsbury and of Woof. He was delighted to hear that his old county had twice beaten Nottinghamshire.

Billy Midwinter died on Wednesday, 3 December 1890, and was buried two days later, among the mourners being a representative for the Gloucestershire club, W.O. Tonge, who had played with him in two county games in 1880.

So vanished one of the most remarkable men who ever entered the arena of international cricket, a man with a sublime sense of the ridiculous which marched with W.G.'s own; a boisterous man, superbly fit, an accomplished athlete who played havoc with the rules and regulations, whose life seemed destined to be one eternal romp until the calm sunlight of his Victorian prime, and yet whose ending was so sudden, so tragic, that Haygarth's *Scores and Biographies* delivers upon him one of the saddest epitaphs in all the recorded annals of cricket:

"May the death of no other cricketer who has taken part in great matches be like his."

CHAPTER IX

GOD'S CLASSROOM ...

One of the more captivating aspects of the Victorian age was its tendency to confuse issues which ought not to have any logical connection at all. Among these the concept of the Gentleman loomed like a cloud over the landscape, permeating every backwater of social intercourse, tilting the balance of debate, affecting conduct and colouring opinion. This beau ideal of the Victorian gentleman owes much to Thomas Arnold, the innovative headmaster of Rugy School, among whose oratorical excesses was the speech in which he placed Gentlemanly Conduct higher than acquisition of knowledge or the possession of ability. As other public schools raced to imitate Arnold's Rugby in the hope of emulating its commercial success, a set of tenets evolved, a complete Gentleman's kit, a *vade mecum* for the well-born and the well-placed without which no man could consider himself in the educational sense quite finished. As the century proceeded, there evolved such things as Gentlemanly dress, Gentlemanly etiquette, a Gentlemanly accent, Gentlemanly opinion, Gentlemanly morality, Gentlemanly religion, all of which were finally gathered together into a single code by that unifying phenomenon, the Gentleman's tour of the continent, after which, having satisfied himself that Europe did not really matter, the perfect Gentleman could settle down to a lifetime of indulgent insularity.

Team games became enmeshed into the Gentlemanly philosophy through the circuitous route of ministerial concern. In 1861 the government of Lord Palmerston appointed the Clarendon Commission to investigate the curious fact that the major public schools appeared to be supplying the nation with a copious flow of imbeciles and philistines. The nation did not ask much from its gentlemen, but it did at least require some vestiges of education. As that astute analyst of the age G.M. Young later commented, what was needed was a gentleman at any rate capable of finding his way to Australia with a boatload of criminals. When the Clarendon Commission finally reported, among its recommendations was the proposal that team games be an intrinsic part of public school education. The thought behind this odd comment was that in some unspecified way, once a young man acquired a mastery of the off-drive and the place-kick, these skills somehow rendered him more efficient in the art of despatching the enemies of the Queen, so that if and when the nation ever found itself embroiled in a war the public school gentlemen would be deadly in the execution of their duties. This correlation of the playingfield with the battlefield was to have tragic consequences when at last the products of the public schools took their men into battle in 1914. Well-intentioned officers often led their men over the top into no-man's-land by booting footballs in the general direction of the German lines and then leading the charge to retrieve them, with a discouraging effect on the length of the casualty lists which need not be specified. Crazed or not, the effect of the Clarendon Commission's recommendation was to make young men of indeterminate intellectual means outstanding at school for their sporting prowess.

So far this admixture of learning and playing is comic but perfectly understandable in its historical context. Where the Victorian recipe for national primacy becomes arcane is in the liberal sprinkling of religion which the headmasters of public schools added to the brew. The exemplar of the type is probably Frederick Farrar, author of *Eric, or Little by Little*, one of the most asinine books of the century. Farrar was one of the leaders of that quaint fundamentalist army which marched so resolutely up the garden path of the epoch, and which so persistently confused the issues of education and salvation as to turn its schoolmasters into divines and its divines into schoolmasters. He was headmaster of Marlborough School, and went on to become Dean of Canterbury. He could certainly consider himself a worldly success by the standards of his day. A later model was Frank Fisher, whose long years as headmaster of Repton School proved so useful an apprenticeship when at last he was transmuted by the alchemy of preferment into Archbishop of Canterbury. It was this marriage of erudition and religion, or (as a more sceptical age might have it) between fact and fiction, which explains, among many other things, both the prevalence of reverend gentlemen on the playing fields of England, and the extraordinary duplication of terminology and symbolism in cricket and Christianity in the Victorian age. As L.C.B. Seaman wrote:

> Cricket was associated with religion: just as freemasons referred to God as the Great Architect of the Universe, young cricketers were taught to think of Him as the One Great Scorer and almost to regard a Straight Bat as second in religious symbolism only to the Cross of Jesus. It was linked, too, with the defence of Empire:
>
> > The sands of the desert are sodden red,
> > Red with the wreck of the square that broke;
> > The gatling's jammed and the colonel's dead ...
> > The voice of the schoolboy rallies the ranks:
> > ''Play up! Play up! and play the game!''.

Of the reverend cricketing gentlemen and their military brothers there will be more to say. Of those Victorian heroes who were neither reverends nor officers but who imagined themselves to be an exotic compendium of both, cricket history knows no more perfect specimen than the man who began as a very small Etonian and ended as a very large nuisance in the councils of the game. In the portrait gallery of English cricket compiled by the pioneer photographers Messrs Elliott and Fry of Brighton, the face of George, Lord Harris, stares out from its monochrome utopia with the assurance of a man who has been born for the express purpose of telling others how to behave. Where most of Elliott and Fry's models turned up for their appointments in playing clothes, Harris is sporting mufti. The polka-dotted bow-tie, nestling in perfect symmetry under the eaves of the white stiff collar, matches the spotted waistcoat, whose slightly debonair effect is nicely balanced by the stern propriety of the single-breasted black jacket. We observe here the features of English cricket administration in its ascendent years. This is one of the men who helped formulate not only the procedures but the etiquette of the game. Undaunted by the heresies of the new, bold with the fearlessness of a man convinced he has nothing to hide, he gazes full-face at a point just behind the viewer's left shoulder, or, to put it in the terminology of the game he loved so dearly, the general area of backward short leg. His hair has recently been trimmed, probably in preparation for the portrait, and under it the bushy eyebrows jut protectively over wide, stern eyes.

And it is those eyes that give the game away. It comes as no surprise to find, even in Wisden's sycophantic obituary, certain veiled references to Lord Harris's tendency to rant and rave whenever the argument was not going his way, to a strength of character unsapped by the slightest inclination to see anyone else's point of view. As one of the indomitable major-generals of British imperialism, it was Harris's duty to give a lead to lesser breeds without the law. Nothing significant remains of his work as Under-Secretary of State for India, under the fleeting captaincy of Lord Randolph Churchill, nor of his time as Governor of Bombay, except perhaps for a long tradition of Parsee cricket. But it is significant that W.G. Grace, who was nobody's fool when it came to judging his fellow men, said of Harris's political career: "It is the only

Lord Harris, a well-intentioned but blinkered autocrat who observed, "My whole life has pivoted on Lord's". Not always to the benefit of the HQ of cricket.

bad thing I know of him.'' From his work as joint-viceroy with Lord Hawke of
English cricket, however, at least one imperial edict survives which tells us that
those half-crazed eyes are not entirely misleading when it comes to an
assessment of his temperament:

> ... to play the game keenly, honourably, generously, self-sacrificingly, is a moral
> lesson in itself, and the classroom is God's air and sunshine. Foster it, my brothers,
> protect it from anything that would sully it, so that it may grow in favour with all
> men.

Before we snigger at such outmoded pietism, it does no harm to admit that
statements of that kind may not seem absurd in their historical context,
particulary if the rhetorician responsible lives a life of diocesan rectitude. To do
Harris justice, he was not quite the insufferable humbug his oratory suggests. A
man may be a loony pantheist and still have a genuine devotion to the welfare
of the serfs. Harris was the first of the patricians to insist that the professional
cricketer has the right to sell his services to the highest bidder, and he later
created the Cricketers' Fund Friendly Society. Yet again, as we peer into the
fronded embrasures of the Victorian conservatory, we encounter a quaint moral
stance and discover that what is wrong is not the ethic it represents but the
failure of its model to respect that ethic, or to realise his failure to respect it.

Sociologically Harris is one of the most revealing figures in English sport. Like
Grace, he embodies certain beliefs and attitudes whose application so far
transcended the sporting arena that they may be said to have affected the course
of national history. The well-intentioned autocracy which public-school,
public-spirited men like Harris brought to the administration of their cricketing
affairs they surely brought also to the administration of the Empire itself. In fact
Harris's blend of self-righteousness, sincerity and blockheadedness is so typical
of its time and place that it will repay closer study. We may find much to explain
the blend of affection and disgust, unique throughout imperial history, with
which the subject races of Harris's day, and particularly the citizens of the
Indian Empire, prepared to throw off the British yoke.

When Harris talked of playing the game, he certainly believed as passionately
in the impeccability of his own bona fides as does the schoolboy who rallies the
ranks in Newbolt's poem. In this sense at least he could claim to be free of the
taint of humbug. But there is such a thing as unwitting hypocrisy, a complaint
from which Harris seems to have suffered grievously. He was indeed so far
insulated from the perception of his own ambivalence that he would certainly
have felt a deep sense of injustice had he been prescient enough to know that a
later age might call his actions into question. We can almost hear him rebutting
the charges with a paraphrase of the magnificent defence of his spiritual sister,
Lady Bracknell: ''Impossible. I am an Oxonian.'' His denials would be
vehement. ''Did I not play the game by the rules, to the best of my considerable
ability, like a true English gentleman?'' He did indeed, and that was the trouble.
The simple fact which neither Harris nor almost any of his class could grasp was
that it was both foolish and hopeless for them to expect that the degree of

benignity with which they wielded their power would mollify those on the receiving end of it. It was not the style of their paternalism but the assumption of the paternalism itself which gave such deep offence to the lower orders. Harris undeniably procured certain material benefits for the professional cricketers of his time. But English history is positively congested with do-gooders, either like Lord Shaftesbury and the Webbs, who were too fastidious to feel any affection for the beneficiaries of their altruism, or like Harris, who not only denied to others the right to reach their own decisions, even to damn themselves to perdition if so inclined, but also failed to measure up to the mark he demanded in others. It is this blend of ethical dishonesty coupled with a perfectly genuine inability to perceive it, a kind of moral imbecility in fact, which makes it difficult not to forgive Harris his trespasses and settle instead for the rich comic relief his antics provide.

Harris took his own innocence for granted. No faint shadow of guilt or self-doubt ever darkened his happy horizon. That he harboured not the ghost of a suspicion of his own transgressions is illustrated once and for all by the comical transparency of his own self-exposure. In 1921 he published a volume of cricketing recollections entitled *A Few Short Runs*, in which he tells "an amusing anecdote". It seems that during an unspecified season in the later 1880s, Harris, leading the Kent eleven on its northern tour, was suddenly confronted by a challenge to his sense of justice. After insisting that "I was always very particular as to qualifications, and very indignant at the lapses from the straight path into which some counties fell," he says he

> ... noticed that Lancashire had advertised to play against Kent S.S. Schultz, an old friend and a member of my team in Australia in 1878-9, but having, I was satisifed, no sort of qualification.

Sandford Spence Schultz (1857-1937) was a useful all-rounder who late in life anglicised his surname to Storey, and who is forgotten today except for one bizarre record which no other cricketer is ever likely to challenge. When Schultz died, the following letter appeared in the *The Times*, with reference to a match played in 1881 between Oxford University and the Gentlemen of England:

> The fast bowler commited such havoc as would have made him famous in these days. The Gentlemen refused to continue, because of the bumpy state of the Christ Church ground. The match was begun all over again the Parks. One batsman, S.S. Schultz, was out first ball each time. Twice first ball in one innings, a record.

This ought to have constituted the beginning and end of Schultz's historical significance, except that Harris bestows upon him further notoriety. Roused by the heinous illegality of Schultz's presence in the Lancashire side, Harris moved into action:

> I wired to Old Trafford that I was surprised to see the announcement, as I understood he had no qualification. On arrival on the ground, my great friend

Albert Hornby and E.B. Rowley came up, and in the most innocent way expressed their astonishment at my protest, and said that Schultz always had played for Lancashire. I admitted that, but pointed out that he had not been born in Lancashire and was not living there.

"Oh yes," they replied, "but his family home is in the county."

"Are you sure?" I replied, "for I understand his mother lives at Birkenhead, and that is in Cheshire."

"Yes," they rejoined triumphantly, "and Port of Liverpool."

The audacity of the claim was so astounding that I never said another word.

There are several revealing points in this account, the most important of which are that there were, after all, circumstances in which Harris would unbend in the face of petty misdemeanours, and that in this case it would have been unthinkable to stand by the letter of the law because both Schultz and Hornby, being gentlemen, were friends of his. Harris's decision to wink at Schultz's ineligibility seems perfectly reasonable, showing a nice sense of proportion. None of the events surrounding the case would have any meaning for the student of cricket were not the circumstances duplicated in another age under vastly differing conditions.

Not long after the end of the Great War, around the time when Harris was compiling his memoirs, a promising young cricketer, his sensibilities alas unrefined by any contact with public school or university, was either overlooked or rejected by his native county and sought the only alternative by registering with another county, where his obvious promise might be better appreciated.

This young cricketer soon won a place in the Gloucestershire side, and by 1922, although still a teenager, was being spoken of as a potential England cricketer. At this point, enter Lord Harris snorting pieties from both nostrils. The County Championship was the County Championship, was it not? If anyone could play for anybody, where was the sense in it? His lordship demanded respect for the law and as usual he got what he wanted, although to a disinterested onlooker it might seem that the passion of his defence of legality was coloured just a shade by the fact that the county from which this talented young man had defected happened to be Harris's own. Walter Reginald Hammond

On the right is A.N. "Monkey" Hornby, of Lancashire and England. Behind him is the slow bowler Alec Watson.

Walter Hammond in full flow, photographed by Herbert Fishwick during an innings of 225 for M.C.C. at Sydney, November 1928.

had been born in Dover, although after the death of his father in the Great War he had attended Cirencester Grammar School. Harris, manfully overcoming his compassion for a boy rendered fatherless by the war, succeeded in his campaign to get Hammond banned from the championship for the rest of the season. In mentioning the case in *Cricket Between Two Wars*, Pelham Warner, scrupulously faithful as ever to the facts, even to the exclusion of the truth, remarks:

> There was some question of his qualification to play for Gloucester – he was born in Kent – and after the end of May he was not seen again that season in the county team.

How sweet the discipline in God's classroom, and how ingenious the methods of enforcing it. Later that summer, evidently assailed at last by twitches of shame, Harris did what any gentleman in his situation would do: he made a public pronouncement denying being assailed by any such twitches of shame.

> I am glad to say that my conscience does not prick me, and I am not aware that my colleagues of the Kent committee are suffering from any contrition because we have done our best to secure respect for the rules laid down by the counties.

If the whirligig of time does not always bring in its revenges, it certainly sometimes causes a man to step very lively in the awareness that the boot has inexplicably worked on to the other foot. Seven years after his enforced removal from the Gloucestershire side, young Hammond came home from Australia having slaughtered the local bowling to the tune of four Test centuries, an aggregate of 905 runs and an average of 113.12. A civic reception was arranged for our hero, and what more appropriate venue than Dover, the young man's birthplace and the traditional threshold of England? And who more indispensable to the welcoming throng than the uncrowned king of Kentish cricket, Lord Harris? Ronald Mason, describing the reception in his biogaphy of Hammond, says:

> And there in its midst was Lord Harris, beaming his congratulations. It would be interesting to know whether he had the iron nerve – I am sure he had – to face Hammond squarely in the eye.

Mason is no doubt correct, but there were some whose social position enabled them to be more frank with Harris than Hammond ever dared. One afternoon not many weeks after the banishment of Hammond, Lord Harris was confronted in the Long Room at Lord's by Lord Deerhurst, president of the Worcestershire county club. "May I congratulate you," said Deerhurst, "on having buggered the career of another young cricketer?"

A much uglier manifestation of Harris's gentlemanly conduct had occurred in 1896, when the responsibility came for selecting the England side to play against the Australian tourists. Here is Patrick Morrah to describe the scene:

> The first test was fixed for June 22–24 at Lord's, and interest centred on whether Ranjitsinhji would be allowed to play for England. The question of qualification for an England side had never been properly settled; in the early eighties W. Midwinter had actually played for both England and Australia in different matches against each other. But in this case the matter rested with the M.C.C.; for teams were selected by the authorities of the grounds on which Test matches were played. And that meant that the decision in practice rested with Lord Harris, whose word at Lord's was law. He had just retired from the presidency, but his dominance depended not on his position but on his personality; what Lord Harris said went. And Lord Harris did not approve of overseas cricketers playing for England. So Ranji was left out.

As it happens, Morrah is quite wrong. Harris had no objections at all to overseas players representing England, if only the circumstances were acceptable to him. Indeed he had made special efforts on several occasions, four to be precise, to ensure they did so. Whatever objection he had to the selection of Ranji, the latter's overseas origins could not possibly have been a factor. For Lord Harris, who between 1878 and 1894 captained England in four Tests against Australia, was born in St. Anne's, Trinidad.

Those seeking the real explanation for Harris's blackballing of Ranji need not travel very far. When a man reacts with such vehemence to petty affairs like the origins of Hammond and the complexion of Ranjitsinhji, it is permissible to wonder if there is not something more profound than the well-being of cricket impelling him. Such punitive fervour, such magisterial wrath, such a show of honour outraged, are surely symptoms of something more than mere chagrin at the thought of all those Kentish centuries irrevocably forfeited to a rival county. When the terrible news was brought that Gloucestershire was wilfully confusing itself with Kent to its own inestimable advantage, who knows what vile spectres leapt into his lordship's brain? In fact he himself unequivocally defined the nature of the beast, in the same published declaration in which he denied the existence of a pang of conscience, as he concluded:

> Bolshevism is rampant, and seeks to abolish all laws and rules, and this year cricket has not escaped its attack ...

with which stupefying statement the enigma of Lord Harris is solved at last. He is neither tyrant nor humbug nor bully nor fraud, only an old fathead, standing forlornly at the corner of St John's Wood Road, peering into the gathering dusk of his own career and awaiting the advent of the armies of the night, while down in the sinister hills of Gloucestershire a young man from Dover conspires with Lenin and the local county committee to bring about the downfall of the Empire.

It requires no great act of the imagination to conceive the sad apoplexies of dismay with which Harris greeted the new age, how uneasily he must have drifted across the shoals of its uncongenial backwaters, above all how denuded he must have felt whenever he sensed that the post-Victorian age was stripping him of all his terrors. J.E. Squire wrote in *The Honeysuckle and the Bee*:

> A night or two afterwards I spent one of the oddest evenings of my life. Another man and I stayed on in Bath, and my eldest son also happened to be there; a message came from T.P. O'Connor, who was staying at the Grand Pump Room Hotel, asking us to come over after dinner. When we got to his private sitting-room we found him with Lord Harris: the incongruity of the pair, although they had age and long political experience in common, was startling – but they had both taken their aged bones to Bath and come together, the impish Irish journalist with his shapeless face and sly eyes, and the tall, austere, aquiline, bewhiskered, correct cricketer and Indian governor. Lord Harris, who was nearly eighty, had recently been making runs and taking wickets on the Fourth of June at Eton, welcomed every attempt to turn the conversation to cricket or imperial history, but T.P. was too much for him and for some hours monopolised the talk with reminiscences of Victorian worthies of the Jubilee Plunger type, and stories of the what-the-lady's-husband-said-to-the-duke sort. Now and again, as he produced an especially impudent piece of ancient scandal, he turned with his brogue and said, "Ye'll remember that, Lord Harris?". Lord Harris was the perfect gentleman, and perhaps he was really enjoying the relaxation from decorum; but his nods of assent were of the slightest and his smiles had a trace of effort in them. It was rather as though an Archbishop should have found himself supping with the chorus, and was making the best of it.

In attempting to take the measure of such a man, and in so doing to stress the abyss which separated his type of Englishman from a mischievous vagabond like O'Connor, it is as well to remember that Harris, through accident of birth as much as through administrative ability, was a man accustomed to wielding absolute power over millions of people, that he was vouchsafed by her Majesty's Government responsibility for an area larger than England, that he enjoyed a

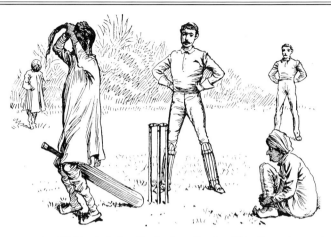

Above and opposite: "Cricket in India: Sketches by a Cavalry Officer" – a characteristically patronising view of the game on the subcontinent.

degree of deference which a more egalitarian age tends to associate only with the potentates of fairyland. Government House at Poona,

> where the Governor of Bombay spent his summers, was built in the chateau style, like a Canadian hotel, and had an eighty-foot tower, a grotto, a lake and innumerable gazebos, arbours and summer-houses. Inside it was burdened with dark wood panelling and chandeliers, feastooned with pictures of kings and maharajahs, crammed with gigantic and lugubrious pieces of furniture. It must have been difficult indeed for the Governor, when wearing his sword for ceremonial receptions, to pass from one saloon to another, but he was used to it all – his other palace, in Bombay, had two dining rooms, one for the dry weather, one for the monsoon.

As Governor from 1890–94 Harris was a little short of a lesser monarch, presiding over a considerable kingdom. Moreover, there was the ever-present, and piquantly exciting sense of danger inherent in the playing of the Great Game to provide the chance of death, of revolt, perhaps even of another Indian Mutiny. Only two years after Harris's return to England, his successor, on Jublilee Day 1897,

> gave a banquet in his palace at Poona, where the summer heat hung heavy over lake and grotto, and great ladies of the catonment conversed stickily with Sassoons. Late that night two British officials, Mr Rand and Lieutenant Ayerst, were saluted into their carriage by the crimson-jacketed footman at the door, and were driven away into the dark; they had hardly left the gate of the Government House compound when a volley of shots rang out from the shrubbery beside the road, and both men were killed.

Evidently the diplomatic touch of administrators like Harris had not altogether resolved the problem of how to communicate with the locals, for the twin assassinations of 1897 had been stimulated by British reaction to plague raging through the province. Troops had segregated the infected from the healthy, destroyed contaminated properties and moved the population around in accordance with medical rather than political logic, all without any explanation to or consultation with the inhabitants. Nationalist propaganda had been mounting for some time, founded on the fact that three hundred million Indians were living ''in slavery, diseased and half-starved''. Soon the murderer of Rand and Ayerst was caught, convicted and executed. The Governor, aping the ethics of his victim, had asserted his powers of life and death.

That sector of the Raj over which Harris presided was a society paralysed with protocol, ponderous in action, stultified in thought, a society long since stiffened by the starch of Victorian pretension, outwardly genteel in the manner of an Eastbourne tea-party, inwardly resolute to maintain both its own ascendency and those minor pleasures of life it took for the symbols of a distant homeland.

> The butler, wearing a sash and turban-band of regimental colours, padded in and announced dinner. Forming up by twos in strictest precedence they went slowly into the dining room. The ladies' high-heeled shoes and the patent-leather pumps of the gentlemen made no sound on the thick red carpet. Behind each chair a servant (for the guests would generally bring their butlers with them) helped the diners to be seated. If the mosquitos were very bad, guests might be equipped with mosquito-boots, but ordinarily a light burning beneath the table was sufficient to discourage the brutes. The table-surface was patterned with ropes of flowers wound between fretwork-designed dishes of marzipan, toffee fudge and chocolate creams. Flower scent hung heavy on the warm evening air and blended oddly with the lavender water of the ladies and the hairwash of the gentlemen. On the walls tigers' heads snarled, the dim figures of a polo team peered out from the heavy blackwood frame. Silver toast racks, boiled egg sets, wedding presents of monumental size, modest trophies of golf and tennis tournaments. The lamps in their great globes shone in stiff crackling shirt-fronts with one or two plain gold studs and on white shoulders and lace and velvet dresses.

It appears from *A Few Short Runs* that this cosy enclave of transplanted English decorum was distinctly ruffled by Harris's determination to flout the gubernatorial conventions whenever they happened to run contrary to his hunger for a game of cricket. Yet it was not the English themselves who objected. They must have known what Harris was up to and must have approved wholeheartedly. Harris had become convinced that cricket offered a short cut to the civilising of

the locals, and had convinced himself that it was the Parsees, with their mercantile tendencies and European pretensions, who were the most likely converts to a cricketing way of life. But Indian newspapers, "the native press" as Harris described them, were scandalised by his belief that a cricket field was a suitable place to ignore religious, moral and social practices evolved over the centuries. He claimed to have been abused by the Indians for trying to lead their youth astray. But Harris pressed on, and contributed greatly to the founding of an Indian cricket tradition. When his term of office was done he returned home to England, resumed his cricketing career, defied the passing of time and the shedding of tradition, played his last game at Lord's in 1929 and made his farewell appearance on the playing fields of Eton a year later when he was 79 years old. By then, haunted by the chimera of revolution, he must have wondered what had happened to the old ideals, to the old Empire, to the Old Country, to the old ways, now that the old Queen was little more than a memory. Confronted with the menace of passing time, he reacted with characteristic defiance. A man who has outfaced an invasion of the pitch by a brawling, drunken mob, as he had done at Sydney in 1879, would not easily be dismayed. He once confided to the editor of *Wisden,* "The only time I was ever afraid was when I was knocked down by a London taxi-cab." At the end of his life, on being complimented for so stoically fulfilling the sad task of reading the Lesson at the memorial service for his wife, his explanation for his courage sounds like a parody of Farrar and yet was utterly sincere: "She never funked anything, and I made up my mind I would not."

It would be uncharitable to linger too long over the spectacle of this aged man in a peaked cap tilting at the windmills of subversion, kinder by far to remember him instead in a setting more conducive to that ideal of dignity he upheld for so long, perhaps in one of the social set pieces at the far end of the long road leading from Upper Sixpenny at Eton, to shall we say the summer dining room at Poona? There we observe him, presiding over the napery of an official dinner party, handing out the tablets of the conversational law to the assembled company, while down at the far end of the table the Assistant District Commissioner's errant sister-in-law coyly requests the adjutant's younger brother to pass the chocolate mints, and through the gauze curtains at the open windows there float across the perfumed night air the drowsy tarradiddles of a regimental band playing selections from "Pinafore". It is 1892 and all's well. The sun never sets, and George Robert Canning, Lord Harris, although so far removed from the Kentish weald, is yet content in a setting commensurate with his own considerable conception of himself. Let us leave him there and steal respectfully away.

CHAPTER X

... AND THE PREFECTS

As the fast-fading figure of Harris merges imperceptibly into the imperial shadows, another looms to take its place. The facial expression is blander, more naive, less apoplectic, perhaps also a shade more self-consciously heroic. In the posed portrait of 1899 there is something about that straw boater, that striped blazer so tightly buttoned, the hands clasped behind the back, the feet placed very nearly in Third Position, which conspire to suggest a weekend flaneur at the lakeside of some Victorian country house, needing only the encouragement of the music's imminent opening chords to embark on a debonair exposition of the "Skater's Waltz". This is Martin, seventh Baron Hawke, son of a country parson who succeeded to the title, much to his own surprise, in the spectacular style of a Thackerayan hero, ennobled only through the failure of two successive incumbents to provide a male heir.

Lord Hawke is a much richer comic character than Harris, because a much smaller man. Where Harris's exploits often betray the presence of something resembling an intellect peeping out from behind the palisades of pomposity, Hawke's remain uncorrupted by the slightest taint of cerebral function. Although hardly worth a place in the

Lord Hawke, famous captain of Yorkshire, strict disciplinarian and the man who booted Bobby Peel out of the first-class game.

VANITY FAIR.

Sept 24 1892.

Spy's portrait of Lord Hawke. Hawke was a stylish off-side batsman, but with a career average of just 20 he flattered to deceive.

great Yorkshire teams on pure cricketing merit, Hawke captained the county for twenty-seven years, maintaining throughout his reign a master-servant relationship with the professionals which by no means lapsed beyond the pavilion gate. Each year the hired hands were invited to tea up at the family seat, and none of the guests would have dared to get married without first displaying the prospective bride to his lordship. Apart from this odd belief in his own ability to read a woman as though she were some kind of top-spinner, Hawke appears to have seen himself as an emissary of God sent down from the Great Pavilion to administer English cricket in general and Yorkshire cricket in particular. Today he is remembered not for his thirteen centuries but for a succession of monumental blunders which fifty years of apologia from his admirers have done nothing to excuse.

His expulsion from the game of the left-arm spin virtuoso Robert Peel for walking on to the field of play too drunk to know in which direction to bowl, and perhaps also, if rumour is to be countenanced, for watering the pitch in a socially unacceptable way, is perhaps understandable. Less so is his remark, made in public some years later, that Peel bore him no ill-will, and indeed respected his captain all the more for the severity of his discipline. In Hawke's calamitous defence of his action there may be discerned striking echoes of Harris after the Hammond affair, the same hand on heart, the same modest assertion of moral courage, the same magnanimity towards the corpse.

> And so I come to the most decisive action of my whole career, the dismissal of R. Peel from the Yorkshire eleven. It had to be done for the sake of discipline and for the good of cricket. Nothing ever gave me so much pain. I did not care that by dispensing with our foremost all-rounder, we were losing the Championship. What hurt me was publicly censoring a valued comrade and a real good fellow. Peel thoroughly proved he was loyal, for he never bore me malice for my decision. We have met as friends many times since, and I was only glad when the *Yorkshire Evening News* engaged him to seek out and coach young players – a job he admirably performs.

Mr A.A. Thomson, who evidently considered his lordship a good sort, once made the startling claim: "Just let anyone try speaking ill of Lord Hawke to an old Yorkshire pro." But it is no use. The acid of Peel's contemptuous irony has been eating into Hawke's official portrait for fifty years now, reducing its grandiloquence to a ghastly parody: "Lord Hawke put his arm around me and helped me out of the ground – and first-class cricket. What a gentleman!"

Hawke always insisted that the Yorkshire side should at all times be a side of Yorkshiremen, even though his very presence on a Yorkshire field was a contradiction of the claim. It was Hawke who invented the rule which has obtained ever since, that no player may represent Yorkshire who was not born within its boundaries. There is of course something to be said for a law which helps preserve the regional aspect of a county club, even though if every first-class county had respected it many outstanding cricketers, from Hobbs, Hayward and Ranjitsinhji to Cowdrey, Dexter and G.O. Allen, would have been lost altogether to the English first-class game. But just as Harris never bothered to explain how cherishing the game was compatible with delaying the entry into it of a young genius, so Hawke has left us no reason why, of all the thousands of cricketers affected by the birth qualification rule, he should have considered it justifiable to have made an exception in his own case. Lord Hawke was born in Lincolnshire.

But the most priceless of all his gaffes involved the best joke in all the history of cricket, and it is only fitting that such a master-comedian as W.G. Grace should be at the heart of it. In a notorious after-dinner speech, Hawke said: "Pray God the day never dawns when a professional captains England." The meaning of those words is perfectly clear. Hawke may have been an idiot, but he was no fool, and knew what he was about. Countless apologists, mortified by the disastrous candour of Hawke's remark, have tried to apply whitewash by explaining that what his lordship really meant was that he hoped the supply of gifted amateurs would never be exhausted. That is not at all what Hawke meant. If that had been what he wanted to say, then that is what he would have said. The joke is that when Hawke expressed his horror at the prospect of a professional ever captaining England, a professsional already had, and his name was William Gilbert Grace. And yet in the matter of Grace's professionalism, a cause which flourished well enough to have tempted one cricket historian to define him as the man who made more money out of cricket than anyone else in history, Hawke's record, like Harris's, is perfectly blank. No report has ever come down to us of lordly admonishment, of censures, of warnings, even of friendly hints to Grace to keep his financial arrangements to himself. The truth is that Hawke and his fellow staff-officers imposed their personalities on the game with such force that any moral inconsistencies were never mentioned in polite society.

No more telling disclosure of Hawke's prestige could be concocted than the obeisance paid by Wisden's *Almanack*, whose editors, impaled on the horns of a dilemma in compiling the 1909 edition, broke with the *Almanack's* conventions in the most farcical way. At the end of the previous season Hawke had been widely congratulated for completing twenty-five years captaincy of Yorkshire. As his technical ability as a player had never remotely matched his prestige, he had never qualified for inclusion in the *Almanack's* annual honours list, "Five Cricketers of the Year". But now that he had endured as a county captain for a quarter of a century the demands on the editors to include him must have seemed irresistible. And yet there was the question of honour. How could Wisden place his lordship in the same category as players like Jack Hobbs and Walter Brearley, who were among their selections that year? So Wisden did what it had never done before and was never to do again. Shamelessly it breached its own tradition, scrapped "Five Cricketers of the Year", and published instead the risible "Lord Hawke and Four Cricketers of the Year". Since his death Hawke has been the recipient of much posthumous abuse, but nothing as derisory as Wisden's well-intentioned insistence on his limitations.

CHAPTER XI

MUSCULAR CHRISTIANITY

W e have seen that, when sufficiently moved to rhetoric, neither Hawke nor Harris was aware of the possibility that the Creator of the Universe might not be much concerned with the future of the County Championship. Their lordships were by no means alone in their faith, nor were appeals and references to God confined to the gentleman-cricketer. It should not be forgotten that it was a professional, the sesquipedalian Albert Knight of Leicestershire, who, on arrival at the crease to open the innings, would address a few well-chosen words to the One Great Scorer before receiving his first ball; that it was a professional, Richard Tyldesley of Lancashire, who once expounded to Neville Cardus the roots of his scrupulous probity as a close fielder: "Westhaughton Sunday School, tha knows"; that it was a professional, Ted Wainwright of Yorkshire, who once remarked of Ranjitsinhji, again to Cardus, "'E never played a Christian stroke in his life". And if, as dullards have sometimes suggested, Cardus was making it all up, then the religious analogy is doubly confirmed, for Cardus was a creative artist probing tirelessly for the most telling and accurate metaphor. Whether or not Cardus was a great reporter or novelist, there is no denying the echo of psalmody wafting through the obituary columns of the late Victorian and Edwardian sporting papers, their columns bristling with sad devotions to the Reverends and Venerables who had delivered their last sermon and struck their ultimate boundary. There we find them, the sporting gentlemen of the cloth, brave diocesan butterflies who, throughout the golden age of the game, came fluttering out, white-flannelled and buckskin-booted, from vicarage and deanery, rectory and close, to play their part in the bizarre and endearing ritual which we know as muscular Christianity.

The Venerable Archdeacon Alexander Colvin, who presided over the meeting which brought into being the Somerset County Cricket Club; the Reverend Henry Giles Alington, who is said to have witnessed every University match at Lord's between 1859 and 1927; the Reverend Arthur Henry Austen-

Leigh, whose technique was eclipsed by his antecendents, among whom was Jane Austen; the Reverend Gilbert Harrison, who so neglected his clerical duties as to find the time to invent the catching practice device known as "The Cradle"; Canon William Benham, a modest Hampshire player who once saw Talleyrand walking down Piccadilly; the Reverend Arthur Gray Butler, who once took muscular Christianity to excessive lengths by leaping across the River Cherwell for no particular reason; the Reverend Canon William Bury, known as "Deerfoot", who made a "a few fugitive appearances for Northants"; the Reverend John Walter Dann, whose misfortune it was to be a poor cricketer related by marriage to the Grace family; Canon the Reverend Edward Rawlins Evans, who represented Warwickshire and was a nephew of George Eliot; the Reverend Walter Fellows, who one day in 1856 while practising on the Christ Church ground at Oxford, struck the ball a record distance of 175 yards; the Reverend Richard Harold Fowler, who, after taking five wickets for Worcestershire against Gloucestershire, was informed by the umpires that "only his cloth had saved him from being no-balled"; the Reverend George William Gillingham, honorary secretary to the Worcestershire county club, who, when the River Severn flooded the county ground, swam across the pitch, reached the pavilion, and swam back with the account books; the Reverend Robert Poole Hooper, who, on being offered a place in the Cambridge side to play Oxford, declined because "I had already made previous promises for matches which I could not honourably throw over"; the Reverend Edgar Thomas Killick, who, while playing for the diocesan clergy of St Alban's against Coventry, ascended to heaven before the match was over; the Reverend Canon Joseph McCormick, who missed a Cambridge Blue in 1855 because "he could not stay in London for the match"; the Reverend Augustus Orĕlbar, who won a quaint immortality by being used as the model for the hero of *Tom Brown's Schooldays*; the Reverend Canon John Henry Parsons, the only cricketing parson to be called Parsons, and the only cricketing divine to appear in the County Championship as a professional; the Reverend James Pycroft, who won immortality with his book, *The Cricket Field*; the Reverend George Barkley Railes, whose allegiances became so confused that while serving as captain of Norfolk he was invited to play for Nottinghamshire; Father William Ignatius Rice, the only monk whose cricket performances were reported by Wisden; the Venerable Avison Scott, whose misfortune it was to score the only double century of his life against a side called the Peripatetic Clowns; Canon the Reverend Charles Theobald, who failed to win his Blue at Oxford because, being one of sixteen children, "the expense of joining the Magdalen Club, membership of which was then considered almost essential to obtain such a distinction, could not be afforded" (oddly, Mr Theobald did not renounce Christianity after this, and lived on until his 99th year); the Reverend Charles Amhurst Daniel Tyssen, who once put on a substantial opening stand with Dr Arthur Conan Doyle for the Authors against the Press Club at Lord's, even though there is no record of his ever having published anything; the Reverend

John Spencer Mullins Walker, whose melancholy distinction it was to have participated in an F.A. Cup semi-final for Clapham Rovers against Oxford University at Kennington Oval in 1874 when only four spectators turned up; the Right Reverend Cecil Wilson, who declined a Blue for Cambridge owing to a previous engagement to travel abroad; the Reverend Clement Eustace Macro Wilson, who enlivened the daily round at Lichfield Cathedral by mastering the art of bowling with either arm; and the Reverend the Honourable Wingfield Stratford Twisleton-Wykeham-Fiennes, all of whose achievements, whether sporting or ecclesiastic, were overshadowed by the length of his name.

Almost all the gentlemen of the cloth who played cricket in the days before the Great War were obliged to retire prematurely because of the Church's disapproval of any of its ministers being connected with a game whose past was so discredited by association with gambling. Those with some knowledge of the history of the Church of England in the eighteenth and nineteenth centuries may be surprised that county secretaries did not disbar their players from association with the Church for the same reason. But those preacher-cricketers who were truly devout required no prompting from their ecclesiastical masters to put aside childish pursuits like the playing of games. One of the more picaresque instances is to be found in *Carr's Dictionary of Extraordinary English Cricketers*, concerning the impressive feats of a Manchester divine called the Reverend Elisha Fawcett (c.1817)

... who devoted his life to teaching the natives of the Admiralty Islands the Commandments of God and the Laws of Cricket. Too poor to purchase a monument to this good man, his parishioners erected his wooden leg upon his grave. In that fertile clime it miraculously took root and for many years provided a bountiful harvest of bats.

Among more easily verifiable cases of religious euphoria overwhelming cricketing technique is the touching case of Charles Thomas Studd, one of six gifted cricketing brothers, five of whom won Cambridge Blues, three of whom captained the university, and one of whom, Charles himself, represented England by virtue of his brilliant all-round gifts. Alas, one day Charles received the call from those ubiquitous evangelical Vaudevilleans, Moody and Sankey,

Literary lion Conan Doyle temporarily cast in the role of cricketing rabbit – dismissed for two in an authors v. actors game at Lord's.

after which he was lost to the game forever. In 1885, still only twenty-four years old, Charles embarked for China, where he worked for ten years with the Inland Mission before being invalided home. He then engaged in missionary work in America and, after 1900, with the Anglo-Indian Evangelization Society. Later, deeply touched by the plight of the natives of the Belgian Congo, he went out to Africa, where he reconciled his twin passions by building a church in the jungle whose aisle measured twenty-two yards from end to end. He died there in 1931. One of the most stunning of all cricketing photographic portraits shows Charles flanked by his brothers J.E.K. and G.B. All three Cambridge captains are capped and blazered, and as they stand there, a resolute brotherhood arm-in-arm, gazing fearlessly into the future, it seems as though nothing could ever sunder them. Charles, taller than his brothers, stands with his left leg slightly forward, with a hint of defiance which contrasts with the hooded eyes and gentle, almost girlish, demeanour of G.B. All three are moustachioed, but only J.E.K. sports an open-necked shirt. Three attractive young men, confident and fortified, it seems, against the whole world by the certitude of brotherly love and loyalty to certain predictable causes. One wonders if, in the moment when the camera clicked, any of them suspected that before long they might be lost to cricket, lost to England, lost to the secular life. George Brown Studd, scorer of a brilliant century against Oxford, will dedicate his life to religious work in of all places Los Angeles. John Studd of the open-necked shirt will evolve into Sir John Kynaston Studd, Bart., Lord Mayor of London and President of the

M.C.C. As for Charles, the most gifted one of all, he will end his days in the wilds of the Dark Continent, where, after much illness and hardship, he will die in the services of God at the age of 71.

A reverend gentleman whose contribution of the evolution of English cricket was vicarious yet profound was John Charles Crawford, born at Hastings in 1849. Known in the cricketing world as ''Parson'' Crawford, his cricket career was divided among a gallimaufry of clubs ranging from Kent and Leicestershire to the Gentlemen of Sussex and the Surrey Second XI. His one moment of glory came when he hit the stumps so hard that he sent one of the bails flying a distance of fifty-one

C.T. Studd, cricketer-turned missionary, flanked by his two talented brothers J.E.K. and G.B. Studd forsook cricket for God's work in Africa.

144

yards. As this incident took place in Dunkirk, it must be assumed that Crawford was willing to travel anywhere in search of a game. In club cricket his renown was so great and his confidence so rampant that on occasion he would take pity on the opposition and bat left-handed to give them a chance of getting him out.

The line of cricketing Crawfords begins in Edinburgh with the birth in 1826 of the Parson's father Andrew Crawford, a moderately talented bowler and a keen devotee of the game who scored his only century in 1926 when celebrating his one hundredth birthday. Having achieved this landmark, Andrew, like all true sportsmen of the period, threw his wicket away almost immediately and was buried the following year at Wimbledon, by which time he had become accustomed to the spectacle of his offspring making their mark on the cricket grounds of the world. Was it heredity, or evironment, or an alliance of the two, which yielded such an astonishing harvest of virtuosity? Within three generations of the Crawford family, aptitude blossomed into high talent, and at last burst into an exfloriation of pure genius. Andrew moved south as a young man and fathered the Parson at Hastings in 1849. Two years later he sired another son, Frank Fairbairn Crawford, who also showed a talent for the game. But Frank was a professional soldier whose opportunities on the cricket field were strictly limited. In 1873 he entered the veterinary department of the Royal Artillery, thus gratifying an affection for horses which was to cost him his life when he contracted fever during service in the Boer War and died at the base hospital at Pietermaritzburg. Wisden describes him as an occasional player for Kent, noted for his fielding at long leg or cover point.

But it is not until the third generation that the Crawfords begin to make history. The Parson and his relations were so prolific that the family became one of those, like the Edriches of Norfolk in a later age, would could field a full eleven of impressive ability. Included in this extraordinary side was Andrew, his two sons, the Parson's two sons, his daughters, plus the occasional niece or nephew to make up the number.

The Parson's first son, christened Vivian Frank Shergold, performed feats so prodigious that even today they stretch credulity. By the time he was sixteen he had become the embodiment of cricket at Whitgift School, and in first eleven and club games in 1895 scored nearly a thousand runs and took over two hundred wickets. In this embryonic stage V.F.S. was primarily a bowler whose batting was spectacular because of his magnificent straight drive of precocious power. What do these statistics of young Crawford imply? One must understand that outstanding cricketers at school in those days were never very far from Test match standard and were certainly up to a reasonable county level. To underline the point it is worth noting that, at the age of sixteen, V.F.S., playing for Richard and District against Surrey, took eight wickets for 35 runs, his victims including Bobby Abel and Ephraim Lockwood. Four years later he scored his maiden century for Surrey, and in the same season took a side down to Cane Hill Mental Asylum, where his father served as chaplain for thirty years, and scored a century in 19 minutes. V.F.S. was one of the great scientific big hitters of his age, and the reminiscences of the Edwardians are full of accounts of his outstanding innings. What is most impressive about these exploits is that they were carried out against bowlers of the very highest class, including C.L.Townsend, Mold and Rhodes. Many of his fours would have been sixes under modern rules, which would raise his already impressive striking rate even higher. In *Hit for Six*, Gerald Brodribb tells us:

> In August 1900 he played possibly his greatest innings. Surrey had lost five for 110 when Crawford came in to hit up 101 not out out of 133 in only 75 minutes and, according to reports, "time after time he sent the ball out of the field of play". E.M. Dowson caught him on top of the Ladies' pavilion. Mold at his fastest was hit into the football stand ... In his innings of 110 against Notts in 1901, he hit Hallam right over the pavilion and into the road ... He never played a more devastating innings of recovery than his 110 for Surrey against Yorkshire in 1901. This particular attack was against Rhodes, bowling from the football-stand end. He hit Rhodes twice right over this stand on to the football pitch. But the most famous hit Crawford ever made was at Bristol in 1900. In going for runs in a match which Surrey eventually lost by 11 runs, Crawford scored 37, including a hit of Paish that sent the ball right over the top of the pavilion to land out of the ground in a garden of a house in Lancashire Road. According to the great historian, F. Ashley-Cooper, the hit-to-pitch distance was accurately measured, and came to 160 yards.

Meanwhile, V.F.S.'s younger brother R.T. was playing for Leicestershire, at the age of nineteen in the 1901 season scoring over 800 runs and taking 40 wickets. Many judges reckoned him to be the most stylish of the cricketing Crawfords. In 1903, V.F.S. joined his young brother at Leicester, where he was appointed county secretary and continued to thrash the county bowlers. In 1910 he retired from cricket and went to live in Ceylon, and in 1922, still only 43 years old, he died from pneumonia. Wisden explains neither the reason for his departure nor his fate during the Great War, saying cryptically that his constitution had been much impaired by the war. In spite of the dazzling style of his cricket, he seems never quite to have fulfilled the prodigious promise of his schooldays, and remains one of those oddly enigmatic figures of the Golden Age.

The youngest of the Crawford brothers, John Neville, was also the most remarkable. Born in 1887, he created such chaos among schoolboy cricketers while attending Repton that at the age of seventeen he was invited to play for Surrey, establishing himself immediately as an outstanding all-rounder, although still attending school. In that season of 1904, drafted into the county side for the summer holidays, Jack Crawford, bowling medium pace with the occasional fast ball and a sharp break-back, took 44 wickets at just over sixteen runs each, coming out top of the county bowling averages. In the following season he finished second in the batting averages; and by the time the 1906 edition of Wisden appeared he had already reduced experienced judges to awestruck metaphoric confusion:

> In all departments Crawford once again is pre-eminent among public school

cricketers, and words fail us when we attempt to estimate his superiority over all public school cricketers of the year. Whether we consider him as a lily, or as refined as gold, the supply of white paint or gold leaf is utterly inadequate for the purpose of painting or gilding his reputation, according to whichever simile may be selected.

Indeed, young Jack Crawford's triumph as a bespectacled schoolboy abroad in a world of famous men reads less like cricket history than the output of a pulp serial writer concocting weekly instalments for his schoolboy readers. Unlike his older brothers, Jack fulfilled all his promise, and his career comprises an astonishing catalogue of sensation and melodrama. In 1907, still only nineteen, he became one of the youngest players in history to be selected as one of Wisden's Five Cricketers of the Year, by which time he had already established himself as one of the strongest, crispest attacking batsmen in the world. People began to throng to the Oval to see young Crawford smashing the ball prodigious distances. In 1907, at home for Surrey against Notts, he drove John Gunn clean through the windows of the Surrey amateurs' dressing-room, very nearly decapitating the Surrey secretary, Mr Findlay. A few days later on the same ground he put a ball through the visitors' dressing-room, the ball crashing full-pitch against the far wall of the room, and making a neat hole in a mirror. In August 1907, playing at home against Kent, Crawford hit 103 in ninety minutes. *The Times* next morning spoke of the ball "soaring away like a bird", and took note of one hit which sent the ball to the top of the highest point of the pavilion:

> Nervous people had mounted to the roof stand to be out of the way of the ball, but Crawford found them with one tremendous overhead drive which scattered them in all directions.

In the winter of 1907-8, Crawford toured Australia with the M.C.C., scoring the fastest century ever seen in Australia, 114 in fifty-eight minutes. The great left-handed Australian batsman Clem Hill was quoted as saying, "there are grand cricketers in this game; and then there is Jack Crawford".

And then, in 1909, having played only four seasons of county cricket, in the course of which he had won twelve England caps, Jack Crawford's career was suddenly breached in the most

J.N. Crawford (centre, back row), whose quarrel with Surrey in 1909 robbed England of a brilliant natural talent and a prodigiously clinical hitter.

shocking way. In the 1910 edition of Wisden we read the bald facts:

> There came the unhappy quarrel with J. N. Crawford. In the absence of Leveson-Gower, Crawford was asked to captain the side in the return match with the Australians, but he refused to act, his reason being that the committee had left out essential players, among others Rushby whose bowling had done so much to win the first match. The committee were much incensed and passed a resolution that Crawford be not again asked to play for the county. At first great secrecy was preserved over the matter, but when the facts came out the correspondence was published and many other letters appeared in the sporting papers. It seemed to outsiders that the quarrel might have been made up very easily, but bitter feeling was aroused.

The crisis arose in July 1909, when the president of the club, one Lord Alverstone, having spent much of the early weeks of the season sending Crawford congratulatory notes on his feats for Surrey, wrote to him demanding that the young man send an apology to Leveson-Gower for refusing, to stand in as captain. Crawford replied as follows:

> I do not understand your letter. I merely declined to accept the responsibility of skippering a team v the Australians which did not include Rushby, Less and Davis. I knew of nothing against any of the three, nor could I learn anything of what you insinuate. I do not know who was responsible for the selection of the second eleven sort of team furbished up for such an important match, but I apologised to the Australians for it, and explained my reasons for standing down. There seems to be some impression amongst a few of the Surrey committee that I am some young professional instead of being a young fellow who has had an experience of cricket that has seldom fallen to the lot of anyone, and my request for an alteration of the team should have had some weight ...

Among the interesting points which arise out of this naive protestation of gentlemanly status from the indignant Crawford is the implication that it would have been quite acceptable had the committee been browbeating one of the hired hands – Tom Hayward, perhaps, or young Hobbs. As to Crawford's epistolary style, it is at least as urbane as his lordship's and indicates a literate and quietly self-confident young man who will not easily be manipulated. This aspect of Crawford's temperament is obvious enough, but it seems not to have been suspected by Lord Alverstone, who responded with predictable irritation: "I much regret the terms of your letter." Crawford came back by return of post, pointing out that whatever the nature of the unspoken misdemeanours committed by the banned players, they seem to have been pardoned, for all three were now back in the county side. Next morning Alverstone returned to the attack, ending his note with a confession to which he must have had recourse many times in his life: "I am wholly unable to understand ... "

At this stage of the guerilla war, with both sides steadily working themselves into positions from which there was no retreat, the Surrey committee decided to call up the heavy artillery. A few days later Crawford received the following comically blackguardly letter from Leveson-Gower:

Considering the line you have thought fit to adopt towards me with regard to Surrey cricket at which I am not only extremely surprised but extremely hurt, I must cancel my invitation to you for Scarborough. The M.C.C. committee who are responsible for the England side to South Africa this winter have asked me to let you know that under the circumstances they will not now require your services.

His honour assuaged, Leveson-Gower, diminutive in stature and in spirit, decided to send a further note to Crawford, which ends with the most revealing remark of the entire postal exchange: ''I shall have to consider the letter I have had from your father on the subject.'' From the moment the incident had escalated into a full-scale war, Parson Crawford had given his son all the moral support he could muster, and we get the impressions that even if young Jack's sinews had required a little stiffening, which in the event they did not, then the Parson would have been there to do his duty. By 6 August, little more than a fortnight after the administrators of the club had appointed Crawford as captain in a prestigious game, the situation was irretrievable. The club secretary wrote informing him that the club would no longer be requiring his services. Crawford then wrote the last sad letter of the correspondence:

Kindly convey to the committee my acknowledgement of their resolution which surely might have been accompanied by thanks for past services. I fail to see why I should practically be branded as a criminal because, as acting captain, I declined the responsibility of skippering a team which did not include three essential players, an independence which I trust will still remain in spite of the awful example made of me to every amateur in the United Kingdom.

Crawford's closing remarks, concerning the freedom of the gentleman-cricketer to conduct his leisure affairs as he saw fit, refer to one of the central problems of English cricket; had Crawford only realised it, the rights for which he was fighting had already been surrendered when he was a very small prodigy at prep school. The case of Herbert Tremenheer Hewett (1864–1921), defines the anomaly of the gentleman so perfectly that it is surprising that more has not been made of it by historians of the game. Altham praises the left-handed Hewett's aggressive batting style but refers to nothing else; Bowen does not even refer to Hewett at all, nor does C.L.R. James. Warner says only that Hewett was ''a kind of left-handed Jessop''. The one contemporary who gives a hint of Hewett's temperament without breathing so much as a word of the symbolic importance of the man is C. B. Fry, whose first overseas tour, to South Africa under the captaincy of Lord Hawke in 1895–6, first acquainted him with Hewett. He described him in his autobiography as ''one of the greatest left-handed hitters of all time''. It was not Hewett's cricket, however, which disclosed his character to Fry, but his behaviour off the field. There were in Hawke's party several men who were accustomed to being treated with due deference, and when the Customs officials at the Transvaal frontier began poking their noses into the baggage, trouble was not long in coming. Fry reports that "Sir Timothy O'Brien had some aristocratically Irish objection to something done to his luggage, and he caused trouble". But the crisis came when Hewett's turn came:

> A Customs official glimpsed what he thought was a revolver in the trouser pocket of H. T. Hewett. The "Colonel", obstinate and imperturbable, refused to be searched. He just said "No", and looked so threatening that the official fetched some more officials. Then followed an altercation, noisily on the part of the officials, silently insistent on the part of the "Colonel". Armed burghers added themselves to the group, and they too, talked. In a word, the most vehement altercation, with the "Colonel" in the middle as obstinate as a cornered grizzly. Lord Hawke had to exercise his diplomatic talent. In the end the "Colonel" succeeded in entraining with the rest of us, with his cylindrical tooth-brush bottle from his dressing-case still in his trouser pocket, unexamined.

A man who will calmly defy an opposition armed with rifles will not easily be intimidated by a mere rabble, and Hewett, defined by Patrick Morrah as "a somewhat cantankerous character", was bound in the end to lose patience with the contradictions of his situation. Amateurs like him, and Fry and Hawke and O'Brien, played cricket because they enjoyed playing, perhaps more than anything else in life. For them it was a wholly pleasurable exercise, like playing snooker or dancing or riding horses. But they constituted only half the equation of English first-class cricket, which had evolved steadily into a form of popular entertainment for which members of the public paid to watch, and whose playing ranks were sustained by a hard core of professionals, employees of the county clubs, men who played partly because they were gifted, and partly to earn a living. But the oil of the gentleman's hauteur and the water of the player's subservience were never likely to mix, and it so happened that it was the choleric Hewett who first gave notice that this improvised accommodation of the paid and the unpaid could not endure indefinitely. In introducing the episode, Morrah states the case for the amateur with admirable succinctness:

> Leading such a life, the amateurs dictated the spirit of the age. Cricket was a game, not a business; and they played it as such. They provided first-class enjoyment for the spectators, perhaps the better for the fact that they recognised no obligation to do so. It was for their own enjoyment that they played.

But suppose the time came when they no longer enjoyed it? A crusty independent spirit like Hewett, wilful and autocratic as well as highly gifted, would certainly not bother to conceal his feelings should the trammels of the first-class game inhibit him. In July 1893 the Australian tourists came down to Taunton to play Hewett's attractive Somerset eleven. The match was due to begin on Thursday morning, but when the time came to start torrential rain caused an official postponement until the following day. That afternoon, however, there was a break in the weather, and the Somerset authorities, overriding the umpires, decided that play could begin. This decision delighted the spectators, who had come from all over the West Country to see the tourists, and dismayed Hewett, who felt that rules were rules and that conditions were not conducive to enjoyable cricket. The Australians won a low-scoring match, and Hewett expressed his disgust with the committee in terms which nobody, not even a committee member, could misinterpret. In 1894 Wisden closed its account of the Somerset year with the announcement that "after the close of the season, Somerset suffered a heavy blow, Mr. Hewett resigning the captaincy through pressure of professional duties".

The pressure could not have been very great, because Hewett continued to extract enjoyment from cricket by turning out for those first-class sides not committed to the championship. This solution to the problem proved short-lived. At the Scarborough Festival in September 1895, Hewett was chosen to lead an England eleven against Yorkshire, and on the first morning the same problem which had spoiled the match against the Australians two years before now presented itself. The start was delayed through bad weather, and when at last Hewett led his side onto the field he was greeted with a torrent of abuse. Wisden describes the insults as "a most unseemly demonstration", and indeed it was unseemly enough to persuade Hewett to take no further part in the match. His action in walking off the field created a furore. For a first-class cricketer to breach the unwritten code in this way was shocking. For a Gentleman to be the culprit seemed literally unbelievable. As events proved, Hewett's retirement from the match was only the prelude of the melodrama. The defence of his actions was taken up by *The Cricket Field*, which put Hewett's case with great sympathy:

> The action taken by Mr H.T. Hewett is likely to direct attention to the question of how far a gentleman who plays a game for his own amusement, is a servant of the public, and at the back of a garrulous and uncomplimentary crowd … The position of the amateur who plays cricket is now apparently this: so long as he is only an indifferent player he may disport himself in comparative privacy and with complete enjoyment in unimportant matches. But as soon as he becomes famous for his skill he enters a higher class of cricket, and thousands gather to see him play. For himself he is still only indulging in his favourite pastime, and is at liberty to play it as he pleases. But the thousands seem to think otherwise; he is, in their opinion, playing for their pleasure and must obey their dictation. He must do as they like; if he chooses to bat steadily when it is their desire to see hitting, they howl and jeer at him. If it is raining smartly and he does not wish to get a wetting they gather round the pavilion and call him names. Mr Hewett saw the logical absurdity of such a state of things, and rather than submit to it, gave up his game. Viewing his conduct in this light, it is hard to find fault with it. The incident serves to remind the crowd that there are gentlemen who will not, merely because they are attractive batsmen, submit to public and unmerited abuse.

At the time those words were published, the writer assumed that Mr Hewett had withdrawn from a match, but in fact he had retired from all first-class cricket. Mr Hewett was never seen on a first-class cricket field again. Neither

Wisden nor any other obituarists ever told how Hewett filled in his leisure time once he had disowned cricket, but when he died in Brighton 26 years later he was still under sixty and presumably capable of putting bat to ball. Whether Jack Crawford, his dignity punctured by the Surrey committee, considered the case of Hewett we have no way of knowing. It is conceivable that he knew nothing of the case at all, since it had occurred when he was still a child. Fortunately for the welfare of the game, the strategy he adopted was very different from Hewett's.

Exactly what Alverstone, Leveson-Gower and company thought they had achieved by their maladroitness we cannot know. Possibly they assumed that after an appropriately chastening spell in the wilderness, their young heir-apparent to the captaincy of the side would duly apologise and return to the fold. Or perhaps the club was content to forgo the services of one of the world's most prodigious all-rounders for the sake of its own authority. Either way, the Surrey committee must be held accountable for a degree of idiocy rarely met with even in the realms of cricket administration. By the time the storm broke, Crawford had been playing for the club for four years, more than enough time for any reasonably endowed group of adults to have taken his measure. The members of the Surrey committee seem to have been astonished as well as dismayed by what now followed. Crawford did not imitate the example of Hewett and retire from the game, but for all the benefits to Leveson-Gower and the Surrey eleven he might just as well have done. Clearly a man who knew his own mind and not wholly convinced that to play cricket for the county of his birth was the only thing in the world which mattered, Crawford adopted the classic ploy of his age and class by remembering John Stuart Mill's definition of Empire and acting upon it with dizzying swiftness. Just as Charlie Studd had disappeared in search of salvation into the darkness of the Congo, just as the errant Gilbert had been bundled off in search of his to the backwoods of Alberta, just as Vivian Crawford was to abstract himself to Ceylon, so young Jack, confronted by a breach in his affairs, looked to the imperial holdings to repair his fortunes. He chose the one continent where his virtuosity would be appreciated, and by 1910 he was working in Adelaide as a schoolteacher and appearing to most impressive effect in the Sheffield Shield. Had he been Australian born there is no question that he would have been selected to represent the colony against England. As it was, he had to rest content with a place in the South Australian side, and such bonuses as might come his way. In 1913–14 he toured New Zealand with an Australian eleven, there playing one of the most astounding innings of his age, 345 in five and a half hours against South Canterbury, an innings which included fourteen sixes and 45 fours. Then came the Great War, to rob him of his best years, after which he returned to England, and made peace with his old county. Although in his thirties, he still played cricket with all the élan of a gifted schoolboy. It was now, in the curiously muted season of 1919, that he played the finest of all his innings, yet again at the Oval, for Surrey against the all-powerful Australian Expeditionary Force side, substantially the official touring side which returned two years later and flattened all opposition. On this occasion it did not quite flatten Crawford. After making over 400 in their first innings, the Australians took the first five Surrey wickets for 26 runs. Enter Crawford at this point of crisis. In the words of Neville Cardus, "he fell upon the advancing Australian attack, and by driving seldom equalled, threw it back". When Rushby, last man in, came to the wicket, 45 runs were still needed to avoid the follow-on. Rushby held his end up for thirty-five minutes, during which time he scored two runs and there were five extras. Crawford added 73 to his score, finally carrying his bat for 144, including two sixes and 18 fours. Particularly memorable was his contemptuous dismissal of the fast bowling of Jack Gregory, "in a swashbuckling manner that no one else ever approached".

But Crawford's dramatic reconciliation with his old county was no more than the briefest of Indian summers. He played only two more first-class games before retiring, surely confident in the knowledge that he had left a permanent mark on the history of the game. There have survived two tributes to his mercurial brilliance which perhaps come closest to conveying the effect of his style. When he destroyed Gregory at the Oval, straight driving him on to the awning at the top of the pavilion, and hooking him away to the tramlines, Collins, the Australian captain, remarked, "it took your eyesight away". And Neville Cardus, summing up the unusual career of this phenomenally endowed player, wrote:

> His break with Surrey must be regarded as a sad deprivation of fame and pleasure to himself, and a grievous loss to the annals of English cricket. It is as certain as anything in a man's life can be confidently postulated, that had he continued to play in English county cricket in the rising of the years to his prime, he would have taken his place amongst the select company of England's captains.

It makes a familiar story, of inherent genius undone by the invincible alliance of autocracy and idiocy. Nobody among the Surrey committee ever seemed abashed by the events leading to Crawford's departure. None of them ever admitted any errors of judgment, or seemed contrite that England should have been deprived of so glorious a cricketer. Sir Henry Dudley Leveson-Gower went on to become president of the Surrey club and chairman of the England selecters. Jack Crawford outlived him by nine years. Parson Crawford, who died in 1925, proved to be the last of the line to concern himself with ecclesiastic affairs, although it was one of his sons who had the most effective impact on the church. When V.F.S. played his great innings against Yorkshire at Bradford in 1902 he hit one low drive with such power that even that prince of outfielders David Denton declined to have anything to do with it and tactfully let it pass. It travelled on, over the boundary and into the crowd, where it finally came suddenly to rest, knocking a spectator unconscious in the process. Upon examination the involuntary fielder was found to be a parson.

CHAPTER XII

THE GALLOPING MAJOR

———————•———————

W hen Lord Harris arrived in India in 1890, he expressed discontent at the fact that only matting wickets were available to him. In his third season as Governor he laid down a grass pitch, an achievement of which he was so proud that he describes it in some detail in his reminiscences, appending the batting and bowling figures of the Residency side. For the first two seasons the names mean nothing, until suddenly, in 1892, the currency of the batting averages is grossly inflated by the arrival of a new recruit who scores over six hundred runs for an average over eighty. The name of this paragon is Captain Poore, who continues to feature in the Governor's side until 1894, after which the details stop. This junior officer with impressive statistics is nowhere else mentioned in his lordship's book, although Harris certainly saw in the young runmaker a most promising cricketer. When at the end of the 1894 season the captain was moved elsewhere on military duty, Harris must have felt the loss keenly, but he makes no mention either of this deprivation or of Poore's subsequent remarkable fortune as sportsman and soldier.

Robert Montague Poore (1866–1938) is the most impressive example in imperial history of the English sporting Gentleman-adventurer, the exemplar of a certain type of long extinct virtuoso who liked to think, sometimes rightly, that his prowess and imposing physique filled the enemy with awe. It is true that Poore's virtuosity was a limited affair when compared with C.B. Fry's, but where Fry excelled at several activities with which a modern age can identify, Poore was a master of those curiously passé turn-of-century pursuits whose faded glories seem to draw him closer to Rudolph Rassendyll in *The Prisoner of Zenda* than to the deliberations of the League of Nations Assembly to which Fry's loyalties eventually led him. Poore is the kind of man who played in the Gentlemen's side at Lord's on the day the leg-spin of A.J. Raffles carried the amateurs to victory. Wisden refers to his "massive frame and powerful limbs", and tells us that he stood six feet four inches and was blessed with an unusually long reach, attributes which must have been useful to him in his advance to the eminence of "one of the most powerful drivers the game has ever known". But what really appeals about Poore, endowing him with his unique Diamond Jubilee flavour, is his personification of the hoary myth, long since discredited, of the English dilettante soldier of fortune who can do anything he pleases better than anyone he pleases merely by having half a mind to do it. If Poore cannot for a moment match Fry's cleverness, he can at any rate echo Fry's conception of the batting art as academic exercise. He claimed never to have taken the game seriously at all until sent out to India with the 7th Hussars. Here he studied text books on the art of batsmanship to such effect that word of his potential reached the new Governor, taking a six-month breather at Poona. Poore is instantly appointed aide-de-camp to the Governor, and begins performing the duties expected of him by achieving a batting average of 80.

By the time he acquired fluency as a batsman, Poore was already in his mid-twenties, which is late for an outstanding cricketer. But then the captain had had plenty to occupy his mind before arriving at the court of the new Governor. He brought with him the reputation of being one of the finest polo players in the Indian Army, the great star of the 7th Hussars side which won the Inter-Regimental tournament in 1891. In 1893 he won the West of India Lawn Tennis title and represented the regiment in shooting competitions. In 1894 he retained the Tennis title, won the Bombay Hunt point-to-point and the Best Man-at-Arms contest. A year later he entered the latter contest once again, this time at Poona, and again was placed first. In 1895 this exemplary military career was most inconsiderately interrupted by one or two imperial scuffles,

when his regiment, transferred to South Africa, became involved in the Matabele Rebellion of 1896 and the Mashona Campaign of 1897. The verdict of history on these little wars has not been too flattering. Undertaken in order that Cecil Rhodes might line his pockets with the gold which he mistakenly believed lay beyond the Limpopo, the Matabele and Mashona escapades have been described since as among "the bloodiest and most ferocious of punitive wars", a scheme by Rhodes "to take over the administration of the area in return for the profits", and, most damningly, as "a chronicle of squalor. There was no style to it all, it was second-rate glory". None of this

The gentleman-adventurer Major Poore, six foot four scourge of the Matabele and county bowlers alike. An extinct imperial species.

155

concerned the Captain, whose professional obligation it was to do or die and ask no questions. For him, the Matabele and Mashona episodes were little more than potential devices for furthering his career. They constituted, so far as he was concerned, a good show. for his bravery during the campaigns the captain was mentioned in despatches and promoted to Major. This promotion was well deserved, but it was in a sense an untimely interruption of Poore's study of the art of batsmanship, which by now had reached the stage where he could put the book aside. When Lord Hawke brought a side to tour South Africa in 1895–6, his bowlers conceded only two centuries. Poore scored both of them. In a stay at Natal of a few months he scored nine hundreds, and by the time he returned home to England in 1898 his reputation had preceded him, largely because Hawke's men had reason to remember him.

The Major was an Irishman, but as a serving officer his residential qualification was for Hampshire, a county which prospered greatly through the accident of possessing within its boundaries the garrison at Aldershot, to which Poore was now posted. In the 1898 season Poore played eleven matches for Hampshire, scored two centuries and impressed most of the experts as a defensive rather than as a destructive batsman. Nobody was prepared for the onslaught of 1899, least of all the bowlers in the counties. Military commitments, plus a few extraneous sporting engagements, delayed his entry into the County championship until 12 June. Eight weeks later the campaign was over and the Major on his way back to South Africa, where a rather less sporting war was now imminent. But eight weeks was all that the Major required. In that brief period he batted twelve times, scored seven centuries, had a highest score of 304, scored 1399 runs and came out with an average of over 116. It was now clear that 1898 had been mere target practice. As to the innate quality of the Major's batting, it may or may not be significant that in that amazing high summer of 1899 his only failures were in those representative games for which he was hastily selected. These bumps in an otherwise smooth progress reduced his average to under a hundred, but did nothing to damage the legend which hung about him. How much longer he would have continued putting the bowlers of England to the sword will never be known, but there must have been many a county trundler who heard of the major's departure for fresh battlefronts with a sigh of relief.

When the Major arrived in the Hampshire dressing-room for his lightning campaign of 1899 he brought with him a trophy cupboard packed with booty, and the most impressive thing of all about him was that while he was smashing all the batting records for his adopted county, he was continuing to spend a considerable amount of time and energy on other aspects of his virtuosity. In his first fortnight home he scored three centuries in succession for Hampshire, including two in one match against Somerset. During this period he also played for the winning team in the Inter-Regimental Polo championships, and, at the Royal Naval and Military Tournament, won the Mounted event for the Best Man-At-Arms in the British Army. It comes as no surprise to learn that this one-man army eventually rose to the rank of Brigadier-General, at which advanced stage in life he was still making life a misery for the bowlers unlucky enough to encounter him. Morrah has written a charming account of Harris's old aide-de-camp in his declining years, mellowed now against the rustic backdrop of an English rural idyll, but still able to intimidate outsiders should occasion arise. One day in 1932 Morrah arrives in the Dorset village of Broadstone, to play for a strolling eleven against the locals:

> The star player on the village side was Brigadier-General R.M. Poore, then over sixty, and his 129 not out was a delight to the eye; to observe his great height and authoritative stance at the wicket, his bat high uplifted in the Maclaren manner, his hard and clean driving, his impeccable forward play and certainty in defence, was to catch a glimpse of the Golden Age in action. The general had a local reputation for caution and steadiness ... but I remember a square leg drive off my humble attempt at a googly which went far beyond the confines of the little Broadstone ground. The village team were a little frightened of him. Certainly he did not suffer fools gladly, and one or two colleagues who were not quite quick enough in responding to his call for a sharp single found themselves blasted in crisp and pungent military phrases. But my pleasantest memory is of his geniality and his reminiscences of the cricketers he had known, over lunch in the village inn.

How had the Major progressed to the rank of general? During the Boer War which had so inconsiderately interrupted his ritual slaughter of England's bowlers he had been Mentioned in Despatches three times and been awarded the Distinguished Service Order. By 1911 he was back in India commanding his regiment. In 1915 he saw service on the North-West Frontier as a Brigadier-General leading the Jhansi Brigade, was Mentioned in Despatches a fourth time and was appointed a Commander of the Indian Empire. In 1921 he retired to Wimborne in Dorset, becoming Deputy Lieutenant of the county and a Justice of the Peace. But about Poore as an individual we know next to nothing. Does such a man ever marry? What was the source of the income which enabled him to spend his retirement by presiding in squirearchical splendour over a rustic English backwater? What of the Matabele and the Mashona, mere stabs of bright colour on the sandwich board of the general's chest? Like many a hero of the Indian Army, the general must have felt at times that his world had completely melted away. He died in July 1938 in his 73rd year, dimly remembered by cricketing antiquarians as the man who, a long time ago, had enjoyed a six-week purple patch which set the country buzzing. A month after his death a professional from Yorkshire called Hutton scored 364 in an innings against Australia to set a new record.

CHAPTER XIII

THE PRINCE
AND THE SCHOLAR

———•———

I n his later years Colonel His Highness Shri Sir Ranjitsinhji Vibhaji, Jam
Sahib of Nawanagar, must have been amused by the way he had been
patronised as a youth by the English cricketing aristocracy, none of whose
members remotely approached him either in rank or expectations. Born in the
province of Kathiaward in September 1872, the prince had been obliged to
endure many a genteel snub from comparatively recently ennobled peers who
had not the remotest idea where Kathiaward was or who the prince claimed to
be, except that he was brown-skinned, and, as the more cynical punsters put it,
beyond the pale. Yet the prince's credentials were impeccable. Like the English
lords, he had been sent to board at a preparatory school, and like them had been
coached meticulously in the morality as well as the technique of the game by a
graduate of Cambridge University, Chester Macnaghton, an expatriate
pedagogue with a passion for cricket. The prince's school imitated the
conventions of its English counterpart even down to the equivalent of house
matches, between the boarders of the northern and southern halves of the
premises. There was a pretty little pavilion, donated by the Maharajah of
Bhownuggar, before which the prince and his team-mates would practice at
every opportunity. While the standards of batting and bowling were modest,
the fielding approached English school standard. And yet for all this, the
prince's counterparts at Eton and Harrow would have dismissed the proceedings as nothing more than a colonial joke. For the aspiring cricketers at the
Rajkumar College performed their practice in native costume.

It happened that English schoolboys, adorned in obtrusively chromatic
striped blazers and tasselled caps, were also inclined to display themselves in
native costume, but the joke eluded most Englishmen of the period, who
regarded young players like the prince as little more than sedulous apes intent
on flattering their masters by impersonating their manners. Mr Macnaghton
imparted as many of the principles of batting, bowling and fielding as he was
able, but by the time the prince arrived in England in 1888, whatever technique

*Parker's Piece, Cambridge, in the 1860s, with the gaol in the distance. The ground nurtured
many outstanding cricketers, including Ranji and Jack Hobbs.*

he possessed was for the most part the fruit of empirical experiment on the lawns of Rajkumar College. He later confessed that in order to condition himself to the English game, he had been obliged to unlearn many of the Rajkumar precepts, and had achieved this by playing club cricket. During the six months following his arrival he attended a London crammer in the hope of preparing himself for the rarefied intellectual atmosphere of university life. Once installed in Trinity, he was unable to make any impression on the local cricketing establishment, and began turning out under the name of Smith for the Cassandra Club. He quickly became one of the attractions of Parker's Piece, on whose plebeian plains he began performing prodigies of such brilliance that it required the bigotry of the varsity blues to overlook them.

The Cambridge captain that year was the Hon. F.S. Jackson, heir apparent to Hawke. One afternoon, while strolling across Parker's Piece, Jackson found himself among a huge crowd savouring the spectacle, rare for those days, of a batsman going down on his knees to play the hook stroke. Jackson later joked about his failure to recognise genius, but there is no evidence that the prince was very amused. Among the aspects of university life which did delight him was that cricket stood as high as any other subject on the curriculum, and that the visiting professors available for hire by undergraduates included Tom Richardson and Ephraim Lockwood of Surrey. As Richardson was thought by many to be the finest fast bowler of the age, and as Lockwood was almost equally renowned, it is no surprise that the Cambridge players tended to be more proficient in coping with fast bowling than with Virgilian hyperbole. Gilbert Jessop, who followed the prince into Cambridge in 1896, and who published a considerable amount of journalism, was as a grown man capable of the most spectacular breaches of spelling and grammar.

The prince's progress was slow, as he shed the old habits and acquired new ones. It was not until 1891 that he began to regard himself as a real cricketer. By now he had entered on the first of his three years as an undergraduate, but it was not until his last season, in 1893, that he found a place in the university side to play Oxford at Lord's. By 1895 he was the ascendent star of the Sussex county side; in the following year, in his first Test match against Australia, he made 62 and 154 not out; in Australia with A.E. Stoddart's side in 1897-8, he made a century in his first overseas Test. In 1899 and again in 1900 he passed the mark of 3,000 runs in an English season, and a year later scored 285 not out against Somerset. From 1899 to 1903 he captained the Sussex side, and in 1904, his last full season with the club, he topped the national batting averages. Yet his progress was not easy. Constitutionally the prince was not a robust man; at the end of his great season of 1896 he had collapsed with congestion of the lung, a misfortune which nevertheless bore literary fruit. In an attempt to beguile the long hours of convalescence, he tried his hand at writing. The result was a sedate classic called *The Jubilee Book of Cricket*, with its spectacular dedication: "By Her Gracious Permission, to Her Majesty the Queen-Empress". As to the full authorship of this work, there remains a faint shadow of contention, but whoever was responsible for the various sections, the book contains observations of unusual insight in the context of the period, particularly the passage in which the writer suggests cricket as a minor art form with emollient qualities:

> Cricket is a first-rate interest. The game has developed to such a pitch that it is worth taking interest in. Go to Lord's and analyse the crowd. There are all sorts and conditions of men there around the ropes – bricklayers, bank clerks, soldiers, postmen, and stockbrokers. And in the pavilion are Q.C.s, artists, archdeacons and leader-writers. Bad men, good men workers and idlers, all are there, and all at one in their keenness over the game. It is a commonplace that cricket brings the most opposite characters and the most diverse lives together. Anything that puts very many different kinds of people on a common ground must promote sympathy and kindly feelings.

Although the prince defines these sentiments as "commonplace", they were not at all so when he wrote them. If he wrote them. In a prefatory note we read:

> In the following work the author has received special assistance from Mr. W.J. Ford; Professor Case; Mr. C.B. Fry; Dr. Butler, the Master of Trinity College, Cambridge; Mr. Gaston of Brighton, and the writers on County Cricket. To these, and to other players of the game and wellwishers of it who have lent him their help, he desires to record his grateful thanks here.

Of those listed, it is probably Fry who contributed most, although perhaps in no more significant role than counsellor. Nobody has ever seriously suggested that there is anything counterfeit in Ranji's authorship of the book.

At the end of the 1904 season Sussex found themselves obliged to struggle on without the prince's services, but in 1912 he made a welcome comeback, returning to England to score over a thousand runs, including one dazzling display against Lancashire at Brighton at the end of July, when he scored 176, including twenty-three boundaries, in such brilliant style that by evening the London newspaper placards were conveying the news to a population which had never forgotten him. And then the prince was gone again; apart from a few gentle outings after the Great War, England saw no more of the first cricketing virtuoso to come out of India and one of the most original sylists ever to pick up a bat. None of his boosters was ever too embarrassed to express their admiration in racial terms. According to the analytical Fry, "What gave him his distinctiveness was a combination of the perfect poise and the suppleness and the quickness peculiar to the athletic Hindu". Neville Cardus, reduced to wonder by Ranji's technique, was moved to far more rapturous prose than Fry, which was understandable. Fry had only shared the crease with this mysterious stranger. Cardus had observed him from the crowd:

> A strange light from the East flickered in the English sunshine when he was at the wicket. When he turned approved science upside down and changed the geometry of batsmanship to an esoteric legerdemain, we were bewitched to the realms of rope-dancers and snake-charmers; this was cricket of oriental sorcery, glowing with a dark beauty of its own, a beauty with its own mysterious axis and balance . . . . .

In more prosaic terms Cardus meant that neither he nor anyone else in England could understand how the prince could so consistently, and so safely, glance round to leg the fastest bowling directed straight at the middle stump.

The curiously disjointed nature of the prince's career in English cricket, with its wonderfully ironic prelude featuring the pseudonymous Smith, the brilliant first movement, followed by a hiatus of eight years, then the second enchanting passage, followed by virtually nothing, seems on the face of it inexplicable, unless this apparent gift for ''esoteric legerdemain'' extended to the prince's apparent ability to appear and then disappear at will. The cricketing public, dimly aware that in a country as quaintly archaic as India some princes still had duties, assumed that from time to time Ranji was obliged to take temporary leave to manage his seraglios, or whatever it was that Jam Sahibs did when not scoring centuries. In the meantime, the cricket world was more than grateful for what it had been given of Ranji. He had enlivened the field of play as no cricketer since W.G. Grace, and in a subtle way had flattered the English into believing that their game was indeed irresistible, a potential world-conqueror. Did it not speak volumes for cricket that so distinguished a personage should come from across the world, dropping all his diplomatic commitments in order to acquire and then exhibit his virtuosity? A closer look at the facts of Ranji's career suggests that the prince never attached to cricket the importance which the English always assumed he did, and that had he not become embroiled in certain political complications at a stage in his life when he was too callow to understand them, he might never have bothered to come to England at all; might never have taken lessons from Richardson and Lockwood; and might never have become an English hero.

There were more than one among the governors of English cricket who would have been truculent at the news that Ranji was not quite of the blood royal after all. As a young Rajput aristocrat he had been adopted by the Jam Bibhaji of Nawanagar, heir to the throne. Students of Indian history of the period may be inclined to assume that the Jam had conjugal access to more than one partner and that Ranji may

Ranji, seemingly about to take wing, is captured for posterity by photographer George Beldam, a tireless chronicler of the Golden Age.

have been the issue of one of these liaisons, a theory rendered considerably less improbable by the sequence of events which brought about the first crisis in Ranji's life. The Jam's patronage having thrust him into the front line of local politics, Ranji found himself at a serious disadvantage when, as a result of a zenana intrigue, his rights of succession were abruptly abrogated. The Jam, although retaining his affection for his protégé, was unable to give him political support, at least for the moment, and indeed found the very presence of Ranji in Nawanager an acute embarrassment. What to do with him? Perhaps it was Mr Macnaghton who came up with the answer. When a prince is unwanted, it would be as well to pack him off to an English university. And so Ranji arrived in an England whose mood was modulating from imperial pride to the stridency of jingoism. Major Poore and his fellow-warriors were at this very moment "punishing" the Mashona and the Matabele in the cause of Cecil Rhodes' bank account, and in any case the young prince could have harboured no illusions regarding the status of a dark-skinned colonial in the Mother Country. Although in later years he was too suave a diplomat to raise the subject, he knew perfectly well that wherever the English went, they were inclined to lord it over the natives as if by divine right and with a degree of coarseness which might have been amusing had it not also been tragic. Ranji's was a life suffused with irony at almost every turn.

The extent of this boorishness was so extreme that it surprised a great many intelligent Englishmen encountering it for the first time. Among their number was Clement Scott, dramatic critic for *The Daily Telegraph*, famous for his opposition to censorship in the Music Hall, notorious for his halfwitted jingo song lyrics, and the object of derision for his dementia whenever anyone mentioned the name of Ibsen. In 1892 Scott arrived in Bombay in time to watch the Parsees defeat Lord Hawke's touring side. Scott relished the experience, but was deeply shocked by his experience of etiquette off the field of play:

> In England at any local cricket match, whether on a village green or in the squire's park, if the squire happened to be playing, or an officer resident in the neighbourhood, or the local solicitor, it would be considered very snobbish if all classes did not sit down together at one common meal in the cricket tent. It is no more infra dig for the gentry to break bread with the artisan than for the lady of the house to lead off with the butler at a servants' ball. But such customs do not prevail, I am sorry to say, in India. On the occasion of which I am speaking, the Parsee captain happened to be a Cambridge graduate, but he and all his companions in the cricket field were not allowed to break bread with an Englishman, or to enter an English club, merely because their skins were dark.

Scott's astonishment at what he found sounds excessively naive, but he was genuinely outraged by this state of affairs, and went on to catalogue other injustices connected with Anglo-Indian cricket. One wealthy Parsee had purchased some land and presented it to an English club for athletic purposes. "But though bought, built and furnished by him, his own daughters were not allowed to enter the ground, because it was an English club, and they were

Parsees". Scott ends his essay, written and published in 1899, with the declaration: "We have won India, we have Anglicised India: let us live with India", sentiments which would have drawn a wry smile from the future Jam Sahib.

Scott's plea for mutual tolerance on the cricket fields of India was based on the assumption that in England no such bigotry was to be found. Evidently he had heard nothing of Lord Harris' opposition to Ranji's inclusion in an England side, and was ignorant of the racial discrimination practiced against the prince at Cambridge. F.S. Jackson, the Cambridge captain who selected Ranji to play against Oxford in the last of the prince's three seasons, later became Governor of Bengal. During his incumbency he modestly confessed that his own enlightenment was the result of his visit to India with Hawke's tourists, where his exposure to the realities of empire had left him with some insights into racial relationships. That Jackson had to go to India before becoming capable of imagining an Indian is hardly surprising in a man who was to occupy the chairmanship of the Conservative and Unionist Party during the deplorable episode of the Zinoviev Letter, but it says something for Jackson's sense of fair play that he did select the prince, even though, in the words of Sir Home Gordon, "there was so much prejudice against a nigger showing us how to play cricket". Sir Home testified that such sentiments were so common that he was threatened with expulsion from the M.C.C. by a veteran who had represented the Gentlemen and had served on the M.C.C. committee, "if he had the disgusting degeneracy to praise a dirty black". Gordon, a sturdy advocate of Ranji's cause, also suggested that the prince's trademark at the crease, a white silk shirt with the sleeves buttoned at the wrist, was evidence of "a sensitive desire to mitigate his dusky appearance". To all this loutishness, and to the courtesies extended to him by more enlightened spirits, Ranji smiled a polite smile and went about his business, which was not, as the English assumed, the game of cricket but the murkier one of politics.

At the end of 1904 a change in the political climate sent him home to Nawanagar, where the chances of his succession to the throne had taken a turn for the better. At last the old Jam died, and on 10 March 1907, Ranji, swathed in jewels, rode an elephant to his installation as Jam Sahib of Nawanagar. In his acceptance speech he said: "I shall endeavour to play the game so as not to lose whatever credit I have gained in another field". Soon after his inaugural triumph he was struck down by fever, but in 1908 he returned to England on political business and once more delighted the crowds at Hove and at Lord's. At the end of the season a banquet was given in his honour at Cambridge, after which he left for India. Four seasons later he was back again, playing for Sussex but in a sense for the whole of England, which was delighted to see him, and which hoped that he would now find the time to devote all his energies to the great love of his life. That is exactly what Ranji did, except that the great love of his life happened to be Nawanager and not English cricket. His 1912 return was a diplomatic mission, a skirmish in his struggle for the rights of his native

The Parsee touring team of 1886. The Parsees were enthusiastic converts to cricket but on this tour won only one of the 28 games they played.

state. Such cricket as he played during 1912 was no more than a pleasant diversion from the stresses of diplomatic special pleading. Had Ranji chosen to proceed with his cricket career, it would have meant long bouts of absence from his throne, an unthinkable tactic in a man who proved to be among the most dedicated and most enlightened of all the princes of the Raj.

When the Great War came, Ranji, now over forty and suffering from severe asthma and bronchitis, served on the Western Front. While on leave in 1915 he went to Filey to enjoy some shooting and was accidentally shot in the left eye by one of his companions. He lost the eye but not the sense of honour which forbids a true gentleman to reveal the name of the culprit. In 1920 he was in England once again, portly and one-eyed but still willing to try his hand with the bat. At Hastings in mid-August the name of K.S. Ranjitsinhji appeared for the last time on a Sussex scoresheet. He batted at number eight against Northants and scored a single before being given out leg-before-wicket to the bowling of C.N. Woolley. After that he took his leave of cricket, but he was never forgotten by those who had seen him bat. A number of his remarks are revealing of the casual outward demeanour which masked a steely courage and a yearning for perfection. He defined his batting procedure as ''Find out where the ball is; get there; hit it'', and on being told of the misfortunes of a fellow-player who had missed the ball and received a bruised rib for his pains, he asked, ''Didn't the poor fellow have a bat?''. Yet Ranji himself lapsed from the ideal at least once. J.B. Priestley fondly recalled that in his first Test, at Old Trafford, ''he finished with a trickle of blood curling down from an earlobe, the price of a rare missed hook against the Australian express bowler Ernie Jones''. Priestley was by no means the only writer to be attracted by the Ranji myth. That passionate lover of cricket James Joyce, who according to his brother Stanislaus, ''eagerly studied the feats of Ranji and Fry'', included the prince in the most esoteric English novel ever published. Those who have trudged through the labyrinth of *Finnegan's Wake* will have found momentary delight in the famous passage which incorporates punning versions of at least thirty-one well-known cricketers. Towards the beginning of this crazy catalogue we read:

> At half past quick in the morning. And her lamp was all askew and a trumbly wick-in-her, ringeysingey.

Joyce's pun is at any rate superior to the effort by *Punch*, remembered as ''Runget-sin-hji'', but hardly more ingenious that the cry once heard from the cheap stand, ''Ramsgate Jimmy''.

More revealing is a novel by John Masters entitled *The Ravi Lancers*, whose hero, an Indian cricketing prince called Krishna Ram, comes to London on the eve of the Great War and scores a brilliant century for Surrey. Krishna Ram is a patent imitation of Ranji, even down to the interlude in which the young prince receives tuition from the great Tom Richardson. But in borrowing so blatantly from reality Masters blundered into one of the most spectacular solecisms in all sporting fiction, more startling in its way even than Ernest Hemingway's memorable observation in *Men Without Women* that ''Down in Australia the English cricketers were sharpening their wickets''. In writing a story about the fighting on the Western Front, Masters made the fictional Ranji a generation younger, which was feasible enough except that in the intervening years an incident had taken place of which evidently he had no knowledge. In a chapter headed ''June 1915'', we find our young prince in the nets at the Oval, batting to the bowling of Tom Richardson, who had by this time been lying in his grave for three years. Richardson had died in obscure circumstances in the summer of 1912, in the French town of St Jean d'Arvey. But whatever the details, Richardson was certainly long since dead by 1915, for which reason Krishna Ram could have claimed to be the first man to live out the poetic fancy of Francis Thompson by batting to the bowling of a ghost.

After 1920 Ranji was finished with cricket. But if the cricketer was dead, the princely diplomat was very much alive and a dominant figure in Indian politics. Although his kingdom was small, his reputation was great, and he was chosen to be Chancellor of the Chamber of Indian Princes. In the words of one writer he was ''perhaps the only genuinely benevolent autocrat who has ever existed''.

Ranji resplendent in his robes as Jam Sahib of Nawanagar. For all his rich cricketing talents, the governance of his tiny kingdom was his chief passion, a fact little realised by his adoring public in England.

At which point we must retrace our steps to examine the vital importance of that coupling by Stanislaus Joyce, "Ranji and Fry". When the prince played for Cambridge against Oxford at Lord's in 1893, one of his opponents was destined to become his lifelong friend, partner in many a record-breaking stand for Sussex, and a loyal supporter in the political wrangles in which Ranji was to find himself embroiled when the Great War ended. Charles Burgess Fry, of Repton, Oxford, Sussex, Hampshire and England, was the most astounding all-rounder of the century, captain of Oxford at football and cricket, scorer of six centuries in successive innings for Sussex, an England cricket captain who never lost a Test, a natural athlete who while still an undergraduate broke the world Long Jump record with a leap of 23ft $6\frac{1}{2}$ inches, a feat which remained unsurpassed for twenty-one years. An accomplished dancer and horseman, acknowledged by his peers as the possessor of the finest academic brain of his generation, Fry ended his days as a journalist and novelist, having devoted most of his postwar energies to the administration of the training ship *Mercury*. It was his friendship with Ranjitsinhji which very nearly transformed a man of startling accomplishments into a figure stranded between a joke and a myth. The episode sprang from Fry's status as a sort of secretary-cum-eminence grise to Ranji during the prince's attendance at the First, Third and Fourth Assemblies of the League of Nations at Geneva. Fry's duties consisted of discussing problems with the prince before meetings with delegates from other countries, and drafting speeches which "would if necessary last an hour". Ranji was a great success at Geneva, being elected chairman of one of the committees, but Fry concedes that both he and Ranji were helped by their cricketing fame, by now so widespread that even the Japanese delegation knew of it. When the prince was introduced to the representative for Poland, it is said that as they shook hands both Ranji and Paderewski murmured, "Aren't you better known for something else?" The story, which sounds more like Cardus than history, at any rate has about it the ring of poetic truth. Yet nothing reads more fantastically than the chain of events which at one point threatened to bring about a unique transformation in Fry's life.

Among the beggars at the diplomatic feast of Geneva was Albania, not a League member but hoping for an invitation. With this end in view they had sent a delegation of three to Geneva. One morning Fry went to visit Ranji, who was still in bed, enjoying his breakfast. Fry takes up the story:

> 'Carlo, would you like to be King of Albania?'
> I accepted on the nail. I was willing to be king of any willing nation.
> 'Well, the Bishop is coming to see me about it tomorrow'.

Ranji then explained the background to his question. When the Great War ended, Albania, ruled by an absconding German prince, found itself kingless. The leader of its Geneva delegation, a bearded bishop who could have been mistaken, according to Fry, for W.G. Grace with the light behind him, decided that the best policy for his country was to "obtain the services of an English

C.B. Fry, cricketer, scholar, diplomat and would-be King of Albania, displays a profile worthy of matinée idol John Barrymore.

country gentleman with ten thousand a year". Fry qualified on the first count but fell woefully short on the second. However, his good friend the prince had more funds than he knew what to do with, and Fry quickly perceived that Ranji "was balancing in his astute mind the relative advantages of finding £10,000 a year and planting me as King of Albania, or of retaining me on his political staff with a considerably less salary, with a view to future political activities in India".

Fry remained rather attracted by the prospect of becoming a monarch, and was never very clear in his own mind why he was never enthroned, although he sensed that Ranji gradually realised the inconvenience of subsidising a king and decided against it:

> How long I remained as the first candidate in the field for the crown of Albania beyond the first fortnight I do not know. If I had really pressed Ranji to promote me, it is quite on the cards that I should have been King of Albania yesterday, if not today. Nor would Mussolini have disposed of me as easily as he did of King Zog.

The episode finally sputtered out in sad anti-climax, but it would be interesting to know whether Fry sensed echoes of his abortive elevation some years later when, accompanied by another England captain, G.O. Allen, he was invited by a third to visit the Hollywood studio where David Selznick was filming *The Prisoner of Zenda*. On the day that Fry came to watch, shooting had reached the stage where Ronald Colman's English adventurer Rudolph Rassendyll, masquerading as King of Ruritania, is crowned in Strelsau Cathedral. Here was an English country gentleman with rather more than ten thousand a year assuming the authority of a distant European monarchy. Fry makes no mention of the parallels in his autobiography, and perhaps never noticed them, but had Ranji provided the wherewithal in Geneva, it is possible that Fry would have proved no more adept at the elusive art of kingship than the hapless Zog, and perhaps a great deal worse. For all his erudition and apparent intimacy with Herodotus and Thucydides, Fry was a dangerous duffer when it came to the politics of the twentieth century. In 1934 he visited Nazi Germany, greatly enjoying a cosy chat with Hitler; five years later, in an autobiography published on the eve of the Second World War, he declared that the discipline of the Hitler Youth, when compared with the Boy Scouts, was "a distinct point of superiority on the German side". Of Nazi Germany as a whole he observed, "the atmosphere of effective discipline strangely appealed to me ... everybody knew his allotted place and went there when called". Fry's notion of the modern state as a sort of cricket team consisting in its entirety of obedient professionals under the command of an amateur whose word is law sounds like the ramblings of an idiot, and yet in the 1920s Fry, who liked to think of himself as a civilised man with vaguely progressive views, twice stood as a Liberal candidate at by-elections, on both occasions polling many thousands of votes. His confession that "effective discipline strangely appealed to me" carries with it a hint of ancient skeletons rattling away in forgotten closets. Years after Fry's death in 1956 there were revelations by ex-apprentices from the training ship *Mercury*, who claimed that life aboard the lugger included regular chastisement personally adminis-tered by the mannish-looking Mrs Fry.

The former England captain who invited Fry and his friends to watch the filming of *The Prisoner of Zenda* was a man who had played the king so many times that, by some obscure process of osmosis, a kingliness now attached to both his profile and his demeanour. Charles Aubrey Smith, Old Carthusian, gifted outside right, and a bowler with a delivery so eccentric that all England knew him as "Round-the-Corner" Smith, became in time the cricketer with the widest fame of all, although not for his cricket. Even as a Cambridge undergraduate, Smith was in love with the theatre, expending much energy on amateur theatricals, although never at the expense of his cricket. He appeared for Sussex between 1882 and 1896, captained a side to Australia in 1887-8, and a year later led England in the first Test match played in South Africa, at Port Elizabeth, where his left-arm medium pace bowling earned him seven wickets. By the time he retired from the Sussex side he was already a rising star of the London stage. In January 1896 theatregoers were flocking to see him as the villainous Black Michael, the would-be king in *The Prisoner of Zenda*, a production so irresistible that the enfant terrible of dramatic criticism, the young Bernard Shaw, accorded it the unprecedented honour of reviewing it twice, saying only that in the role of Black Michael, "Mr Aubrey Smith suffices". At the end of the year Shaw returned to the same theatre to watch *As You Like It*, and to find that Smith's appearance as the Duke "was so magnificent that it taxed all his powers to live up to his own aspect".

Smith's fame as a cricketer followed him through the years, not always to his own advantage as an actor. When Shaw suggested him as a suitable Professor Higgins in the first production of *Pygmalion*, Mrs Patrick Campbell reacted with "Really, Joey, what nonsense. I could never act with a cricket bat". However, by 1920 Smith, a "kindly man, but pompous and without humour", was the only leading man in London willing to endure Mrs Pat's tantrums, and he was found acceptable as Higgins, even though he seemed unsure of his lines. Mrs Pat, whose own sense of humour was also limited, enjoyed twitting the ex-England captain at rehearsals by greeting him with, "Good morning, Aubrey dear, have you brought your cricket bat with you?"

Mrs Pat might have been surprised to learn that the answer to her rhetorical question would always be "Yes". Smith always brought his cricket bat with him, even to the barren plains of Hollywood, where, from a home high in the hills called "The Round Corner", he administered the Hollywood Cricket Club and enjoyed the unique honour of having a cricket ground in Los Angeles named after him.

Smith was the leader of that colony of

A caricature of C. Aubrey Smith, and his inimitable 'Round-the-Corner' bowling action, in a one-day game between authors and actors.

C. Aubrey Smith with his beloved Hollywood Cricket Club on a visit to Vancouver in 1936.
Errol Flynn lounges on the end of the front row next to Nigel Bruce, familiar to film fans as
Dr Watson to Basil Rathbone's aquiline Sherlock Holmes.

British expatriates hired by the studios to man the ramparts of the last beleaguered outpost of Empire. When Fry arrived in Hollywood at Smith's invitation, he was soon walking through a North-West Frontier village left over from *Lives of a Bengal Lancer*. One afternoon he found himself playing for Smith's side against one of the local clubs. Smith's eleven that afternoon included A.J. Raffles (David Niven), Sherlock Holmes (Basil Rathbone) and Dr Watson (Nigel Bruce). In discourse with another player, Frankenstein's Monster (Boris Karloff, a keen and adroit wicketkeeper), Fry reached the conclusion that Karloff's great success as a monster was "easily explained by his earlier career as a Greek scholar and Indian civil servant".

David Niven recalled that when Smith summoned you to the cricket field, you obeyed the command. And you maintained some sort of decorum even in the face of absurdity. A.A. Thomson has told how Smith, fielding in the slips, dropped a catch, stopped the game and called for his butler, who was instructed to bring the captain his spectacles. The butler returned with the spectacles and the game continued. A few minutes later Smith dropped another catch, and was heard to curse, "The damn fool brought my reading glasses".

By the time Smith dropped those catches he was an unofficial ambassador-at-large to the courts of the movie moguls. Whenever a producer required the services of a blueblood, out went the cry "Send for Smith". In *The House of*

Rothschild and *Sixty Glorious Years* he was the Duke of Wellington; in Tolstoy's *Resurrection* he was Prince Korchagin; in *Romeo and Juliet* Lord Capulet; in *Lloyds of London* the Marquess of Queensberry; in *Kidnapped* the Duke of Argyll; in *Madame Curie* Lord Kelvin; in *An Ideal Husband* Lord Caversham, bringing to all these roles the same bristling patrician authority for which his Colonel Sapt in *The Prisoner of Zenda* is so fondly remembered. But it may be that the ubiquitous Smith's greatest contribution to the evolution of cricket as a world game came about as a result of illness contracted during the 1888–9 tour of South Africa. One of Smith's companions on the tour was an amateur cricketer, Monty Bowden, an impetuous type who thought he saw in the volatile society of Johannesburg, in a frenzy of speculative excitement after the discovery of gold, an opening for a pair of enterprising young English stockbrokers. The firm of Smith and Bowden began operations, pausing only for a moment to wave their fellow-tourists farewell as the boat sailed for England. But then the stock market collapsed and so did Smith, stricken with typhoid. He became so gravely ill that one local paper published his obituary, fifty-nine years too soon. Once Smith had recovered, he began to involve himself with local cricket, and soon became enthusiastic about the potential strength of Johannesburg cricket. During the English tour the Kimberley side had been awarded a new trophy, called the Currie Cup, for their outstanding performances against the all-conquering tourists. Smith now decided that he would muster the strongest available eleven from the Johannesburg area and issue a formal challenge to the Kimberley side, with the Currie Cup as the prize. Smith's Transvaal eleven won the cup easily, but the real importance of Smith's challenge lay in the establishment of an annual contest for the Currie Cup. That annual contest has continued to this day, exactly one hundred years after reports of Charles Aubrey Smith's death were exaggerated. ''Round-the-Corner'' Smith was knighted for his contribution to Anglo-American relations in 1944. Four years later, about to embark on the role he had coveted for so long, Old Jolyon in *The Forsyte Saga*, he died in his 86th year. He lies in the churchyard of St Leonard's in Hove, within hailing distance of the ground on which he made his county debut in a match between Sussex and Derbyshire in June 1882.

CHAPTER XIV

APPEARANCE AND REALITY

The mechanics of spinning a cricket ball are straightforward enough. If a right-arm bowler places his fingers across the seam and turns his wrist from right to left at the moment of release, the ball will spin through the air in an anti-clockwise direction and, on hitting the grass, will continue on in the same direction, away from the right-handed batsman. Because such a delivery moves into the batsman from the leg-side, this ball is known as the leg-break. On the other hand, if the bowler turns his wrist from left to right, the same process will occur in reverse, the ball travelling through the air while spinning in a clockwise direction and cutting into the batsman from the off-side. This ball is called an off-break and, because of the anatomy of the human arm, wrist and fingers, is easier to control than the leg-break. It follows from these apparently immutable laws that a batsman, faced by a spin bowler, would be well advised to master the art of "reading the arm", or deducing the way the ball will turn from the movement of the bowler's wrist at the moment of delivery. Some great batsmen have even claimed to study not the bowler's wrist but the movement of the ball as it comes towards them. Ranjitsinhji said that he "watched the seam", for the accuracy of his eyesight was legendary in the days of his primacy.

The exactitude of these methods of spinning a ball made batting an easier art than it might otherwise have been. An accomplished batsman need never select the wrong stroke to deal with any given delivery, for he would know even as the ball began its flight through the air what it was likely to do once it hit the ground. This certitude on the batsman's part was at the basis of all his attacking play. It nurtured the grandeur of the cover drive, the spectacular flourish of the straight drive, the sly cunning of the leg glance, the dashing hook off the back foot. A clever bowler might still contrive to mislead a batsman by varying his flight through the air, or adjusting his pace so minutely that the batsman might be induced to play too soon or too late. But naturally the chief weapon in the spin bowler's armoury was spin, and where the axis of spin was so predictable,

174

the outstanding batsmen of each epoch were usually able to deal comfortably with all but the very greatest slow bowlers. This obeisance of cricket to the laws of the solid, three-dimensional universe, whether by accident or design, matched the solid pragmatic philosophy of the Victorian age. With Johnsonian obduracy, Grace and his contemporaries knew that just as, if you attempted to kick a stone you hurt your foot, so, if you assumed that an off-break might turn the other way, you would damage your batting average. It was an ordered universe.

But although no cricketer ever fretted over anything so abstract as the *zeitgeist*, cricket has, in its own way, reflected the intellectual changes taking place in the wider world. Joseph Wells was bewildered as well as delighted by his son's speculative ideas on the behaviour of Time. The idea that Time might be induced to travel the wrong way was ridiculous and unthinkable, which was precisely why *The Time Machine*, published in 1895, was instantly acknowledged as one of the most thrilling romances of the century. Some years later a German mathematician working in the Academy at Zurich, gave rise to much hilarity and mirth by announcing his discovery that Space was curved. Einstein's Theory of Relativity astounded those who tried to understand it, but once again due credit must be given to the slightly dotty Reverend Dodgson, who, in an otherwise indifferent novel, *Sylvie and Bruno*, postulated the case of a war on a very small planet in which the defeated faction, retreating before the triumphant opposition, withdrew so far and so fast that it came upon the enemy from behind and won a glorious victory. If such things were possible, if Space really was curved, if Time really were a dimension, what of the iron laws of physics which governed the axis of a spinning cricket ball? After centuries in which the appearance indicated the reality, something might very easily be in the wind. That something duly arrived with the new century.

Bernard James Tindall Bosanquet (1877–1936) was an archetypal monied Edwardian sporting bachelor. His only son, born when B.J.T. was in his fifties, once described the comfortable routine of his father's life: "He would arrive at a country house weekend in time for dinner on Friday, spend the next day either playing billiards, riding or playing cards until it was time for the cricket match. After the match, back to the house for dinner, the same routine on Sunday, and then on Monday morning he would give the butler a two-guinea tip and move on to the next invitation". When he was not disporting himself in this way, Bosanquet played cricket, for Eton, Oxford, Middlesex and at last for England, a triumphal progress which delighted his father, Lieutenant-Colonel B.T. Bosanquet, a keen club cricketer who began bowling at his son when the boy was no more than six years old. Selected for Eton as a fast bowler and a hard-hitting batsman "with no grace of style to recommend him", he proceeded to slaughter the Harrow bowlers, hitting them for 120 in two hours. Between 1898 and 1900 he played three times for Oxford against Cambridge, performing merely respectably. He graduated easily into the Middlesex side, twice scoring two centuries in a match. On the second of these occasions, against Sussex at

Lord's in 1905, one of these hundreds was not out, and he also took eleven wickets. This kind of all-round success would have satisfied most cricketers of the day. But Bosanquet came from a very unusual family, and it is when we examine his environment, linked with the forces of heredity, that it becomes a little less surprising to us that somewhere inside the complacent soul of this tall, elegant bachelor, there was a heretic trying to get out.

The Lieutenant-Colonel's brother was one Bernard Bosanquet, a neo-Hegelian philosopher, the man largely responsible for the revival of interest in England of the doctrines of the German philosopher G.W.F. Hegel. Bosanquet published several books in support of Hegel's ideas, which were shared by his more renowned colleague Francis Bradley. Central to Bosanquet's philosophy was the belief that aesthetics can reconcile the natural and supernatural worlds and that there is a relationship between the object and the content of human thought. The fashion for his theories declined before his death in 1923, when they were superseded by the even more abstruse theories of Bertrand Russell.

While the more eccentric members of the family were busying themselves with what might lie behind the beyond, young B.J.T. went about his lack of business with a commendable energy and skill, becoming one of the most attractive cricketers of his day. But for all his success, he did not seem to enjoy the fast-medium style of bowling which brought him modest reward. He disliked trundling away in this fashion on hot afternoons almost as much as he became bored by wet mornings. At some time in the early 1890s he began experimenting with a device which might solve both problems at once, rid him of the need to exert himself so strenuously while bowling, and help to make life more interesting indoors when it was raining. Soon his inventive mind, genetically related to the mind which conceived the idea that there is a relationship between the object and the content of human thought, had solved both problems with the invention of a new game which he named "Twisti-Twosti", the sole object of this game being to bounce a tennis ball on a table so that his opponent, seated at the far end of the table, could not catch it

> After a little experimenting I managed to pitch the ball which broke in a certain direction; then, with more or less the same delivery make the next ball go in the opposite direction.

Meanwhile, the cricketers of the world, blissfully unaware that the *zeitgeist*, Messrs Hegel, Bradley and Einstein, and the terrible confusions of the twentieth century were about to bear down on them, manfully thrust the front foot forward, swung the blade in a splendid arc, relishing the cover drive, the straight drive, the drive over the bowler's head, the hooks to leg and all the rest of their weaponry.

It was not long before B.J.T. decided to introduce the fundamentals of "Twisti-Twosti" to a larger arena. And so, just as his uncle might move some empirical experiment on to a new plane of speculation, B.J.T. began practising his new methods with a soft ball in the open air, at stump-cricket. For two or three years the experiments continued, with Bosanquet gradually increasing his control over the consistency of the new delivery. At last, in July 1900, playing at Lord's for Middlesex against Leicestershire, Bosanquet decided to risk ridicule and disaster by bowling his new style of spin delivery in a first-class match. In the event, ridicule and disaster were both his, along with amazing success. The left-handed batsman Samuel Coe, having reached 98 not out, was contemplating the pleasurable experience of making a century at the headquarters of cricket when a singular event occurred. Bosanquet, known throughout the game as a purveyor of fast-medium, came to the crease, swung his arm over, worked his wrist into a curious and uncomfortable-looking position, and released a delivery which was no delivery at all. The ball, describing a lazy arc, came to earth halfway down the pitch, bouncing three more times before reaching the mesmerised Coe, who stepped out, missed it altogether and was ignominiously stumped.

B. J. T. Bosanquet demonstrates the grip for his Googly – an off-break bowled with a leg-break action – the bowling wonder of the Golden Age.

What had Bosanquet discovered? Simply that the wrist, placed in position to deliver the leg-break, will impart degrees of spin on the ball acccording to the point in the turning of the wrist when the ball is released. If I release the ball so that the back of the hand is facing mid-wicket on the on-side, I will produce a leg-break. But suppose I drop the wrist and delay the release of the ball by a fraction of a second? By the time the ball is on its way, the back of the hand is actually facing the ground and the axis of spin thereby amended. On contact with the ground, the ball will spin in a direction diametrically opposed to the normal leg-break, even though superficially the wrist-action is the same as the leg-break action. Furthermore, if I manage to control the delivery which is neither the conventional leg-break nor the new-fangled imposter, but some-thing midway between the two, then I have gained an additional weapon of camouflage, the ball which does not break in from the leg, nor break in from the off, but simply goes straight on. I have, in other words, added to the armoury of the leg-spinner a delivery known as the top-spinner. Two factors now decide the fate of this mystery delivery. Can I achieve sufficient control to eliminate the fiasco which preceded the dismissal of the hapless Coe? For unless I can do this, my new delivery will be useless. And second, once batsmen in the game have been put on their guard against the new delivery, will its effectiveness last?

The first of these problems Bosanquet mastered by the simple expedient of constant practice, but it was the second which stimulated in him all the deviousness which comes of being born into a family of Idealist philosophers. As the news of Bosanquet's freak deliveries spread through the cricketing world, its creator began to play a remarkable game of double-bluff. Not only was he attacking batsmen with a ball which appeared not to obey the known laws of the universe, but once having performed this feat, he would compound the crime by acting out the charade of his own bafflement, convincing the victim that the whole thing had been a lucky accident and not the fiendish stratagem it was suspected of being. Of course Bosanquet could not sustain this pantomime indefinitely, but when men are placed in the situation of having either to believe a tall story or reject the laws of the world as they know them, the tenacity with which they will adhere to the tall story can be surprising. Two years after the Coe incident, Bosanquet employed his secret weapon in more elevated company:

> The first time it was bowled against the Australians, at Lord's late one evening in 1902, was when I had two overs and saw two very puzzled Australians return to the pavilion. It rained all next day and not one of them tumbled to the fact that it was not an accident.

In the following winter Bosanquet toured Australia with Lord Hawke's side, and waited until the last encounter with the local hero Victor Trumper before unveiling his secret delivery. In the second innings of the match between Hawke's eleven and New South Wales, Trumper opened for the home side and began batting with his usual fluency and grace. Bosanquet then came on, baited the trap and caught his rabbit:

… Trumper batting, having made about 40 in twenty minutes. Two leg-breaks were played beautifully to cover, but the next ball, delivered with a silent prayer, pitching in the same place, saw the same graceful stroke played, and struck the middle stump instead of the bat.

Bosanquet's graphic account of this ensnaring of the world's greatest batsman illustrates the perils to which he, as well as the opposing batsman, was being exposed. First the trap is set with two conventional leg-breaks, pitching around the off-stump. Playing with the spin, Trumper is able to stroke them through the covers on the off-side. Then comes the disguised delivery, which Bosanquet must pitch in the same spot, otherwise in spinning the other way it might turn too far and go wide of the leg stump. And suppose when the trap is about to be sprung Bosanquet's control over a very difficult type of delivery lapses, and Trumper is able to treat the ball with the same disdain with which he had despatched the two previous balls? Not only will Bosanquet have failed to take a wicket, but he will have chanced the disaster of having given the game away. Coe and Trumper were only two of a generation of batsmen reduced to disarray by Bosanquet's elevation of the art of double-bluff to the level of a deadly weapon. When the Nottinghamshire veteran William Gunn ran halfway down the pitch in his attempt to smother the spin and found himself nearer to the bowler than to his own crease, he missed the ball and was stumped. His teammate Arthur Shrewsbury then complained that such bowling ''wasn't fair''. In the Gentlemen-Players match at the Oval in 1904, Bosanquet took some wickets in the second innings before being presented with a challenge he could not resist:

> One of the Pro's came in and said, 'Dick Lilley's in next; he's calling us a lot of rabbits, says he can see every ball you bowl. Do try and get him and we'll rag his life out'. Dick came in. I bowled him two overs of leg-breaks and then changed my action and bowled another leg-break. Dick played it gracefully to fine leg and it removed his off stump. I can still hear the reception he got in the dressing room.

This is perhaps the most revealing anecdote in Bosanquet's career as the propagator of the new ball. First, he invents the bluff of a ball which spins the wrong way, building it into a double-bluff with the pretext that the whole thing is as much a mystery to him as it is to the batsman. Then, with the sceptic Dick Lilley attempting to unravel the mystery, he hoodwinks him into expecting the mystery ball before totally misleading him with a conventional leg-break. A triple-bluff, worthy indeed of a scion of the family of Bernard Bosanquet, the champion of Hegel. On two occasions Bosanquet routed the Australians to win a Test match virtually singlehanded, after which batsmen slowly learned to come to terms with the threat, known in England ever since as the Googly, and in Australia as the Bosey.

After 1908 Bosanquet ceased to bowl, but continued to devote most of his time either to cricket or ice hockey or billiards or, in his younger days, hammer-throwing. After his retirement an odd thing began to happen to him. He had misgivings about the wisdom of what he had done, and grew angry at the frequent accusations levelled at him that because of his invention, strokeplay in first-class cricket had been forever ruined. Batsmen who once had stepped into the spin bowlers and, having "read" the spin, thrashed them to all parts of the ground with utter confidence, now began curbing their aggression, poking speculatively at the ball just in case it might turn out to be not what it appeared. Even the greatest batsmen were likely to be fooled by the Googly. The Australian spin bowler Arthur Maily, who worshipped his fellow-countryman Victor Trumper, mastered the mystery ball and bowled Trumper with it in an inter-state match. Later he said that he felt as if he had shot a dove. But Bosanquet managed to convince himself that there was nothing deceptive about the Googly, and that it was not his fault if batsmen had lost the confidence to attack. At last, in 1924 he took the unprecedented step of publishing a defence of himself in *The Morning Post*, in which the tone of outranged virtue never quite convinces. This essay so impressed those who read it that Wisden reproduced it in its 1925 edition, thus perpetuating what might otherwise have been a passing burst of outraged irascibility:

> Poor old Googly! It has been subjected to ridicule, abuse, contempt, incredulity, and survived them all. Deficiencies existing at the present day are attributed to its influence. If the standard of bowling falls off it is because too many cricketers devote their time to trying to master it. If batsmen display a marked inability to hit the ball on the off-side or anywhere in front of the wicket, it is said that the googly has made it impossible for them to attempt the old aggressive attitude and make the scoring strokes.

At which point Bosanquet, straining to minimise the effect of his invention on the art of batsmanship, makes a comically dishonest attempt to rationalise his actions:

> What after all is the Googly? It is merely a ball with an ordinary break produced by an extra-ordinary method.

In his attempt to turn the attack, Bosanquet is being comically disingenuous, and soon finds himself slipping deeper still into the mire:

> It is not difficult to detect, and, once detected, there is no reason why it should not be treated as an ordinary break-back.

In other words, Bosanquet is claiming to have expended years of experimental drudgery in perfecting a subterfuge which is "not difficult to detect". And then he relents, with the following abject note:

> However, it is not for me to defend it. If I appear too much in the role of the proud parent, I ask forgiveness.

By the time Bosanquet died at his Surrey home in 1936, the Googly was just one more familiar feature of the art of spin bowling. But speculation lingered long after his death. The enigma of the Bosanquets and the influence they had on attitudes to the relation between Appearance and Reality in at least two spheres of human thought prompted letters to *The Times*.

13th May, 1965:
Sir,

Do you want to be torn to pieces by nettled Bosanquets? That family claims two major innovations: 1) The introduction into Oxford of Hegel and German 'Idealism'. 2) The introduction into cricket of the googly. It is obvious that 2) was merely the sporting consequence of 1) But just as Bradley must be granted to have helped with the philosophical juggle, so must my mother, dear mother (nee Louise Bosanquet), be allowed her share in the bowling one.

As a little girl she hero-worshipped her cousin BJT, and paid for it in the 1890s by being made to stand at one end of a lawn for hours, retrieving his experimental googlies, A tennis ball was always used. "*Not* a billiard ball, a *tennis* ball', were among my mother's last words to me.As she knew nothing about German Idealism, I must append the following highly significant dates off my own bat:
1886. Publication of B. Bosanquet's "Introduction to Hegel's Philosophy of Fine Art".
1890. The googly idea conceived by B.J.T. Bosanquet.
1893. Publication of Bradley's 'Appearance and Reality'.
1893–1900. Intensive work, helped by my mother, to hide the reality behind the googly's appearance.
1903. The Ashes regained by the Googly – German Idealism's first and last sporting victory.

Yours Faithfully,
Nigel Dennis.

Substantiation for Mr Dennis' claims was not long in turning up. Five days later the distinguished novelist's letter was followed by one from an equally distinguished theologian, the future Dean of York:

18th May, 1963.
Sir,

Nigel Dennis rightly points out the connexion between Hegelian Idealism and the philosophy of cricket at the turn of the century. It was well understood that the game was a necessary incident in the evolution of the Absolute Idea, in which all differences are reconciled, and that in every cricket match the Absolute was achieving self-realization. You will recall the lines of Andrew Lang, which indicate the ultimate reality behind the invention of the googly:

> If the wild bowler thinks he bowls,
> Or if the batsman thinks he's bowled.
> They know not, poor misguided souls,
> They too shall perish unconsoled.
> I am the batsman and the bat,
> I am the bowler and the ball,
> The umpire, the pavilion cat,
> The roller, pitch and stumps, and all.

Yours faithfully,
Alan Richardson.

The poem by Andrew Lang, straining for metaphysical comic effect, is echoed in the most prosaic way by one of the outstanding bowlers of all time, the Yorkshireman Wilfred Rhodes, the only bowler in history to take over four thousand wickets, and who also managed to find the time and the skill to score nearly 40,000 runs. Rhodes was a modest professional from the West Riding village of Kirkheaton, famous for having produced the two greatest all-rounders of the first half of the twentieth century, Rhodes and his Yorkshire team-mate George Hirst. The sheer length of Rhodes' career, extending from 1898 to 1930, once caused Neville Cardus to lose his head by comparing the ups and downs of Rhodes' cricketing life to "the surge and thunder of 'The Odyssey'". More to the point, on at least two occasions Rhodes delivered an epigram on the bowling art which no batsman should ever forget, and one of them has close application to the puzzle of Appearance and Reality. In stating that "You can't flight a ball, only an over", Rhodes was shaping a truism into a memorable saw. But his other venture into apothegm paraphrases everything Bosanquet was trying to do, and rather more than Andrew Lang was straining to versify. Once asked about the art of slow bowling, the wily Rhodes observed, "If a batsman thinks ball is spinning, it *is* spinning".

None of this was much help to batsmen faced with the prospect of untangling the nets which the googly bowlers laid for them. But there was a lone exception to their wails of woe, a batsman who not only refused to acknowledge the problems set by the googly but also scorned its spell in the only effective way open to him, by smashing it to all points of the ground and advising others to do the same. This was Gilbert Jessop (1874–1955), one of those rare virtuosi for whose technique and the havoc it wrought there is no rational explanation. Jessop was a Gloucestershire and Cambridge player who was steered into the county side by one of his greatest admirers, W.G. Grace, who regarded the stupefying heresies of Jessop's batting methods as one of the best jokes he had ever encountered. Jessop, known as 'The Croucher' because of his eccentric stance at the crease, and whose match-winning century in the 1902 Oval Test against Australia remains the fastest ever scored in a Test match, was no slogger but a scientific hitter. Some idea of his power is conveyed by reference to the list of the fastest-scoring batsmen in history. Bradman and Compton scored at an average rate throughout their careers of 47 runs an hour. Ranji achieved the very high mark of 50, while his nephew Duleepsinhji surpassed his uncle with 52. Trumper and Frank Woolley scored at a rate of 55 runs an hour. Only three men achieved a rate of 60, Percy Chapman, Maurice Tate and Percy Fender. Jessop tops the list with 79 runs an hour. This is what he thought of the Googly:

> Whether it be that the ordinary run of batsmen are still uncertain as to what direction a particular ball will turn, this type of bowling is treated with a courtesy which, in my opinion, is scarcely deserved. Instead of cramping the game, which apparently it has done for some time now, the googly ought to produce just the opposite effect. To act on the defensive is the very thing which a googly bowler desires, for the more latitude allowed him in pitching the ball well up, the greater

G.L. Jessop on-driving. Jessop, known as 'The Croucher', was the most ruthless of scientific hitters and a lethal fieldsman.

his chances of producing the unplayable ball which gentlemen of this kidney do at times roll up.

Jessop's term of derision for the Googly bowlers was "pifflers", especially after the 1907 Test series against South Africa, a nation whose bowlers had studied Bosanquet so assiduously that included in their ranks were four men, Faulkner, Vogler, Schwartz and White, who, between them represented the complete range of esoteric spin from the Googly through the top-spinner to the orthodox leg-break. In the Lord's Test England collapsed to 158 for five wickets. Jessop then strode in and hit 93 in 75 minutes. On at least two occasions writers have conveyed something of the overwhelming effect of Jessop in full cry. One of these testimonies was factual, the other fanciful, and it is impossible to say which is the more effective. C.B. Fry, coolly analytical, said, "No man has ever driven a cricket ball so hard, so high, and so often in so many different directions. No man has ever made cricket so dramatic an entertainment". In 1899 the schoolboy Neville Cardus attended a match at Old Trafford between Lancashire and Gloucestershire:

> I might have thought that Old Trafford was being bombed, except that the possibility of bombs on cricket fields had not yet occurred to us. Towards lunchtime I left my seat to buy a bottle of ginger-beer before the crowd swarmed into the refreshment room. I was placing my money on the counter, standing on tiptoe to reach, when suddenly there was a terrible noise and crash. Broken bottles and splinters of glass flew about everywhere, and I thought that the end of the world had come and that Professor Falb had been right after all. A man in the bar soothed my fears. 'It's all reight, sonny – it's only Jessop just coom in to bat".

CHAPTER XV

SIR JACK

E pochs in a game like cricket do not generally succeed each other with abruptness, but rather melt one into the next with an imperceptible grace. Occasionally some dramatic or even melodramatic event, like the admission into the ranks of the first-class counties of four new clubs, Derbyshire, Essex, Leicestershire and Warwickshire in 1894, or the replacement of the five-ball over by the six-ball over six years later, or the abolition of the distinction between Gentlemen and Players in 1963, or the introduction of one-day matches a year later, might herald either the dawn breaking on a new era or dusk falling over an old one. But more often than not the sporting generations evolve by a succession of overlapping arches, each one representing the careers of outstanding individuals. The case was once put to perfection by an American writer called A.J. Liebling in *The New Yorker*. Liebling happened to be discussing professional boxing at the time, but the analogy with cricket is so exact that it is worth digesting his theory, and the charming whimsy with which he expresses it:

> It is through Jack O'Brien, the Arbiter Elegantiarum Philadelphiae, that I trace my rapport with the historic past through the laying on of hands. He hit me, for pedagogical example, and he had been hit by the great Bob Fitzsimmons, from whom he won the light-heavyweight title in 1906. Jack has a scar to show for it. Fitzsimmons had been hit by Corbett, Corbett by John L. Sullivan, he by Paddy Ryan, with the bare knuckles, and Ryan by Joe Goss, his predecessor, who as a young man had felt the fist of the great Jem Mace. It is a great thrill to feel that all that separates you from the early Victorians is a series of punches on the nose. I wonder if Professor Toynbee is as intimately attuned to his sources. This book is joined on to the past like a man's arm to his shoulder.

Converting Liebling into cricketing currency, W.G. Grace played with Rhodes, who played his last matches in the season that Don Bradman first came to England. Bradman played against Trevor Bailey, and was it not just the other afternoon that we watched Bailey holding the bridge against the Australians? It is a poetic stroke more outrageous than any poet would attempt that in the last season when W.G. Grace qualified for inclusion in the first-class batting averages by playing ten innings, he should have begun that campaign by playing in the same match which saw the debut of his successor as the world's most complete batsman. In April 1906 at the Oval, Grace led the Gentlemen of England against Surrey. The home side's batting opened with Tom Hayward and a young protégé of his called John Berry Hobbs, of whom Wisden had this to say: "Nothing in the game was quite so good as the batting of Hayward and Hobbs". The master scored 39 and 82, the pupil 29 and 85 not out. Those runs were followed by nearly 60,000 more in the course of the next twenty-eight years, and all were accumulated with a matchless grace.

Hobbs was a quiet man, modest to the point of reticence, but fortunately he took to literature in his prime, just as Grace did, and it was on a morning in 1978 that *The Times* staged a cultural debate of some profundity, the bone of contention being the literary technique of the well-known author John Berry Hobbs. The argument centred around two of his most popular works, *The Test Match Surprise* and *Between the Wickets*, originally serialised in that quintessentially chauvinistic periodical *Chums*. The indecisiveness of the correspondence could not conceal the near-certainty that Hobbs the author was, like Grace before him, helpfully haunted by a company of ghosts, a spectral convocation which flourished so prolifically that the newspaper's literary editor speculated that there may well have been enough of them to raise their own XI. No reference was made during the exchanges to *My Life Story*, but it is worth noting that one J.T. Bolton acted as ghost to Hobbs for a period of more than twenty years which ended in 1950. As *My Life Story* first appeared in 1935 in the wake of Hobbs' retirement from first-class cricket, the implications are clear enough. But whoever was responsible for compiling the book in its final form, the voice it raises is certainly the authentic voice of Hobbs. Both in its quiet decency, verging at times perilously close to Mrs Grundy, and in a humility so excessive as to be very nearly ostentatious, *My Life Story* is clearly a performance deriving from one of the most self-effacing men ever to become a national hero. It can hardly be said that the prose is bejewelled, or its psychology original, or its disclosures sensational. Hobbs was simply not that kind of man. Nevertheless, the existence of the book is important, not just because Hobbs is far too important a figure in the evolution of cricket for his image to be allowed to become blurred, but also because the link with a vanished English which the book represents ought to be a priceless asset to the social historian. Perhaps the most demanding challenge facing any student of the past is that of locating and then accepting the validity of the intellectual and moral viewpoint of the people concerned. The sophistication of hindsight can be a very damaging thing, and a great many of the remarks Hobbs makes in his 1935 summation of his life, while they might easily pass for lampoon in our own disenchanted times, were certainly normal enough a century ago.

Hobbs was born in December 1882. General Gordon was alive, Sherlock

Contemporary cricketers take note. Jack Hobbs, the complete English batsman, neat, relaxed and perfectly still at the crease.

Holmes unborn. Tennyson was Poet Laureate to a monarch yet to be corrupted by the idolatry of two Jubilees. *The Mikado* was unwritten, Kipling a name unknown to any but its owner, and the most sensational new book of the season was *Treasure Island*. It was a world without the Maxim gun, the battleship, wireless telegraphy, X-rays. The message of Charles Darwin had hardly begun to percolate down into the consciousness of the honest poor. Mr Gladstone resided at 10, Downing Street. It is against this essentially Victorian background that we have to digest certain episodes in the boyhood of Jack Hobbs, that he sang in the church choir, forsook his amateur status for ever by accepting a fee of threepence for rendering "I'se a Little Alabama Coon", joined the Band of Hope and not so very long afterwards enlisted in the cause of Temperance.

So resolutely evangelical an environment for the child was sure to leave its mark on the man, whose brush with Temperance left him with the opinion that the best tipple was soda-and-milk; that when all's said and done, East, West, home's best; that *East Lynne* is "a fine story"; and that however far short of his own ideals he may have slipped from time to time, he has sincerely "tried to be good". But before the modern world smiles behind its hand at such touching lack of worldliness, let us admit that there is an engagingly gastronomic mitigation of all this pietism, especially in the early years, when his consideration of the divine mystery of Creation is influenced by a touching concern for his appetite. One of his choirmasters, understanding the juvenile mind better than some of his fellow-toilers, was in the habit of inviting his young singing birds home to tea, where he would deliver a religious homily, probably not altogether in ignorance of the fact that the real attraction for young Hobbs was not the reflections but the refreshments: "Never in my life have I tasted such delicious bread and butter and jam". Again, when his father takes him to see Ranjitsinhji bat for the first time, what sticks in the memory is not the silken shirt nor the leg-glance, but the hot pork pie devoured in the stands. Later, when he is old enough to help his father perform his duties at the Jesus College ground, what truly animates him is the occasional opportunity to enter the tea-tent and to devour plum pie and custard.

Cricketers may wonder what connection any of this has with Hobbs the master-batsman, although Hobbs himself evidently considered it relevant enough to include in his autobiography. When he claims always to have tried to be good, he is thinking about the cricket field as well as the parish church and the purlieus of Kennington. Whatever his technical status, Hobbs was one of nature's gentlemen, an athlete so pristine in his honourable intentions that he became famous the world over for walking when convinced of the legality of his own dismissal, sometimes absolving the umpires from the embarrassment of an awkward decision. In the thirty seasons he played in first-class cricket, never once was he heard to utter an uncharitable word about a fellow-player, nor ever to engage in a brush with authority, nor to show dissent, nor to aspire to the fleshpots of the Leagues. Nor was he ever in dispute with his county, nor ever grieved his family through some public indiscretion, nor ever sailed closer to the winds of scandal than the time in Australia when a famous actress chastely kissed him in an impulsive gesture of tribute. But a true gentleman, although he might occasionally kiss, never tells, and Hobbs withheld the actress' name.

He was born into a sporting hierarchy whose administrative methods were a quaint compromise between autocracy and theology. Victorian parallels between Jehovah and the President of the M.C.C. are too familiar to require proof. As late as 1921 Lord Harris likened a game of cricket to a lesson in God's classroom. It was against this background of cricket as an allegory of the good Christian life that Hobbs scored more centuries in his career than any other batsman before or since, and more runs, and, until the enchanted summer of Denis Compton in 1947, more centuries in a season than any other player. And although his fifteen centuries for England is a total which shrinks by the year as the proliferation of Test matches induces an ever-rising statistical spiral, we should note that twelve of those centuries were scored against Australia, a record which is in no immediate danger, and which begins to look more impressive than ever when compared with Walter Hammond's nine and Herbert Sutcliffe's seven.

But although Hobbs was usually the best player in the England side, and always the best batsman, it never occurred to him to indulge in the fatal syllogism: I am the best player: the Captain is the leader: I should be the captain. Hobbs, raised in that climate of pantheistic dottiness exemplified by Harris' theological excesses, accepted the authority of his patrician betters, although not quite without a murmur. In the Old Trafford Test match against Australia in 1926, the England captain, A.W. Carr, contracted tonsilitis in mid-battle. Hobbs, being the senior professional, was asked to step into the breach. At first he demurred politely, pointing out that there remained one fit amateur in the side in the person of G.T.S. Stevens. The selectors said that yes, they had noticed that, but would Hobbs lead the side all the same? And so he did, the point being that at the time of the Great Crisis, Stevens, aged twenty-five, was playing against Australia for the first time. On that day at Manchester, Hobbs was forty-three years old and had represented his country on twenty-nine previous occasions. And yet the passage in which Hobbs describes the incident is lit with an ambivalence which seems to suggest that he was not opposed to professional captaincy, only captaincy by himself. As he reminds his readers, there are moments when the insistence on a Gentleman-leader constitutes both a cricketing absurdity and a social affront to the professionals.

This refusal to take himself seriously as a leader is typical of a man who always appreciated the greatness of others so generously that he never reached the stage where he quite took his own measure. One of the most touching moments in Hobbs' autobiography comes when he explains why his great hero, mentor and father-figure Tom Hayward was not present among the guests when young Jack took a wife at the end of the 1906 season. Some people, not knowing their man, thought they detected in Hayward's absence from the celebrations an element of professional jealousy on the part of the junior partner. On the contrary, the bridegroom had all his life gone in such awe of the great Tom that he felt that to send so distinguished a figure an invitation amounted to insufferable pretension. To be sure, 1906 was Tom Hayward's year, a

triumphant progress in which he set a new seasonal record aggregate of runs which stood until Compton finally lowered it more than forty years later. Even so, Hobbs too was in the runs that year, nearly 2,000 of them, and that so prominent and respected a professional should be too shy to extend a social invitation to his batting partner per-haps tells us as much about the man and his diffidence as all the biographies in the world.

Hayward was a Cambridgeshire man, like Hobbs, and it was within the boundaries of that county that Hobbs' career was born. Today the student of such affairs may travel to Cambridge and wander across the homely turf of Parker's Piece in the knowledge that it was here, in 1901, under the scrutiny of Tom Hayward's expert eye, that the most complete English batsman of all

Tom Hayward, a doughty opener for Surrey and England and the first batsman to follow W.G. Grace to 100 hundreds.

time first impressed a great cricketer. As in all biographies of extraordinary men, there comes a moment when the tyro is transmuted into the virtuoso, after which the drama of his story tends to fall away. And, like every virtuoso in every field, Hobbs can tell us nothing technically enlightening about his art. He was a natural batsman, and any analysis by him of how he performed at the crease was really a rationalisation after the event of a series of intuitive actions. This is not to say that he never practiced, never agonised, never worked, never thought deeply about his cricket, simply that he was born to be a batsman and found his vocation with a swiftness to hearten even the most abject pessimist. There is in his confessional one moment of rich unintentional comedy, when he attempts to describe how to extract the sting from a Googly. It will be remembered that Hobbs had hardly begun his first-class career before the sensational arrival in the Garden of Eden of Bosanquet's serpent. At a stroke, the canons of classical batsmanship were overturned, causing those hearty extroverts, the front-foot drivers, to become so many buckskin-booted Hamlets sicklied o'er with the pale cast of thought. The Googly, harbinger of that Decadence where nothing is quite what it seems, was a gauntlet flung at the feet of the very finest batsman of the age, and he promptly used those feet to achieve a fresh dimension of mastery:

> When I suspected the googly, I played well forward, so that the break might be smothered, or I played back and watched the ball right on to the bat.

There we have it, the greatest batting technician in world cricket telling us how to repel the most cunning challenge of the new epoch. Either play forward or play back. We can derive a little more enlightenment, but not much, from Cardus:

> Immediately the bowler begins his run Hobbs seems to have some instinct of what manner of ball is on the way; rarely does he move his feet to an incorrect position. His footwork is so quick that even from behind the nets it is not always possible to follow its movements in detail.

But if Hobbs is ineffectual as a spokesmen for his own batting method, he is positively mute when it comes to his style as a writer. Neither he nor the best of his biographers, Ronald Mason and John Arlott, mention the works of fiction published under his name, an omission which needs to be rectified. Here is an example of how valiantly those journalistic ghosts laboured in the Hobbsian cause on the occasion of the appearance in *Chums* of the new serial, "Between the Wickets":

> "Fennell", Greystairs said very clearly, "you're the worst kind of cad I've yet met". Fennel became scarlet as to face. He had no opportunity of replying to the accusation, for just then Greystairs felt a hand on his shoulder.
> "Trying to freeze you out, old top?", said Drake. "Well, there's two sides to that. I've been talking to Lorimer, the School cricket skipper, about you. He's over at the School net and he wants to have a chat".

Any last lingering doubt that Hobbs was indeed the author of this stirring stuff is dispelled by the italicised sentence at the bottom of the page, "Another topping long instalment soon", buttressed by a snapshot of a distinctly uncomfortable looking Jack in mufti, sitting "at the desk on which 'Between the Wickets' was written". What the Band of Hope would have made of that kind of disingenuousness one shudders to think, but it is revealing that when the same publication ran serials by J.W. Hearne, Patsy Hendren, Charlie Buchan and Andy Wilson, every one of those eminent authors seemed to have derived stylistically speaking from Jack Hobbs. But Jack, who could just about bring himself to pose as a writer seated at his desk, drew the line at anything more spectacular. Arlott tells us that England's greatest cricketer "was slightly alarmed by the invitation to play the lead – with a suitable leading lady – in a film; and "that when Sir Oswald Stoll offered him £250 a week to appear in a cricket 'Scena' at the Coliseum, he backed hastily away from both". There was, however, one exalted moment when Hobbs trod the boards. The occasion was the Royal Command Performance at the London Palladium on 22 May, 1933. The official programme, maddeningly cryptic, says only that the show was to be climaxed by a Finale featuring Evelyn Laye, Jack Hobbs and Roy Fox and his Band.

That his world is already remote is underlined by countless incidents: his departure for a Test series in South Africa on a donkey-cart; his night out at a Soho restaurant – gastronomy again – where he exults in eight courses for half-a-crown; the team outing to the Canterbury Music Hall when the audience called for him and he almost crawled under his seat. The world of Jack Hobbs is a world long lost, and the devil's advocate might well be justified in asking why anyone should bother with so ancient a testament as the life of a bygone cricketer. Therein lies one of the several peculiar charms of cricket, the evocative power of its literature. We can never hope to see Hobbs now, moving through time and space to the pitch of the ball as he once did. But somehow, once we become familiar with his conversational nuances, study his photographs and digest his statistics, he begins to swim within the range of the imagination, not least because the game at which he excelled invites long loyalties. Men have been known to grace the first-class game through as many as five decades. Hobbs himself scored half his hundreds when past his fortieth birthday, which means that although the young Jack who graduated from Parker's Piece to the great arenas of the world is as remote from us as a halfpenny bun, the knight who reported cricket in his retirement is no further removed from us than some kindly blue-serged, watch-chained great-uncle. Many middle-aged gentlemen in the 1980s are smug in the knowledge that somewhere at the back of the old wardrobe in the loft is the cricket bat they were bought one red-letter day in childhood, on a visit to Jack Hobbs' shop in Fleet Street, and that the great man actually inscribed the blade for them, shook them by the clammy hand and wished them the joy of many centuries destined never to come. The shop survived into the 1960s, a last metropolitan reminder of the physical presence of a modest master of his craft.

"The Master" in old age, presiding with unassuming good humour over his Fleet Street sports shop in 1952.

In such ways does the unassuming sporting hero retain the affection of generations literally still unborn. Just as Grace was the Great Cricketer, so Jack Hobbs was the Great Professional, a man who mastered the art of batting on the plumb matting of the veldt, but also on wickets misty with imminent English summer rain; a man who scored the last of his 197 first-class centuries not long before his fifty-third birthday and who retained so powerful a hold on the national imagination that nearly twenty years after his retirement, he was knighted for services to cricket. His life is a proposition, laid out with Euclidean punctilio, that the hired hand may, through application, technical genius and stoic decency, rise as far as he cares to. His age is past and his type extinct. The loss is cricket's. Ours too.

CHAPTER XVI

SHOWING THE FLAG

————— •—— —————

W hen the British left home to colonise the world they took with them certain items of baggage whose usefulness would have commended itself to no other imperial adventurers in history. Venturing out on to the deep and perilous waters of tropical speculation, comically eager to get under way and yet utterly convinced of the ineffable superiority of their own civilisation over any other they might encounter on their travels, they clasped to themselves, in an endearing blend of messianic jingo frenzy and respect for creature comforts, as many of the artefacts of their own indiosyncratic culture as they could contrive to stow into the baggage holds:

> The specialist outfitters of London offered all kinds of ingenious devices for defeating the equatorial climates – patent ice machines, spine pads, thornproof linen, the Shikaree Tropical Hat ... the Union Jack Patent Field Boot Container, the Up-Country Mosquito Net, the Unique Anti-Termite Matting ... puttees (against snakes) and neckpads (against heatstroke).

Included in this clutter of the practicalities of daily life, among the portable writing desks and the canvas camp baths, the shoe-trees and the diamond shirt studs, the sauceboats and the chandeliers, the grand pianos, ukeleles, monogrammed kerchives, embossed cutlery, soda siphons and bars of Pear's soap, there were some items of a subtly differing nature without which few itineraries would have been considered complete: Billeness and Weeks' Automatic Wicket, "adapted for ship's deck cricket"; F.H. Ayres' Billiard Tables, "specially designed for hotels and clubs"; the William Curtis Scoring Tent; Szaley's Pneumatic-Grip Dumb-bells; Vigon's Home Horse Exerciser; and the tennis shirts, croquet hoops, shin guards, hockey sticks, lawn boots, sand boxes, jumping sacks, scoring books, badminton nets, fives gloves, squash rackets, club ties, coloured caps, medals, badges, cups, shields, bowls and vases which distinguished the English from all the other predatory Europeans wandering the surface of the planet in search either of God's work or increased dividends or a happy combination of both.

They sailed down the sealanes of the world, out from Liverpool, down the Bristol Channel, into Southampton Water, away from Tilbury: the brevet colonels flushed with the proud apoplexy of a recent mention in despatches; horse-faced captains whose toothy sibilances would soon be whistling across the remote and dusty townships of the Sudan; staff majors grimly pursuing the succulent carrot of a K.C.I.E.; ruddy adjutants whose leaden gallantries would in a month or two be rattling the bone china teacups of some remote hill station; missionaries dedicated to the export of their religion to areas which had known their own faiths when the English were still daubing their rumps with berry juice; and smooth-cheeked young men who had prepared themselves to serve as Collectors and dispense justice over tracts of land half as big as Wales in the manner of school prefects or house captains. All of them were resolved somehow to reconcile the opposing ideals of playing the game and playing it on someone else's territory, and miraculously they succeeded, at least in part. Off they ventured, across the spacious and still unpolluted plains of the nineteenth century, carrying with them not only the Gatling gun but the polo mallet, not only prayer books but scorebooks, not only cartridge belts but belts to keep up the cricket whites.

Inside the baggage train as it bounced and rattled its way down the dusty imperial road, jostling the Bibles and the bayonets, were cricket bats bearing the imprint of Mr Dark: "I have always found your bats as good as anyone would wish to play with, Yours truly, W.G. Grace"; tucked away inside the handstitched termite-proof luggage were the handstitched termite-proof cricket balls, perhaps John Wisden's "Special Crown Brand; London County C.C., Crystal Palace, Oct 27th, 1900; Dear Sirs, Your cricket balls again gave great satisfaction. Please send me half a gross for next season at your earliest convenience, I am, Yours truly, W.G. Grace". Cricket had now become a kind of recreational paraphrase of the ability to act like a Christian gentleman and a good empire-builder, a sentiment espoused by Sir Henry Newbolt in that bathetic pearl, "Vitai Lampada", where he solemnly fuses the images of fast bowling in a poor light, jammed guns and the chance of laying down's one life for the honour of the flag.

It would be foolish to assume that to the gentleman-cricketers of the late Victorian age all this was no more than a game. Had it been no more than what the imperceptive Kipling said it was, an elaborate device for these flannelled fools who preferred to fritter away precious energies better spent on imperial pursuits, then W.G. Grace would have been no more than a gifted athlete, instead of what he undeniably was, the Eminent Victorian Lytton Strachey mercifully forgot. But if cricket was not just a game, exactly what else was it? It seems to have been a typically English compromise between a religious manifestation and an instrument of policy, occupying a misty hinterland in which ethics and biceps merged into a third entity, an exquisite refinement of that other imperial concept, the White Man's Burden. And if the mystical pole of this odd and starkly original hybrid is ideally represented by Lord Harris' solemn invocations to God in his grassy classroom, then the political pole is just as precisely defined by Trevelyan, observing, with a censorious glance across the English Channel, that cricket had saved the English from bloody revolution.

The case for cricket as an instrument of imperial policy has been well proven, but the difficulty still facing a baffled post-imperial age is to decide how far the use of team games as a political expedient was calculated and how far fortuitous. If only we knew the solution to that conundrum, it would tell us a great deal more about our great-grandfathers than we already know. But the question remains unanswered, and perhaps always will. Certainly team games have proved to be by far the most durable of all Victorian inventions. It is one of the richest jokes we can enjoy at the expense of the empire-builders that while all the mighty monuments they erected collapsed decades ago, sport still stands. Not the vice-regal lodges, nor the plumed tricornes, nor the standing armies nor the dreadnoughts nor the sewage systems nor the statuary nor the constitutions nor the cathedrals, but the bats and balls. The far-flung battle-line has marched deep into the recesses of history, leaving the flannelled fool in possession of the field. As the Oxford History of England puts it: "Organized games may on any reckoning rank among England's leading contributions to world culture".

But the triumph of team games is no proof that this was what the English intended, or hoped for. "Sport was their chief spiritual export, and was to prove among their more resilient memorials. They took cricket to Samoa and the Indians took it up with enthusiasm". This begs several questions: why did the English take cricket with them to the South Seas, and to what extent were they gratified by the reactions of the natives? Was the pacifying, colonising, apostatising potential of team games a lucky stroke or a gambit of diabolical cunning, sheer good fortune or political acumen, happy accident or grand design? There is evidence to support both arguments, which is not surprising as both appear to be half-truths. The most relevant fact of all is that the ruling classes of Harris' day acknowledged no limits to their jurisdiction. As they stare glassily at us down the vista of a hundred years, they seem to be telling us that as their knowledge is infallible and their good taste unquestioned, there is no good reason why they should not exercise their authority over the whole of life.

The Victorian equation of Cricket and Christianity went to such absurd lengths that it also embraced Sex. Having confused virtue with abstinence, and having convinced themselves of the practicality of sexual sublimation, the Victorians came to believe that cricket consumed potentially dangerous surplus energy in the most chaste fashion. In the aftermath of the Indian Mutiny, the British, intent on remaining aloof from the locals, grasped at the straw of team games with comically misguided faith: "Sweat the sex out of you" was the watchword as more and yet more games of football were arranged through the long hot weather. In the summer of the Grace Testimonial Fund came the crash of Oscar Wilde, followed by a stampede of fearful males anxious to establish their sexual bona fides: "There was trembling in the City and even at Court. In the country, bachelors gave up painting water colours and started to play cricket". Long before this upheaval the Victorian Establishment, diligent as always, had already succeeded in battering its own logical processes half to death with the bludgeon of false syllogism: Christianity means Chastity; Cricket is Chaste; Cricket is synonymous with Christianity.

The rulers of Britain had always had great difficulty in controlling their own countrymen; how much more difficult might it not be to control those foreign subjects who were not inhibited, as the British were, by a common stock of religious fear and superstition? To put it another way, how could you hope to cow into conformity a native so barbarous that he didn't even have enough education to be frightened of General Wolseley? It is true that the imperialists first exported cricket in an attempt to beguile the long summers and to simulate the landscapes of home, but they must soon have realised that cricket presented their own culture in a highly flattering light. Its very illogicalities were endearing, and as for the tight formalism of its rules and regulations, what better engine to train subject races in the etiquette of polite submission? The empire-builders had no sooner run up the flag than they started rolling out a pitch, confident in the knowledge that before long the natives gawping at them from the boundary would soon be responding to instruction in the execution of the cover drive. Arthur Grimble, who went out to the Gilbert Islands in the palmy days of the Edwardians and rose to be Resident, inculcated the right spirit into the natives with such success that it was from them that he received one of the most accurate and affecting definitions of the charm of the game:

> I like best of all the dictum of an old man of the Sun clan, who once said to me, "We old men take joy in watching the kirikiti of our grandsons, because it is a fighting between factions which makes the fighters love each other". His remark meant that cricket stood for all the fun of fighting, and all the discipline needed for unity in battle, plus a broad fellowship in the field more valuable than anything the old faction wars had ever given his people. I doubt if anyone of more sophisticated culture has ever summed up the spiritual value of cricket in more telling words.

And Grimble, who wrote those words in 1952, adds: "'Spiritual' may sound over-sentimental to a modern generation, but I stand by it, as everyone else will who has witnessed the moral teaching-force of the game in malarial jungle, or sandy desolation, or the uttermost islands of the sea."

There are indeed worse concepts to instil into a savage than that there should be rules and that a gentleman is someone who never fails to observe them. And so Playing the Game acquired a mystical significance transcending the technicalities of the game to which it referred. A member of the staff of Harrow School once observed, so long after the close of play as to suggest metaphors of chickens dancing about after their heads have been cut off:

> Cricket has added a new conception of fairness and chivalry to the common stock of our national ideas, since everyone English knows at once what is meant by such statements as "this is cricket" and "that is not cricket".

195

To which one might be tempted to add that there is not much point in people understanding that a new conception has been added to the common stock of national ideas if, having understood it, they then ignore it.

Nevertheless, the schoolmaster had a point. There had once been such a code, incorporating several tenets which, if only they had been adhered to, would certainly have eased the cares of Government House. These rules of conduct said that the umpire was always right, that a true gentleman would strive at all times to observe the spirit as well as the letter of the law, and that a man should always conduct himself with modesty and dignity, even in the face of outrageous injustice. A rigorous code indeed, one to try the patience of a saint. But the vital point about it is that when Victoria's indomitable major-generals carried the tablets of this dotty law to the outposts of empire, they had in mind exclusively the conversion of savages to Christianity. The creed was admirable, certainly, but only for the natives. It was for export only. To have taken codes of gentlemanly conduct to the Athenaeum or to Horse Guards Parade would have been palpably absurd; everyone knew that there was no need for a true English Gentleman to behave like one, because he already was one. It was very different for the natives, who had so much to learn. The patricians therefore remained unperturbed by the stringency of the code, confident in the knowledge that they were expected only to administer it, not to live up to it. The code was an account of their own conduct, not as it really was, but as they liked to imagine it, and perhaps in some extreme cases of moral dementia, sincerely believed it to be. When the code was breached by one of your own, you did not cast him out if you could help it, any more than one policeman on point duty would dream of arresting another for jaywalking. Instead you closed ranks to conceal the nature of things from those too poor and ill-educated to understand it. We have seen how Harris and Hawke manipulated the birth qualification law when it suited them and how Doctor Grace took money and continued to enjoy the esteem which went with amateur status. The English taught that it was more important to compete than to win – and would then stop at nothing to get a result. The English taught that on the field of play all men were equal, and were still insisting on white captains for West Indian sides nearly forty years after Grace's death. The English taught that it was a gentleman's code never to traffic with the ignoble, but for long decades never selected a black player to play against South Africa. Even so, it is unwise to conclude that such evidence, and there is much of it, constitutes proof of a conscious plan on the part of the major-generals to say one thing and mean another. On the contrary, it is this very unwittingness of much of its hypocrisy which renders the history of English cricket's golden age so irresistibly comic. But the best joke was still to come.

There is nothing unusual or unexpected about the flourishing double standards which applied in English cricket. If the rest of the society practiced such duplicity, why not cricket? It would be foolish to look for much in the way of mature enlightenment from a society which ennobled an Edward Carson at the expense of an Oscar Wilde; which winked at the Prince of Wales' adultery but not Parnell's; which could keep a straight face when Lord Salisbury announced that while aristocrats dominate government, "the struggles for ambition are not defiled by the taint of sordid greed"; and a nation which could shed rivers of tearful pride at the relief of Mafeking, the only siege in modern military history where the besieged outnumbered the investors. In the midst of so much self-deception, why should the image of cricket not seem just as absurd when held up to the mirror of history? But in going about their business of inculcating into breeds without the law a sporting morality which many of them were congenitally incapable of respecting themselves, the empire-builders were exposing themselves to one terrible danger which must always rank as an occupational hazard for the professional hypocrite. As the cricketing major-generals criss-crossed the globe, scattering the earth with the seeds of imperial mission disguised as assorted sporting goods, it could hardly have occurred to them that there was one threat against which they had not provided. Fearful of the consequences of a second Indian Mutiny, aware of the unsporting envy of France and Germany, haunted for a century by nightmares about the Russian Bear, and conscious that the whole vast edifice of imperial glory was balanced precariously on a tightrope pegged down at one end at Gibraltar and at the other on the Suez Canal, they prepared their defences accordingly. They knew that if insurrection were to rear its ugly head at two or three outposts simultaneously, then their resources, already stretched to the limit, might snap altogether. There were only so many Major Poores available. The answer, they felt, lay in a combination of psychological warfare, discipline and decorum, good manners and plenty of churches, propaganda by polite pretext – a campaign in which one quarter of the earth might be transformed into a vast public school where sweet reason and the prefect system prevailed, and the crackle of the firing squad was superseded by the thwack of leather on willow, all of which might explain why so many England cricket captains were born on the outposts: Harris and Warner in the West Indies, G.O. Allen in Australia, Jardine, Cowdrey and E.R.T. Holmes in India. History knows of no more extraordinary strategy, conceived in a bumbling idealism compromised from birth by rapacious commercial intent, and excited with a typically English blend of audacity and feeble-mindedness, of determination and indecision, of gentility and ruthlessness, of disgusting greed and heroic altruism, of Disraelian cynicism and Arthurian idealism, a monumental contradiction which Santayana was smiling over when he suggested that perhaps the English would one day be found guilty of being the sweetest conquerors of all. Thus, if you were a patriotic and well-off young man, you joined the ranks of the major-generals, and, armed with the poisoned darts of loyalty, honour and fair play, sailed away to distant shores, prepared to trek to the interior and bring to any Africans, Polynesians, Caribs and Indians you might happen to meet on the way the astonishing news that a gentleman always plays the game, that it is better to compete than to win, that the Empire was embodied in the Umpire. But there was something which nobody anticipated. Suppose the natives believed you?

CHAPTER XVII

PALM AND PINE

—•—

England is not ruined because sinewy brown men from a distant colony sometimes hit a ball further and oftener than our men do.

J.B. Priestley

S ixteen miles off the South American coast, on the eastern rim of the Gulf of Paria where Nelson once came looking for Villeneuve, the island of Trinidad stands like so much jetsam flung overboard from the Venezuelan mainland. For three centuries after Columbus bumped into it, ownership was disputed by the European powers until the day in 1797 when the Spanish surrendered their authority to the British fleet and the island's future was made safe for cricket. Ten years later the British abolished the slave trade. After this route march along the road to practical Christianity, the British then stopped for a much-needed breather, spending the rest of the century working the rum and sugar trades, in return for which they attempted the import of their own peculiar blend of religious dogma and Big Side morality, entrusting the running of this vital operation to a small army of Oxbridge barristers and divines, soldiers and administrators, who imposed on the island an unconsciously amusing parody of the metropolitan whirl they had left behind them.

Their task could not have been easy; to anyone less egocentric than a monied mid-Victorian gentleman it must surely have seemed downright impossible. In an average year-round temperature of 80 degrees Fahrenheit, the tropical flora and fauna was fed by generous rains falling from July to November, and which were often punctuated by the terrifying hurricanes which came roaring in from the Atlantic to rake the foreshore of the entire archipelago. The English eye, nurtured on meticulously barbered ancient lawns and the decorous pastels of domestic horticulture, suddenly found its optic nerve assaulted in the most disconcerting way by frangipani and bougainvillea, palm and hibiscus. Humming-birds and chatterers swarmed in the balmy air, the monkey and the mongoose vied for the settlers' attention with iguanas, scorpions, lizards and poisonous snakes, an exotic backdrop against which the locals expressed their creative urges in the un-Ruskinian pursuits of Limbo, Carnival and Calypso. On the face of it not the most auspicious soil in which to transplant precepts hammered out by a country doctor in a Gloucestershire orchard. What was it that fertilised that unlikely soil so effectively that less than fifty years after the country doctor's death, English cricket was seen to be a feeble echo of what the natives were contriving to do with bats and balls?

There were two principal ingredients, the printed word and the Team ethic expressed through the agencies of English religion and English education, both of which spread across the entire Caribbean with such speed that before the end of the century the evangelising process was complete. Some idea of the success of the British in drumming into the locals the touching delusion that they were not Caribs at all but residents of some unusually torrid West-Country shire may be gauged from two recollections of island reading habits:

> Every mail brought parcels of books, "The Times" and weekly papers like "The Spectator", and "The Illustrated London News", "The Field" and Wisden.

> Our bookseller spread his wares ... "The Review of Reviews", "Tit Bits", "Comic Cuts", "The Strand", "Pearson's", sixpenny classics, "The Boys' Own Paper".

While it is true that between those two lists there yawns the gulf of an intellectual discrepancy, and that those who followed *The Field* might have been a little less abreast of cultural events than readers of *Comic Cuts*, there is no denying that the two itineraries share a common cultural heritage. And while it is fair to add that the first list refers to the 1880s and the second to Edwardian days, by far the most revealing thing about them is that the first was composed by the son of Trinidad's Attorney-General, the second by the small black son of the island's proletariat living a few miles from Port of Spain with a pair of pantomime puritan aunts. When two cultures so hopelessly antipathetic as those represented by Sir Pelham Warner, of Rugby, Oxford, Middlesex, M.C.C. and England, and C.L.R. James, Marxist club cricketer and fiery advocate of Trinidadian independence, have converged so rapidly and so peaceably, it is time to ask how so remarkable a marriage of opposites ever came about. The answer is the same one wherever the Victorians are concerned – books and team games as the pragmatic expressions of Religion and Education. James' grandfather, an employee on a sugar estate:

> went to church every Sunday morning at eleven o'clock wearing in the broiling sun a frock-coat, striped trousers and top-hat, with his walking stick in hand, surrounded by his family.

The churchgoer having achieved an incongruous echo of a Forsytian elegance, it remained for his son, James' father, to match it with no less incongruous an echo of a Forstye's comparative literacy by becoming a schoolteacher. James himself completed the process of emulation by making physical contact with the English ruling caste, neither through piety nor erudition, but because of a gift which the English have always respected more wholeheartedly than a mere commonplace willingness to pray or con by rote, the ability to pitch a good length. One day James performs well for his college eleven, after which:

> Mr Warner, the warden, a brother of Sir Pelham's, sent for me to congratulate me on my bowling.

This was Aucher Warden who, a few years before, had made his own considerable contribution towards the completion of a bridge stretching from Port of Spain to St John's Wood by captaining the first West Indies side to tour England, a fact which the studious and cricket-mad young James would certainly have been savouring in that moment when the hand of a Warner grasped his own. James would have known also the dates carved on the other milestones along the road of West Indies cricket history: first inter-colonial match, 1865; first inter-colonial tournament, 1891; arrival of first English touring side, 1894. Perhaps James would have heard also of the knockabout comedy of 1897, when not one but two English touring sides arrived on the island, an absurdity easily explained by the fact that one of them was led by the Yorkshireman from Lincolnshire, Lord Hawke. All the pre-tour parleys to avert the fiasco failed because of what one commentator called Hawke's "mulish-ness", the spectacular thickness of his lordship's skull proving once more to be impervious to the insertion even of the most rudimentary logic.

Not only on his paternal side was James exposed to the intellectual light of the English tradition. His mother, convent-educated and a puritan down to her button-boots, read omnivorously, and gave him the chance, which he eagerly grasped, to read Scott, Dickens, Thackeray, Shakespeare, Stevenson and the Brontes. By his teens he had developed the habit of reading *Vanity Fair* at regular intervals, and had also become addicted to the schoolboy habit of filling scrapbooks with clippings from the pages of the sporting prints:

> Me and my clippings on W.G. Grace, Victor Trumper, and Ranjitsinhji and my "Vanity Fair" and my puritanical view of the world. I look back at the little eccentric and would like to have listened to him, nod affirmatively and pat him on the shoulder. A British intellectual long before I was ten, already an alien in my own environment among my own people and my own family.

Something extraordinary was happening to James, something much more dramatic than the customary sundering which must always dog the heels of any son infinitely better-read than his father; indeed, James' is one of the most remarkable stories in the annals of the British Empire. For James' testimony, shedding the dry light of its ratiocination on Grace and company, vastly enlarges the shadows of those pioneers to the point where the Atlantic shrinks to the proportions of a country stream and lifts the imperial significance of cricket on to a new plane of speculation. Here is James, born into the Empire at the turn of the new century, a small black boy who accepts with the blind faith of the innocent the facts of life on a tropical island. He begins to notice that three in every hundred inhabitants of this island have white skins. And that this minority is infinitely wiser, richer and braver than everyone else, a fact which must surely be so, otherwise why would this tiny élite be the lawgivers, the peacekeepers, the makers of manners and morals? The boy accepts the authority of this breed of supermen, even though he sees that their presence on his island is the height of comic absurdity. Some of these white men are very good and some are very bad; the good tower like massive oaks among the bougainvillea, and are no less impressive; the bad are as unfortunate as an outbreak of foot-and-mouth disease in paradise, and no more accountable. But good, bad or indifferent, the authority of these men is absolute. They are English, mysterious, maddening, illogical, hypocritical, loveable, ridiculous.

And yet, not so ridiculous as all that. As he matures the boy comes to realise that somehow the English have stumbled on a way of imprinting on to an alien subject population the desire to observe, voluntarily, the canons of an imported code. They have, in fact, wrought the great imperial miracle, injecting the vanquished with a passion for conducting themselves according to a code of imposed rules, or Civilisation, as it is modestly defined by the conquerors. It was a triumph unparalleled in history, and compromised not in the least by the fact that it was unintentional. For the joke at the heart of the comedy of empire is that the conquerors failed where they tried, succeeded where they didn't, and appear never to have had the faintest idea of what they were supposed to be doing, or later, after they had done it, exactly what it was they had done.

Every attempt the conquerors made to push their panaceas failed: in the classrooms and the lecture halls, where the hunger for self-determination rose inexorably out of subjunctive clauses and the pretty fables of an alien history; in the courts, where juridical tutelage illustrated, as it always must, not the infallibility of the law but the fallibility of those who administer it; in the polling booths, in the pulpits, in the streets, in the factories; it even appeared to fail in the cricket pavilions where, in spite of constant assurances that on the greensward all men were equal before God, the captaincy always had a funny way of ending up in white hands. But then the evangelising of the natives is always a doomed exercise, because people will always prefer to go to perdition under their own steam than hitch a free ride to utopia in the baggage train of a conqueror. But the failure was an honourable one, because the task the British were attempting was impossible. In order to grasp the crazy magnitude of the moral crusade on which they were embarked, we have only to sample the abject testimonial of a true supporter of the code:

> Before long I acquired a discipline for which the only name is Puritan. I never cheated. I never appealed for a decision unless I thought the batsman was out. I never argued with the umpire, I never jeered at a defeated opponent, I never gave a friend a vote or a place which by a stretch of the imagination could be seen as belonging to an enemy or a stranger. My defeats and disappointments I took as stoically as I could. If I caught myself complaining or making excuses I pulled up. If afterwards I remembered doing it I took an inward decision to try not to do it again. From the eight years of school life this code became the moral framework of my existence. It has never left me. I learnt it as a boy. I obeyed it as a man, and now I can no longer laugh at it. I failed to live up to it at times, but when I did I knew, and that is what matters. I had a code, and I cared, I couldn't care more.

Whose voice is this, and from what ivied cloister does it echo? Is this one of Thomas Arnold's muscular prigs? Or some dropsical old general, perhaps, heavy with medals and megalomania? The address of the school captain, returning from a Lieutenant-Governorship to compose his valedictory for the school magazine? Or is it a Flashmanesque parody of the type? If it is indeed a parody, then its flavour is utterly authentic, with its admixture of Dean Farrar and a penitent at a revival meeting. But it is neither parody nor the reminiscence of the ghost of some forgotten Victorian blade, but a coolly considered statement by C.L.R. James, made after a lifetime of Marxist commitment and political campaigning for Trinidadian independence. And the vital thing about it is the drift from the general to the particular, from cricketing rectitude to the birth of moral passion in the larger sense, a transition from what used to be called King Willow to the fervour of its closing cadences, all of which illustrates a revealing point about the attempt by the Englishman to evangelise the planet on his own behalf. The attempt never failed after all; it succeeded in the one arena which nobody thought was important, on the playing field. In its unassuming way, James' confessional is one of the most astounding tributes the empire-builders have ever received, and the fact that sociologists and historians have never referred to it may provide a hint as to why more people are interested in cricket than in sociology or history.

Why team games should have succeeded where the New Testament, the Houses of Parliament, and the British Army failed, is one of those riddles still unaccounted for. But fail they undoubtedly did:

> The striking thing was that inside the classroom the code had little success. Sneaking was taboo, but we lied and cheated without any sense of shame. I know I did. By common understanding the boys sitting for the valuable scholarships did not cheat. Otherwise we submitted, or did not submit, to moral discipline. But as soon as we stepped on to the cricket or football field, all was changed. We were a motley crew. The children of some white officials and white businessmen, middle-class blacks and mulattos, Chinese boys, Indian boys, and some poor black boys who had won exhibitions or whose parents had starved and toiled to give the eldest boy an education. Yet rapidly we learned to obey the umpire's decision without question, however irrational it was. We learned to play with the team, which meant subordinating your personal inclinations, and even interests, to the good of the whole. We kept a stiff upper lip in that we did not complain about misfortune. We did not denounce failures, but "Well tried", or "Hard luck" came easily to our lips. We were generous to opponents and congratulated them on victories, even when we knew they did not deserve it. We lived in two worlds. Inside the classroom the heterogeneous jumble of Trinidad was battered and jostled and shaken into some kind of order. On the playing field we did what ought to be done ... Eton or Harrow had nothing on us.

The testament grows more remarkable with every phrase, and finally achieves the pinnacle of irony with the witness' insistence that even his realisation that the code was riddled with imperfections came from within the code itself:

I laughed without satiety at Thackeray's constant jokes and sneers and gibes at the aristocracy and at people in high places. Thackeray, not Marx, bears the heaviest responsibility for me ... What interests me is that as far back as I can trace my consciousness, the original found itself and came to maturity within a system that was the result of centuries of development in another land, was transplanted as a hothouse flower is transplanted and bore some strange fruit.

English culture had become the central truth of James' life, and cricket the central truth of that culture. His friendship with Learie Constantine gave him a part to play in the rise of West Indies cricket in the twentieth century, a rise so meteoric that its beginnings have already been forgotten. James reminds us that L.S. Constantine, father of Learie and a player good enough to be selected for the first West Indies tour of England in 1900, ''often played with bats made of coconut branches and balls of adaptable fruit''. It was the elder Constantine who participated in a legendary match at Bristol where the visitors learned how much ground remained to be made up. James tells how Jessop thrashed the bowling with such force that he ''reduced the fielders to a mild form of hysteria'', and how, with the slaughter at its height, one of the West Indian bowlers requested permission to make an amendment in his dress:

On June 28th, 1900, in a match against Gloucestershire at Bristol, a West Indian bowler went to his captain and asked permission to take off his boots. The captain, Aucher Warner, a brother of Sir Pelham, asked him why; he replied that he could bowl properly only when barefooted. Woods was making the best

The West Indies touring team of 1906. E.H.D. Sewell wrote of them: ''It is a most extraordinary thing that the side can't get going ... I cannot help thinking that they may one day do something surprising''.

203

Genius in action. Learie Constantine, extravagantly gifted all-rounder, who rarely lingered more than an hour over a century.

response he knew to a truly desperate situation. Gloucestershire had won the toss and batted. Three wickets fell rapidly. Then Wrathall, followed by C.L. Townsend, followed by G.L. Jessop, all made centuries. Jessop hit 157 in an hour. Woods was a bowler and nothing else, so that his emotion prompting a return to nature can be understood. Warner promptly refused the request. Woods returned to the bowling crease. Jessop despatched his first balls over the boundary, out of the ground, on to roof-tops.

By the next generation, the local fast bowlers were more sophisticated; the greatest of them, George John, might have become an international star but for the Great War. Had he done so, however, it would have meant his leaving the islands and selling abroad the one marketable talent he possessed, his gift for cricket. James tells how Constantine's son Learie, having had a good elementary education and acquired wizardry at the typewriter, performed a succession of menial clerical jobs but could get no proper work because of his colour. Even as a great cricketing figure, there was nothing for him. He was, says James, a national hero without a nation. So Constantine made the decision which altered his life and the history of West Indies cricket. He decided that when he came to England with the 1928 touring side, he would perform so well that he would be invited to stay and earn his living as a professional cricketer:

> I believe that if Constantine had had not only honour but a little profit in his own country he never would have settled abroad ... What he did become was the

result of personal choice arising from national neglect. Had his skin been white, or even light he would have been able to chose a life at home.

The plan worked, and in 1929 Constantine became a professional for Nelson in Lancashire. Two years later, James, by now committed to the cause of West Indian independence, had followed him. At Constantine's invitation, they formed an alliance with independence as the goal. Constantine struggled on with his law books, while James picked up what commissions he could as a freelance writer. One day he wrote an essay about the great bowler Sidney Barnes, who had played in a match at Nelson and created a vivid impression on James. Constantine read the essay and advised James to send it to his friend Neville Cardus:

> All I asked was that Mr Cardus should recommend to me a provincial paper which might publish the article. Much to my astonishment, Mr Cardus replied that the "Manchester Guardian" would publish it. Also, he would like to see me when next I was in Manchester. I went, we talked, and he told me he wanted someone to deputize for him when he was engaged otherwise.

At last James could support himself without Constantine's charity, but it was many years yet before he realised that the twin crusades of his life – to bring political pressure to bear in order to gain independence for the West Indies, and to bring sporting pressure to bear to make it possible for the West Indies cricket team to be captained by a black player – were really one and the same cause. Before he came to England James had worked as a schoolteacher, under a principal called A. M. Low:

> a man of pronounced Tory, not to say chauvinistic ideas, who amazed me by the interest he took in me. Once, in an expansive moment, when discussing work prospects, he muttered a phrase. "We do our work, and in time you people will take over".

And so they did.

CHAPTER XVIII

CASUALTY LISTS

⸻•⸻

On the afternoon of 4 August 1914, Jack Hobbs once again asserted his primacy among batsmen by scoring a double century, his second of the season, against Nottinghamshire at the Oval; the innings was enjoyed by a crowd of 15,000 Bank Holiday celebrants. At Derby the home side was being bundled out twice in a day by the Essex bowlers, while at Lord's, young Howell of Repton, tipped by many as the great batsman of the next generation, scored 78 not out for The Rest against Lord's Schools, mercifully unaware that this was to be the last half-century of his brief life. Perhaps a sombre premonition clouded the mind of the Leicestershire player A.T. Sharp, playing in the match against Northamptonshire. In the first innings Sharp seemed preoccupied, scoring only two runs before being given out leg-before-wicket. It was a modest enough performance, but at any rate more effective than what followed. The scorecard for the Leicestershire second innings reads:

A.T. Sharp ...... absent, 0.

On the evening of the 4th, Sharp had packed his bags and walked out of the ground to join his regiment.

The years following that fateful day, have fostered the impression that first-class cricket expired with the British ultimatum to Germany. In fact the County Championship continued virtually undisturbed almost to the very last rites of the season. Two of Surrey's home games had to be removed to Lord's while the military mind performed its mysterious convolutions at the Oval, and the fixture arranged for 10 August between Somerset and Northants was cancelled, although Somerset went on to fulfil subsequent championship engagements. Not until 27 August did Dr Grace's muddle-headed command to the sportsmen of England to join the colours appear in the pages of *The Sportsman*:

There are many cricketers who are already doing their duty, but there are many more who do not seem to realise that in all probability they will have to serve either at home or abroad before the war is brought to a conclusion. The fighting on the Continent is very severe, and will probably be prolonged. I think the time has arrived when the county cricket season should be closed, for it is not fitting at a time like this that able-bodied men should be playing day after day, and pleasure-seekers look on. There are so many who are young and able, and are still hanging back. I should like to see all first-class cricketers of suitable age set a good example, and come to the help of their country without delay in its hour of need.

In spite of this pathetic attempt by the Doctor to interfere in matters so tragically beyond his comprehension, the county programme staggered on for several more days. In retrospect, it is hard to comprehend the mentality which announces its discovery that cricket is incompatible with patriotism, and that war is a condition of affairs in which pleasure is a regrettable business. Every cricketer should join the colours immediately, thought the elders, without stopping to consider who might be the beneficiaries of this surge of unco-ordinated gallantry. It is arguable, and has indeed been argued already by more than one historian, that the flood of volunteers unleashed by the brand of fustian of which Dr Grace's letter was typical, did more to embarrass the war effort than to assist it. A.J.P. Taylor has observed:

> Kitchener had expected to get perhaps 100,000 volunteers in the first six months, and maybe 500,000 altogether. This was all, and more than all, that the existing factories could equip with rifles and uniforms. These modest plans were submerged by the wave of patriotic enthusiasm. 500,000 volunteered in the first month. Altogether, Britain raised more than three million volunteers. This vast army was not produced by design; it was thrust on a Government and War Office which did not know what to do with it. There were few camps and little equipment. All through the winter of 1914–15, men lived under canvas and drilled in civilian clothes with walking sticks for rifles. It was the beginning of their disenchantment.

It seems that A.T. Sharp might safely have lingered long enough at Northampton to enjoy his second innings without imperilling the Empire.

At the heart of Grace's invocation was his belief, shared by the great majority of Englishmen, that warfare was an extended version of sport, and that the practised athlete must therefore by definition be a deadly soldier. Even Douglas Haig, whose only known sporting accomplishment was pulling strings to further his professional fortunes, finally made football compulsory for the troops, with every platoon issued with a regulation ball. One society lady raised a Sportsman's Battalion of the Royal Fusiliers, ''upper and middle classes only, for persons used to shooting, hunting and outdoor sport''. The idea that team games and the ritual slaughter of animals was lighthearted preparation for the Greatest Game of All had long before received its sanction from the philosophers who, as usual, spoke the greatest nonsense of all. In the light of what was to happen to the young men of Europe in the years between 1914 and 1918, it is interesting to recall that half a century earlier John Ruskin had written in *The Crown of Wild Olive*:

I use a test which I have adopted, of the connection of war with other arts. I reflect how, as a sculptor, I should feel if I were asked to design a monument for Westminster Abbey, with a carving of a bat at one end and a ball at the other . . . I had rather carve it with a shield at one end and a sword at the other.

It may be that Ruskin's asininity was born of the attempt by a Victorian hero called Frederick Gale to convert the famous critic to the cause of cricket by dragging him to the Oval in 1882 to see the Australian tourists. No record has come down to us of Ruskin's reactions, but as *The Crown of Wild Olive* was published in 1866, possibly his good friend Gale believed there might be a chance of conversion. At any rate, Ruskin's preference for warfare is characteristic of the frame of mind of the White Feather brigade. Such was the mood of the intrepid armchair warriors of the Yorkshire County Committee, performing even then its customary appropriation of the moral consciences of its employees, that it announced that all their professionals would be engaged on war work: "This was made a strict condition of their future employment".

For the moment the County Championship ground on, like the rush to war, simply because no machinery existed to stop it. Not even the approaching thunder of Armageddon had any effect. On 28 August 1914, Paris came under the authority of the military governor, Gallieni; that afternoon, at Lord's, Kent were being skittled out for 67 by Nigel Haig and J.W. Hearne. On the 29th General French displayed his peculiar tactical genius by moving the British Expeditionary Force (B.E.F.) away from the fighting towards the French coast, leaving a yawning gap between the French Fifth and Sixth Armies; that afternoon, at Bournemouth, Hampshire romped to an innings victory over Essex. On 1 September, Kitchener, outraged by French's pusillanimous tactics donned the mothballed fancy dress of a Field Marshal's uniform and went over to Paris to browbeat Sir John into doing his duty. Meanwhile, still at Bournemouth, Charles Mead was doing his by scoring a century against Kent. That night the French cabinet, casting around for a way to instil confidence in the people of Paris, hit on the bright idea of entraining for Bordeaux. The following day the German Army was reported to be only thirty miles from the capital, and therefore presumably not much more than a hundred and fifty from Brighton, where Sussex were striving, without success, to bowl out Yorkshire. The great all-rounder George Hirst stood across their path and at close of play was still there, on 18 not out. That night the B.E.F. took up its positions on the Marne.

The opening phase of the war was now over, and so, for the duration, was first-class cricket. The edition of Wisden which appeared, deceptively chubby, in the spring of 1915, dealt with events upon which the ironies of circumstance had already bestowed a measure of antiquity, except that its obituary columns comprised an odd and pathetic mingling of peace and war. Alongside the ancient reverends who had died that year in bed in slumbrous rectories, and the blue-blooded old bucks who had lived all their lives in the same draughty country house, were the young men destined never to enjoy the passive pleasure of declaiming that the game had gone to the dogs: "... who was killed in action near Ypres, was in the Eton eleven of 1904 ... killed in action on the Aisne, was in the Bradfield side of 1895 ... died of wounds received at Mons, in the Wellingborough sides of 1911 and 1912...". Sometimes the images of peace and war imitated the Reverend Dodgson's bowsprit and rudder, and became inextricably tangled, as in the case of that man of peace, the Reverend Archibald Hugh Conway Fargus, a Haileybury boy who played twice for Cambridge against Oxford, became a naval chaplain and was reported as having gone down in HMS *Monmouth*, flagship of a long-forgotten admiral, in a long-forgotten action in the Pacific. Throughout the kingdom headmasters addressed the school on the glorious sacrifice of so-and-so who, I am sure many of you will remember. At Clifton and at Tonbridge, at Eton and Harrow, at Cheltenham and Haileybury, Fettes and Marlborough, Highgate and Charterhouse, heads were bared and responses muttered, a scenario later apotheosised in one of the most popular novels of the century, and later, a motion picture:

> Every Sunday night, in the chapel after evening service, Chatteris read out the names of old boys killed, together with short biographies. Very moving, but Chips, in the back pew under the gallery, thought, "They are only names to him, he doesn't see their faces as I do".

The death lists were by no means confined to public schoolboys, but the editor of Wisden, and his gentlemanly editorial team, inspired by the harmless vanity of self-recognition, were inclined sometimes to pay excessive deference to the dead young cricketers. But the death notices covering the early months of the war included one name which, if it evoked recollections of no great deeds in the higher reaches of the game, at least represents a record which still stands today. On 11 November 1914 Lieutenant Arthur Edward Jeune Collins was killed in action, his fate to be remembered ever after as the Clifton schoolboy who, over five days in June 1899, scored 628 not out for his house eleven in an otherwise insignificant match against a local side.

The next four editions of Wisden were reduced to less than half their usual size. And yet, even in their shrunken state, those annuals recording the years of the fighting are by far the most dramatic books in the canon of sporting literature. Indeed, it is their very emaciation which renders them sensational, like a portly matron suddenly fallen on hard times. Although the contents of the *Almanacks* between 1916 and 1919 are limited, they are almost unbearably poignant. No longer a yearbook devoted to the documentation of cricket, Wisden becomes a yearbook devoted to the deaths of cricketers. Had it not been for the slaughter in the trenches, there would have been precious little with which to fill the pages. The Public Schools section alone bore any resemblance to its peacetime predecessors, although even here familiar appearances were deceptive. The sixth-formers honoured by Wisden were now learning to live with the almost certain knowledge that before long the bats and pads of summer term would be exchanged for a bayonet and a bag of bombs. Small wonder that the young athletes of 1914–18, plucked from back street or quadrangle and dumped in the mud and blood of Flanders, clung to the old sporting images, dreaming of bats and balls. The pathos of their predicament, underlined by what has since been defined as "the ridiculous proximity" of the old life proceeding less than a hundred miles away, was later exploited in a thousand works of fiction. In a diary entry of 1917, Arnold Bennett confided that an officer "had breakfasted in the trenches and dined at his club in London". In such unreal circumstances, truth became distorted. Peace, which might be a mere season away, or a few miles of shell-churned earth, was a world removed in terms of experience, an irony which became so melodramatic as to become a marketable literary device. Stacy Aumonier, a celebrated short story writer of the day now totally unread, wrote a tale whose sentimental impact is achieved by the stressing of the lost glories of matches from a distant past, featuring ancient champions long since vanished from the face of the earth; the surprise ending of the tale lies in the fact that this catalogue of remote deeds refers to the cricket of the previous summer of 1914. Such was Aumonier's way of defining the contrast between the plump Wisden of 1915 and its starveling successors.

One war casualty exemplifies the case of a man with greatness posthumously thrust upon him. On 22 July 1916, Percy Jeeves, of the Royal Warwickshire Regiment, was killed in that military obscenity, the Battle of the Somme. Jeeves was a Yorkshireman who, having failed to convince the locals of his bowling skills, migrated to Warwickshire and there developed to such impressive effect that had the Great War not destroyed him, he would almost certainly have

represented his country in a less pitiless game than the one played out at his expense by Douglas Haig. But Percy Jeeves can claim possession of the most widely known name of any cricketer with the possible exception of W.G. Grace, not because of technical ability or a freak of statistics, but through the sheer fluke that shortly after his death a writer of short stories who had once opened the bowling for Dulwich College, and who now found himself groping for a suitable name for a gentleman's gentleman, remembered him. That same author did not invent, although he might well have, an occasional cricketer whose death was lamented in the Wisden of 1918.

Percy Jeeves, killed on the Somme in 1916, whose names lives on in the shape of P.G. Wodehouse's peerless gentleman's gentleman.

GEORGE TUBOW 11, King of Tonga, the last of the independent kings in the Pacific, died April, 1918, aged 46. Very fond of cricket, gaining his love of the game while at school in Auckland. His subjects became so devoted to the game that it was necessary to prohibit it on six days of the week in order to avert famine, the plantations being entirely neglected for the cricket field.

The creator of Jeeves, scanning the casualty lists, must one day in 1916 have been deeply saddened by an item refering to the death in action of Lieutenant K.L. Hutchings in September of that year. Hutchings, of Tonbridge, Kent and England, had been one of the outstanding schoolboy cricketers of the 1890s, had scored his first century for Kent when he was twenty, and, in a Test at Melbourne on the 1907–8 tour, established a record which has stood ever since, scoring a century in boundaries out of a total score of 126. His career was short but brilliant, and after 1912 he dropped out of the county side

Another casualty of the Great War, K.L. Hutchings, the Kent amateur, who once scored a century in two hours against Australia.

through loss of form. Even so, he was the most famous cricketer to have died in the war, a lugubrious distinction soon to pass on to one of his team-mates. But the death of Hutchings, blown to pieces by a shell, no doubt sent P.G. Wodehouse's mind racing back to a June day in 1899, when Hutchings and his brother, F.V., scored more than half of the Tonbridge total against Dulwich, at which point Wodehouse dismissed both of them before running through the rest of the side.

A year later an even more renowned Kentish star died in France. This was Sergeant Colin Blythe, the slow left-arm virtuoso from Deptford, whose sensibilities were so finely attuned that not long before the war he had renounced Test cricket because of the strain on his nerves. Blythe, who played the violin as a hobby, took 2, 509 wickets, and although by 1914 his career was coming to its close, he had still enjoyed a successful last peacetime season. At the age of 35 he had taken 170 wickets at just over fifteen runs apiece. He took thirteen or more wickets in a match fifteen times, including seventeen in a day at Northampton in 1907; for England he claimed exactly one hundred wickets for eighteen apiece, and it seems likely that had he survived the war, would have taken a few more on being recalled at a mature age to the depleted national side, just as his great rival for the primacy among left-hand slow bowlers, Wilfred Rhodes, was to be. Of all the deaths of cricketers ever recorded in Wisden, one in eight was a casualty in the Great War, although it must be said that the editors of the *Almanack* included obscure schoolboy heroes not for their prowess but for their old school ties and their patriotism. Even in these instances, a melancholy poetry rises up from the entries, conveying something of the spirit which animated the sportsmen of 1914–18. Among the casualties on the Somme was Lieutenant Henry Webber. Eighteen months later Brigadier-General Roland Boys Bradford, VC, MC, followed him. Neither of these two men had been distinguished cricketers. Webber had once played for Tonbridge School and run up some big scores in club cricket; Bradford had sometimes found a place in his regimental side. What can posterity learn from the deaths in that terrible war of two such modest men, an obscure lieutenant and an ancient general, a young

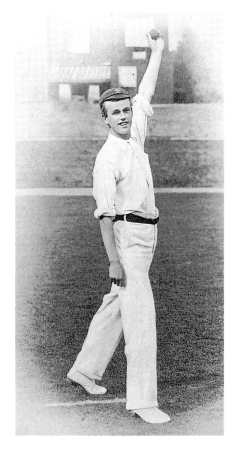

The highly-strung Colin Blythe, violin player and superb left-arm slow bowler for Kent and England. He was killed in France in 1917.

sprig of 25 and a venerable sport of 68? Little, except that it was the general who was 25 and the lieutenant who was 68. With almost comic irony their sad fate was not shared by the Reverend Hugh Fargus, whom we left aboard the stricken *Monmouth*. For, the Wisden obituary columns notwithstanding, the reverend did not after all go down with the ship in November 1914. Returning from leave, he missed his train, was unable to rejoin his ship, and was appointed to another, where, if he was an honest man, he preached with irresistible passion that the Lord is our shepherd.

CHAPTER XIX

FURTHER LOSSES

I t may be that in spite of the ritual slaughter on the Western Front, the deaths in the war most resonant with history were not connected with the fighting, but with three heroes who never wore a uniform. On the night of Easter Saturday, 3 April 1915, the sometime secretary of the Neasden Golf Club went to his bedroom and blew his brains out. Beset by financial difficulties at a time when his marriage seemed to be collapsing and his health failing, the 52-year-old ex-secretary decided on the only escape open to him. Even though the country had too many other deaths to mourn, this suicide attracted great notice, because of the heroic status the victim had once enjoyed. Andrew Ernest Stoddart had played for Middlesex for fifteen seasons, captained them in 1898, represented England sixteen times, made two centuries against Australia, been appointed captain of the side in the 1894–5 and 1897–8 series, scored dozens of tries as a wing-three-quarter for Blackheath and won ten international caps. In a haunting posed photograph taken at Lord's, he resembles one of the dashers who frequented Boulter's Lock on the Victorian Sundays de-

A.E. Stoddart, whose raffish life fell apart after his playing days were over The only English captain to have committed suicide.

scribed by Jerome K. Jerome. He wears a striped blazer and a straw boater, and in his left hand carries the indispensable symbol of masculinity of the period, a pipe. His upper lip is pendulous with a bushy black moustache, the expression in his eyes boyish and slightly wistful. The beau ideal of the gifted athlete, a gentleman and a virtuoso. That so distinguished an athlete should have come to so pathetic an end shocked an England already half-mad with grief. It was *The Pall Mall Gazette* which best expressed reactions to the suicide:

> The tragic death of Mr Stoddart has drawn a sigh from thousands. Could nothing have been done? Thousands remembered him and his glorious batting and Rugby play; and in how many country houses is his portrait at this moment hanging with those of the other great sportsmen of our time? Had his admirers but known of his difficulties would they not gladly have ended them? Something forbade it, perhaps pride. It is all too sad for words.

Six weeks after Stoddart's remains were cremated, the best-loved Australian died in a Sydney hospital. His name was Victor Thomas Trumper and he was 37 years old. The death certificate gave the cause of death as Bright's Disease. Although it is impossible to make comparative judgments on cricketers who died before the cinematograph could give even a sketchy impression of their

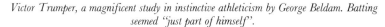

Victor Trumper, a magnificent study in instinctive athleticism by George Beldam. Batting seemed "just part of himself".

technique and style, it seems likely that Trumper was one of the four or five greatest batsmen of all time, not just because of the runs he made, but for the grace and brio with which he made them. The possessor of an orthodox technique, Trumper could, when conditions demanded it, revert to brilliant heresies while other batsmen were floundering. On the sticky wickets of England in 1902 he made twelve centuries, reducing the schoolboy Neville Cardus to such raptures that later, attempting to convey his emotions at the time, he wrote of the beauty of the batsmanship he had seen in terms of "the leaping strings in a Straussian orchestra, flights of seagulls, from roses that rear to spikes of great nobility". Torn between patriotic excess and aesthetic passion on the eve of a Test match, the young Cardus presented a petition to God: "Please God, let Victor Trumper score a century today for Australia against England – out of a total of 137 all out". He quotes A.C. Maclaren, the England captain who had the task of trying to "keep Victor quiet". Plots were conceived, stratagems perfected, traps laid, in an attempt to stop Trumper wrecking the England attack. In the event, Trumper scored a century before lunch on a waterlogged pitch. Maclaren, reproached for negligence, replies; 'I set my heart and brain on every detail of our policy. Well, in the third over of the morning, Victor hit two balls straight into the practice-ground, high over the screen behind the bowler. I couldn't very well have had a man fielding in the bloody practice-ground, now could I?" The aspect of Trumper's technique which commends itself to connoisseurs is the fact that although raised on Australian wickets, he could come to England and display instant mastery in completely unfamiliar batting conditions. It is this all-enveloping mastery which has tempted so many Australian commentators to nominate Trumper, and not Bradman, as the finest all-round batsman ever produced by their country. Writers like Ray Robinson and Jack Fingleton, by no means enamoured of Bradman's personality, have used Trumper as a stick with which to flog the man who, in one of the crassest defences against failure ever offered by a great cricketer, likened the experience of batting on a turning wicket to that of playing billiards on a table with a torn cloth, a simile of almost sublime imperception. In his biography of Trumper, Fingleton ends with this sentence: "Bradman rightly contends that runs are the name of the game; in judging batsmanship, however, equally important is how they are made". Cardus, in his attempt to measure the two men, likens Trumper to a bird, Bradman to an aeroplane. Philip Trevor makes the interesting point that being a true artist, Trumper never enjoyed repeating himself, and adjusted his strokeplay accordingly:

Once, in a match at Lord's, Schofield Haigh, then the best bowler of the day on a rain-damaged wicket, bowled Victor three balls in succession, each of which was a perfect length, and all three pitched practically on the same spot. They were the opening balls of the match. Trumper put the first into the gallery of the hotel. The second he lay back and cut for four behind point. He danced into the third and lifted it into Q stand with a fine on-drive. If you had bowled W.G. a series of half volleys in the off, and he found that he could get each one of them through the covers for four, he would have gone on getting them through. But Trumper's artistic temperament fought against repetition.

There is another factor to be considered in assessing Trumper. Every one of his idolaters takes pains to register the man's modesty and sense of fair play. It would have been unthinkable, for example, for Trumper to have stood his ground at the crease knowing he had been fairly dismissed; and equally unthinkable for him to have trumpeted his own greatness to journalists, or taken commercial advantage of his great fame. One of his teammates, Frank Iredale, although convinced it was impossible even to attempt to describe Trumper to those who had never known him, nevertheless offered the following observation:

> To be near him seemed to me to be an honour. His was one of those natures in whose presence you felt it good to live. His loving nature made many friends. I never knew anyone who practiced self-effacement as he did. If by any chance a player coveted a bat he gave it to him. It became embarrassing for his friends to avoid his favours. If there was a bad seat in a train, he was in it. If the sleeping compartment happened to be over the wheels, Victor would change his place to take it. Children loved him because he was so easily approachable and so adaptable.

When he was thirty years old Trumper suffered an attack of scarlet fever which some of his friends later thought might have been the beginning of his physical decline. Seven years later, in the Australian season of 1914–15, he played all day one Saturday, and next morning noticed that his ankles were swollen. His wife sent him to the doctor, but he returned from the visit dismissing the idea that there was anything wrong with him. Six months later he went for a holiday with his wife and children. After two days the holiday was over. Mrs Trumper saw that the sea air was too strong for him. At the beginning of March a specialist put Trumper to bed, where he stayed for the next three months. At the beginning of June he rose from his bed and instantly caught a chill. The swelling returned. He was sent into hospital, where, much to the astonishment of the staff, he died on 28 June. There are a thousand ways of measuring a man's eminence, but perhaps the most telling in Trumper's case is to consider a small social event which took place in London at the end of the great season of 1902. In an attempt to raise funds, the Cricketers' Benevolent Fund Society held a public auction of 44 cricket bats donated by their famous owners. The prices fetched by the various items are immensely revealing. The bat of the great Lancashire batsman Johnny Tyldesley fetched £3. The bat of Tom Hayward, the second man after W.G. Grace to score a hundred hundreds, fetched £4. C.B. Fry's went for five guineas, Ranji's for thirteen guineas. The bat donated by Victor Trumper went for £42.

England's honour was saved when, after a flurry of telegrams and telephone calls, Grace's bat was knocked down for £50. It must be remembered, however, that had the positions been reversed and the bats of Trumper and Grace been auctioned in Australia, the outcome would have made a colonial holiday.

Australia had mixed feelings about the Doctor. Ever since the tour of 1873-4, the colony had been immune to the hero-worship which the English lavished on their champion. During that tour one local newspaper had written:

> It may be confessed, if only in a shamefaced fashion, that in Australia we did not take kindly to W.G. For so big a man he is surprisingly tenacious on very small points. We duly admired him at the wicket, but thought him too apt to wrangle in the spirit of a duo-decimo attorney over small points of the game.

Large points also. Australia had not forgotten Grace's mercenary aproach to cricket, and would have preferred something more akin to the discreet charm of Trumper. But at home Grace's prestige grew with his bulk. Since his retirement in 1908, the Doctor, unable to resist the blandishments of competition, had devoted himself to the raising of a national bowls team, whose first captain he became. By all the natural laws, his last years should have been spent in the county of his birth. Instead, he was a resident of the Kentish village of Eltham, largely owing to the tactlessness of the Gloucestershire county committee, whose secretary, at the opening of the 1899 season, wrote to the Doctor asking him to be specific regarding the matches for the county in which he intended to appear. Grace responded wrathfully, the dispute got out of hand, and within weeks the Doctor had accepted a contract from the Crystal Palace to run the London County side, which he did for a few years with intermittent success. The breach with his native county was sad, but the historian may detect something symbolic in the move from the country to the city. In 1851 Britain had become the first nation in the history of the world to have more townees than countrymen, and in a whimsical sort of way it was only proper that its greatest athlete should reflect this drift in his own life.

In October 1915, not long after the bloody battle of Loos, Doctor Grace was working in his garden when he suffered a stroke. He dragged himself into the house, but once put to bed found he was unable to get up. He told one visitor how much he hated the Zeppelin raids. "How can they bother you", asked the visitor, "when you played all the fast bowlers of your time with ease?"; to which the invalid replied, "Ah, I could see those beggars; I can't see these". A few days later he made an attempt to leave his bed, fell, and was put back to bed, where he died on 23 October 1915. Reasons for his death varied. The Germans claimed that he had been the victim of a Zeppelin raid. The doctors said that over-exertion in the garden had caused the stroke which led to his death. Others felt that Grace had lived too strenuous a life and overtaxed his body. There was a modicum of truth in all these theories, but not according to Arthur Conan Doyle, Grace's good friend, who had played with and against him on many occasions. Doyle was convinced that Grace had died at the comparatively early age of 67 because his heart had been broken by the barbaric nature of a war far beyond his grasp, and which was killing so many of his fellow-athletes every day.

By the time of Grace's death, few of his fellow-countrymen harboured illusions about a short war and a swift return to the status quo. The past was past and victory – if it ever came – would propel the world into a new and less comfortable age. Too many landmarks, faces, and habits had disappeared. The death of the most famous sporting figure of all time seemed to punctuate an age. The Liberal editor A.G. Gardiner, who, in his more rustic moods, masqueraded as ''Alpha of the Plough'', wrote an essay describing how one evening he walked to the country railway station near his home, in the hope of picking up the evening newspaper. He stood there under the dim light of an oil lamp, reading the war news, when a voice behind him said, ''W.G. is dead''.

> At that word, I turned hastily to another column, and found the news that had stirred him. And even in the midst of world-shaking events it stirred me, too. For a brief moment I forgot the war and was back in that cheerful world where we greeted the rising sun with light hearts and saw its setting without fear.

CHAPTER XX

A LAND FIT FOR PIERROTS

———•———

To the English, peace is not peace without a game of cricket. After four years of war, the public of 1919 looked forward to the sweet renewed pleasure of whiling away an afternoon at the county ground, or, at the very least, of opening their morning newspapers back-to-front and basking in the emollient of the county scorecards. It would have been unthinkable for the authorities not to have provided some sort of first-class programme, but when it came it had a faintly bogus look about it. The price of admission reflected the inflationary aspects of war finance, and the new Entertainments Tax.

Much more disturbing was the experimental reduction of county games from three days to two, a departure guaranteed to wreck both the cricket and the financial good health of those who provided it. In good weather, two days was woefully insufficient to reach a decision; on the other hand, bad weather on the first day would make a mockery of attendances on the second. The editor of Wisden, who in the 1919 edition had dismissed the new scheme as "a sad blunder", was proved quite right, and in the 1920 edition Mr Pardon cited another reason why the two-day game was a mistake. The problem was the freakishly long hours of play. Play continued to half past seven each evening, but "before that time the craving for food had as a rule become stronger than the passion for cricket. To put the matter in a prosaic way, the advocates of the two-day match overlooked the needs of the human stomach". The two-day match, so hastily adopted, was just as hastily discarded and has never been heard of since.

A deeper-seated problem concerned the finances of the counties. The professionals, for so long fobbed off with niggardly salaries and no retirement security, were now being tempted much more than before by the Leagues, which could afford to offer a more inviting wage and a much less demanding itinerary. To balance this looming threat, there was the great surge of public support which greeted the re-opening of the county grounds. This surprised nobody apart from those responsible for the administration of cricket, who had

219

glumly assumed that, in some obscure way, four years of deprivation must surely have killed the public's enthusiasm. Instead, the cricket grounds of 1919 were thronged with delighted spectators, many of whom must have eagerly anticipated the imminent resumption of Tests against Australia. The tour of 1920–21 would show finally that peace indeed had come. The English authorities were promised huge crowds and a warm reception, two factors which did much to assuage the selectors' fears that English cricket was not yet ready for so rigorous a trial of strength. But the fears were put aside and a touring party led by the Olympic Boxing Middleweight champion of pre-war days, the Essex all-rounder J.W.H.T. Douglas, set sail for Australia, with results even more calamitous than the pessimists had feared.

English cricket was not altogether devoid of the old names, but age and accident had taken their toll. R.E. Foster had died in 1913, and his namesake, F.R. Foster, had been crippled by a motorcycle accident. C.B. Fry, now playing for Hampshire, Spooner of Lancashire and his teammate John Tyldesley, were all past the age when the rigours of Test cricket were congenial. Among the bowlers, Blythe and Jeeves lay in premature graves, and Wilfred Rhodes had apparently lost his appetite for bowling now that he was an accomplished batsman. Gilbert Jessop was not only too old but a semi-invalid since 1916 when the British Army, in a hamfisted attempt to cure his lumbago, had very nearly boiled him alive. On the credit side, there was the emergence of young Herbert Sutcliffe in Yorkshire. But neither he nor his county partner Percy Holmes was invited to tour. To make matters much worse, the Middlesex batsman J.W. Hearne dropped out of the side early in the tour owing to illness, and Douglas, struggling desperately to make a contest of it, became the first England captain to lose a series 5–0. He was, however, retained for the 1921 rubber, even though, as his contemporary Fry later wrote, "From Douglas's captaincy no idea ever emerged". Predictably, Australia won the first Test comfortably, at which point the England selectors invited Fry, now 49 years old, to return to the command. Fry accepted but then withdrew with an injured finger, advising the selectors to turn to the Honourable Lionel Tennyson, a grandson of the Poet Laureate who claimed to remember his ancestor as "a beard at the foot of the bed". The Hon Lionel was something of a poet himself, publishing a volume since forgotten called *From Bed to Verse*. However, his grasp of poetic principles was sketchy, and he was the only known propagator of the theory that his grandfather was the author of *Hiawatha*. Tennyson was also the only county captain in history to employ his wicketkeeper as his valet, or possibly his valet as his wicketkeeper. This dual-purpose menial, by name Livsey, would run his lordship's bath as well as his short runs, lay out his clothes as well as his ready money, and ask for batting instructions from Tennyson much as he might take orders for luncheon. No doubt Tennyson would have been delighted to have had him at his side in the England eleven, but this was not to be.

Tennyson came into the side for the second Test at Lord's, where the authorities, still blithely unaware of the ever-growing demand for Test cricket,

Mad Dogs and Englishmen. Suitably clad against the noonday sun, Lord Tennyson and Bill Edrich go out to bat against Sind during a tour of 1937.

made a notorious botch of the arrangements. Among the witnesses of the chaos outside the ground was the essayist Robert Lynd, who penned, "Disgraceful Scenes at Lord's":

> That is the only heading that could do justice to the feelings of thousands of folk who had bought tickets and who were still attempting to blaspheme their way into the ground nearly an hour after play had begun. It was not the players, or the public, or the police who behaved disgracefully: it was the authorities at Lord's. They had sold thousands of reserved seats, but had made no arrangements for admitting ticket-holders or for informing them where they could be admitted. They seemed to have kept the secret even from the police, who were as much at sea as anyone else.

The chaos outside the ground on that first morning of the first postwar Lord's Test was a clear indication – ignored at the time – that the nature of cricket, and its place in the national life, had changed radically since 1914. What had once been a sporting pastime supported by patronage had grown into a form of popular entertainment, much to the astonishment and perhaps also the dismay of the M.C.C. As the tour proceeded, it became painfully obvious even to the most arrant chauvinist that the home side was no match for the Australians. There were a few consolations, particularly the batting of the Kent left-hander

Frank Woolley, but although the visitors had to be satisfied with draws in the last two Tests, it was conceded that deaths in the war and the absence for four seasons of an arena in which rising talent might sharpen its wits had grievously weakened English cricket.

In their despairing attempts to devise a winning formula, the England selectors called on no fewer than 30 players, and Wisden complained that those who chose the team "lacked settled policy, and were inclined to clutch at straws and be influenced too much by the latest form". Mistakes were made: the omission of Mead of Hampshire until the fourth Test; the failure to acknowledge the existence of the eccentric Nottinghamshire batsman George Gunn; and the refusal to offer a chance to Louden of Essex. But even more serious than any of these blunders was an oversight so blatant that later generations failed even to notice its occurrence. Only one factor could have saved the host country from debacle, the presence in the side of a genius. Every historian, looking back to that season, explains that, being short in this department, the selectors could have done nothing to remedy the lack. As it happened, this was shamefully untrue, and the self-deception is ironically demonstrated by this apologia for the performance of the England bowlers:

> We had not recovered from the war of 1914–18, in which we lost such fine cricketers as Blythe, Jeeves, and Booth, all killed in action. Moreover, S.F. Barnes had retired from first-class cricket and F.R. Foster had broken a leg and could not play at all. We therefore lost five bowlers during the war period.

That account was composed by the distinguished casuist Pelham Warner, whose version of history is coloured, as usual, with half-truth. In order to locate the cool insolence of the lie, it is necessary to look back across the abyss of Flanders to a time which must have seemed positively arcadian to the sad-eyed men who survived the war.

In the winter of 1901 the Lancashire captain A.C. Maclaren was invited to take an England side to Australia and accepted. However, on selecting his men, he soon found himself opposed by that bear of little brain, Lord Hawke, who refused to allow either Rhodes or Hirst to accept Maclaren's offer, on the grounds that a winter's rest – that is, a winter's unemployment – was what his two star bowlers required if they were to do their best for him in the following season. Finding himself in difficulties, Maclaren embarked on one of the most inspired gambles of his life by inviting a relatively unknown bowler to make the tour. The popular anecdote regarding this remarkable stroke of perception by Maclaren is that he took a bowler called Sydney Francis Barnes into the nets and was soon being thumped on the thigh and the gloves from good-length balls. Barnes then attempted to apologise, to which Maclaren replied, "Don't be sorry, Barnes. You're coming to Australia with me". The story sounds dubious if only because the idea of Barnes apologising to anyone for anything seems too laughable for words. A more feasible explanation may be found by referring to Wisden for 1902, where, in the section devoted to Lancashire in the

Frank Woolley of Kent and England, one of the great all-rounders who in the 1928 season scored 3,352 runs and took 100 wickets.

Championship, the report on the last game of the season at Old Trafford, against Leicestershire, shows that in the visiting side's first innings one bowler dominated:

> A feature of the match was the successful appearance in the Lancashire eleven of Barnes, the Burnley Club bowler, to whom Maclaren afterwards gave a place in his team for Australia.

This dramatic advent sounds less like a cricket report than an extract from some boys' paper serial. In fact Barnes did not spring from nowhere, a fully-armed master bowler. Born in Staffordshire, he appeared in the Warwickshire side from 1894 to 1896 without attracting much notice. He then performed the act which was to become his trademark. He walked away from first-class cricket and vanished into League cricket. A season in the Birmingham District League was sufficiently successful to attract the attention of the Burnley Club, who signed him on. By 1899 word had reached Old Trafford that he was a likely prospect, and he represented the county twice in that season, although not until Maclaren became his patron did he become a county regular. In that speculative Australian tour, Barnes justified all Maclaren's faith in him by taking thirteen wickets in the second Test, after which his knee gave way and he took no further part in the tour. In the 1902 season he was back in the county side, but disappointed by taking only 82 wickets. Wisden sounded a little puzzled: "... it cannot be said that he by any means fulfilled the hopes formed of him ... there were many days on which he proved quite ineffective ... he lacked the perseverance and resolution that would have enabled him to make the most of his natural gifts ... only at his best by fits and starts". Even in 1903, when he did much better with 131 wickets at less than eighteen runs each, was it noticed that "the difference between his best days and his worst was almost immeasurable". The *Almanack*, evidently believing it was closing its account with this remarkable player, now made the greatest gaffe in its long history:

> Before the summer was over, Barnes' connection with the Lancashire Club came to an end. He declined to sign the usual form promising his services for 1904, and in consequence he was left out of the team in the last match. It was stated that he had accepted an offer from the Church Club, and would return to Lancashire League cricket. His defection caused quite a sensation and was commented on in rather bitter terms. Temperament is a great thing in a cricketer, and in this respect Barnes has always been deficient. If he had possessed the enthusiasm for the game that characterised Barlow and Briggs he might have made a great name for himself, his natural gifts as a bowler being so remarkable.

The accumulation of error and imperception in this brief passage would be comic were it not also so tragic in the context of Barnes' life. The first thing to be said about this unique cricketer is that no bowler in history ever worked so tirelessly to acquire that complete mastery which the editors of Wisden so blandly define as "natural gifts". Nor could it be said of a man who for forty years played the game at the very peak of its artistic possibilities that he lacked either enthusiasm or resolution. As for the apparent mystery of his fluctuating form, the official eye had been conditioned from birth not to see the solution. For the truth was indeed too awful to contemplate. There were occasions when Barnes, being supremely indifferent to the unwritten law that a true sportsman gives of his best at all times, simply never bothered to try very hard. It was not that he was immoral but rather that he subscribed to a different morality, that of the artist, who will only give of his best when the circumstances challenge his virtuosity. In the last overseas tour undertaken by an England side before the Great War, to South Africa, Barnes took 49 wickets in the first four Tests and then declined to play in the fifth, having decided that so one-sided a game was not worth the candle. Knowing what we do about him, we perceive that the attempt of the Lancashire committee to bring him to heel by refusing his terms was as misguided as the conclusions drawn by Wisden. Barnes left Lancashire never to return, preferring to exhibit his genius in the more lucrative and less arduous backwaters of the North Staffordshire, Lancashire, Bradford, and Central Lancashire Leagues. To those who accused him of wasting his sweetness on the desert air, he would have replied by pointing to his wage packet. For Barnes was an extraordinary Victorian case, a self-made man whose determination not to be dictated to by committees, nor to be patronised by lesser men, nor to be fobbed off with anything less than what he considered to be just reward for his gifts, smacks more of the latter years of the twentieth century than the fag-end of the nineteenth.

Henceforward his appearances in county cricket were limited to Minor Counties games, where he represented Staffordshire for 22 seasons. How grimly he must have smiled when in 1907 he was recalled to the England side. Four years later he took 34 wickets in a series against Australia; in the 1912 Triangular Tournament involving England, Australia and South Africa, he took another 34 wickets. After the Great War, and well into middle age, he continued to play for Staffordshire to devastating effect. Yet nowhere is his name mentioned again as a possible England player in the calamitous postwar years, with England struggling to make a game of it and apologists chanting in unison that it was the war which had decimated the local bowling strength. Yet nobody ever bothered to ask Barnes. Was it because he was now considered too old to be effective? In his twenty years with Staffordshire, he took 1,432 wickets at eight runs each; in thirty-eight summers in the Leagues he took another 3,741 at under seven each. In 1934, in his sixty-second year, he took 86 wickets for Staffordshire at less than eleven runs each; in 1928 the West Indian tourists encountered the old boy in a club match and decided he was the best bowler they had seen all season. C.L.R. James defined him as "the greatest of all bowlers". Neville Cardus agreed. In 1930 that dedicated student of the bowling arts, Ian Peebles, was given an audience with Barnes:

> ... one of the great hours of my life. Barnes was most expansive and, given a cricket ball, demonstrated the whole technique which was of his own invention, and which has never been wholly or successfully imitated.

Exactly what was this mysterious technique? Having begun as a fast bowler and sacrificed speed for control, Barnes, once his art came to full flower, was a fast-medium bowler whose control of length, flight and swerve could make him unplayable. Long supple fingers, a tall frame, a shrewd analytical mind, and a ruthless determination to destroy the batsman, conspired to render him all-powerful even at the very highest level. At Melbourne in 1911 he opened the bowling for England. In no time Australia were 38 for six and Barnes' figures read: 11 Overs. 7 Maidens. 6 Runs. 5 Wickets.

His most deadly weapon, known as "the Barnes ball", pitched on the stumps between leg and middle and then turned sharply to threaten the off-stump or find the edge of the bat. In other words, by ceaseless application during those early years in the Birmingham League, Barnes had achieved the great dream of every bowler, the ability to deliver an accurate leg-break at true pace. And yet

The implacable Sydney Barnes (left) and the durable Wilfred Rhodes as portrayed on cigarette cards. The artist has softened Barnes' austerely hostile features but there is still a hint of the baleful glare which terrified teammates and opponents.

in the lean years of the early postwar period, when for Australia to score four, five or even six hundred became a commonplace, nobody ever thought to send for Barnes, a remarkably curious oversight by the selectors.

The explanation can only be that those responsible for the selection of England sides feared Barnes so much that they decided that ignominious defeat at the hands of the Australians was infinitely preferable to reliance on this cussed man. Cardus goes some way to depicting his essence when he suggests that there was something Mephistophelean about him: "He was the living image in flannels of the 'Spirit of Denial'". Patrick Morrah says of Barnes that "he was not remarkable for joie de vivre. He was dour, intense, unsmiling, quick to take offence". Certainly in the portraits which have survived there is something ominous about the way Barnes gazes out at the world, fearless, appraising, coolly superior, a glint of icy derisive humour in his eyes. In the photograph showing him standing squarely with hands in overcoat pockets, watchchain and white stiff collar, peaked cap over dark hair, he looks less like an athlete than one of those police inspectors who are said to have followed in the wake of Mr Sherlock Holmes. Even his idolators found him too testy to be absorbed into the context of a cricket side. Cardus says that "it was a case of Lancashire with Barnes, or of England with Barnes". Even Maclaren, who plucked him out of obscurity to place him on the centre stage of Test cricket, quickly came to question his own wisdom. On the ship travelling out to Australia, passengers were warned that high seas put every one in danger, at which Maclaren, seeking for crumbs of comfort, murmured, "If we do go down, that bugger Barnes will go down with us".

The most vivid and impressive sketch of Barnes the man comes from outside the charmed circle of international cricket and professional criticism, from a man whose father captained Staffordshire in the balmy era when Barnes was running through sides day after day, year after year, and who himself played alongside the great man in the same side. Bernard Hollowood is better known as an editor of *Punch* than as a professional cricketer, but his career with Staffordshire was an honourable one. In his essay on Barnes he opens with a remark which expresses perfectly the contradictory emotions which the man inspired: "My father regarded Barnes as the greatest bowler of all time, though he invariably spoke disparagingly of him in other contexts than cricket". Hollowood senior defines Barnes as "as mean as they come". His son suggests that had he bothered with politics, "he might have been a Keir Hardie or a George Lansbury", for he was "forever kicking against the pricks and quarrelling with the Establishment". Hollowood recalls that when put on to bowl at the wrong end, Barnes would "scowl and sulk and develop mysterious physical disorders, sprains and strains". And he finally comes to the heart of the enigma of the postwar years when he talks of the disarray to which Barnes could reduce not only his opponents but his own teammates:

> His colleagues admired his skills, but were terrified of incurring his displeasure and found games with him a sore trial. So there was no great outcry when the selectors omitted the name of Barnes from their national elevens. I suspect that on these occasions – and they were numerous – all the more easy-going Players and most of the Gentlemen breathed a sigh of relief. I was frankly afraid of Barnes, afraid of his scowling displeasure, his ferocious glare, his crippling silences and his humiliating verbal scorn, and I played with him and against him only when he was beginning to mellow! "There's only one captain of a side", he used to say, "when I'm bowling – me!"

What Hollowood is saying is that grown men went in such fear of Barnes that they would rather lose matches than have anything to do with him. But for a grown man to admit this fear is hardly commensurate with his assumption of maturity, of authority, of sportsmanship. Some sort of evasive euphemism must be found, and it was Pelham Warner who expressed it when he so shamelessly misled his readers into believing that Barnes "had retired from first-class cricket", disdaining to explain why, if retirement from first-class cricket

Wilfred Rhodes, recalled to play for England against Australia in 1926 at the age of 48. He clinched the rubber with figures of 4 for 44 on the final day at the Oval.

disqualified a man from selection for England, Barnes of Staffordshire had represented his country to such brilliant effect from 1907 to 1914. In those years he had been by far the greatest bowler in the world, a figure so awesome that rising young batsmen would seek out encounters with him in the spirit of dedicated students attempting to pass the last examination, a genius who husbanded his resources with such care that visiting cricketers had no hesitation in naming him as England's premier bowler through the 1920s. As for the claim that by then he was too old for the hurly-burly of Test cricket, it is revealing that

Barnes in 1921 was a year younger than Wilfred Rhodes when Rhodes made his famous international comeback in 1926. Both these immortal cricketers lived on into extreme old age, Rhodes reduced by blindness, Barnes as upright as ever into his nineties, still working as a master-calligraphist for his county council, inscribing his immaculate copperplate on illuminated scrolls. Barnes and Rhodes, Rhodes and Barnes, talismans of the Golden Age, two indestructible survivors in an epoch utterly removed from that of their heyday. They watched cricket till the end. One day they were spotted at a Test by the poet-cricketer Alan Ross, whose evocative verse reminds us that in old age the jagged, unyielding contours of Sydney Francis Barnes softened to a degree which would have amazed his old enemies:

> Then, elbows linked but straight as sailors
> on a tilting deck, they move. One, square-shouldered as a tailor's
> Model, leans over, whispering in the other's ear:
> "Go easy. Steps here. This end bowling".
> Turning, I watch Barnes guide Rhodes into fresher air,
> as if to continue an innings, though Rhodes may only play by ear.

CHAPTER XXI

PLAYING THE GAME

T he historic match in which the veteran Yorkshireman Wilfred Rhodes made his Test comeback began on 14 August 1926, by which time the English were beginning to despair of ever again winning a series against Australia. During a summer disrupted by the General Strike, the two cricketing nations sparred and feinted through four drawn games before the host nation, gambling on a new young captain in A.P.F. Chapman of Kent, and on an aged spin bowler in Rhodes, finally won, thanks to a famous opening stand by the great partnership of the decade, Hobbs and Herbert Sutcliffe. The seemingly irreversible tide had been turned at last, as in cricket it always is, as the generations flow on. Even the seemingly everlasting marks made by W.G. Grace were being erased by new heroes. In the year before the great Test triumph at the Oval, Hobbs had gone down to Taunton and, by scoring 101 in the first Surrey innings, equalled Grace's record of 126 first-class centuries. In the second innings, chasing a winning total of 183, Hobbs, partnered by his gifted friend Andrew Sandham, scored 101 not out to set a new mark. By now Hobbs was himself a veteran, but there were few fears for the continuing high quality of English batsmanship. Walter Hammond, free at last of the uncharitable attentions of Lord Harris, was performing prodigies for Gloucestershire. Within one week in August 1928 at Cheltenham, he scored a century in each innings and took ten catches against Surrey, and then took fifteen wickets in the game against Worcestershire.

Although the regaining of the Ashes, the apotheosis of Hobbs and the rise of Hammond were rightly seen as great events, later generations of cricketers would probably be inclined to select someone much less celebrated as the true hero of the time, someone whose deeds have influenced in a most benign way the destiny of every professional in England, even though the name of this important figure is all but forgotten. In 1902 the Kent eleven included for the first time a young batsman called James Seymour, whose playing style, productive rather than classic, soon made him an indispensable member of a

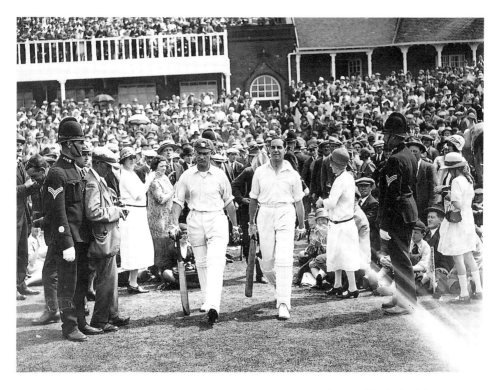

*Hobbs and Sutcliffe, the greatest of English first-wicket partnerships: Hobbs the classicist
and Sutcliffe the pragmatist with a cool big-match temperament.*

side already blessed with an embarrassment of batting riches. Like all of his
generation, Seymour (1879–1930) found his career sundered by the Great War.
In the first half of his career with Kent, the county side ranked among the most
exciting in the championship, which they won in dazzling style four times
between 1906 and 1913. Yet Seymour, playing for a club which could call on
the likes of Alec Hearne, J.R. Mason, C.J. Burnup and Frank Woolley, was
never in danger of losing his place. After the war he was even more effective, and
by 1927 when he finally retired, had scored 53 centuries and represented the
Players against the Gentlemen three times. In a period less richly endowed with
batting virtuosity he would surely have won more representative honours, not
simply as a batsman but also as one of the outstanding slip fielders of history. In
a match against the South Africans at Canterbury in 1904, he took six catches
in an innings. It was natural enough that so loyal a servant of the county should
receive as his reward the privilege of a benefit match. The moment came for him
in 1920, and he chose the match against Hampshire at his favourite ground,
Canterbury, and by so doing unwittingly altered the course of cricket history.

The institution of the Benefit Match had evolved long before Seymour's entry
into the game. It was a custom rather than a law, with no specific rules for
qualification, although it was generally understood that ten years service was
obligatory. The essence of the award was that it should be uncontracted, and

231

that any expenses incurred in the administering of the benefit match should be deducted from the sum handed over to the beneficiary. This rule-of-thumb arrangement occasionally gave rise both to anomalies and to unlooked-for good fortune among the professional ranks. A player who claimed unusually long service might invoke the ten-year convention and enjoy a second benefit, which often happened. But because there was no contractual obligation on the part of the club to grant him a benefit, a player whose relations with the committee had been stormy could expect no such gift. Nor was there any guarantee of profit from a benefit. If the beneficiary was unfortunate enough to choose a game subsequently washed out, then he could expect little in the way of a nest-egg. There were frequent cases in the early years of the century when professionals, invited to choose a benefit match, refused on the grounds that they couldn't afford it. Nor was their caution misplaced. As late as 1935 Wisden could record the doleful fate of a Leicestershire professional called Alan Wilfred Shipman (1900–1979), a loyal all-rounder who in seventeen seasons with the county scored fifteen centuries and took over 500 wickets.

> Gates were extremely disappointing. Indeed, on the occasion of Shipman's benefit, the attendances were so poor that the player found himself some £60 out of pocket as a result of the match.

Fortunately for the hapless player, the arrears were cancelled by the proceeds from a charity match, and Shipman ended his days as a modest but solvent publican. More remarkable is the case of Albert Trott, the wayward Australian who first came to England from Victoria in 1898 in a fit of pique after being inexplicably omitted from the Australian party to tour England. Trott joined Middlesex, entering the history of cricket by becoming the first, and last, player to hit a ball over the Lord's pavilion. This stupendous event occurred in 1899 after which Trott, an excellent batsman, degenerated into a mere big hitter forever aspiring to repeat himself.

It was as a bowler that Trott's real gifts shone through. A medium-pace stylist with a sharp off-break, he also had in his repertoire an effective out-swinger and a cleverly disguised fast ball. In 1899 and again in the following year he took over 200 wickets, but as the new century opened he began to decline, taking fewer wickets and growing progressively plumper, probably because of the thirst he seemed unable to assuage. By 1907 he seemed to be

Albert Trott, the emigré Australian whose liking for the bottle destroyed a great natural cricketing talent. He killed himself in 1913.

playing largely from memory, at which point his club, sensing that the time was approaching when they would have to dispense with his services, granted him the richly merited reward of a benefit match, adding an extra sweetness to the dish by assigning him the unfailingly well-attended Whitsun fixture against Somerset. Trott performed modestly with the bat, scoring 1 and 35, and in Somerset's first innings bowled only five overs for ten runs with no wickets. On Whit Monday, Somerset went in with 264 to make to win the match. Beldam and Mignon opened the bowling for the home side, but were soon replaced by the two Australians, Tarrant and Trott. What followed was high comedy for everyone but Trott and his bank manager. Tarrant took two quick wickets, at which Trott came on and had A.E. Lewis leg-before. The next man in, E.S.M. Poyntz, was then cleaned bowled first ball. Sammy Woods came in on a hat-trick and was also bowled first ball, to be followed by Robson, whose stumps went down with a crash, once again first ball. Trott, by taking four wickets in consecutive deliveries, had wrecked the Somerset innings. Tarrant then took another wicket, by which time Somerset had lost seven wickets without reaching 100. Trott took the ball again and instantly had Mordaunt caught. Off his next ball the Reverend A.P. Wickham, remembered for his predilection for brown pads, failed to get them in front of his stumps and was bowled. The last man, A.E. Bailey came in and was caught by Mignon, first ball. Trott had performed the freakish feat of taking four in four and three in three in the same innings, returning figures of seven for 20. No more glorious benefit-match swansong exists in the annals of cricket, and the affair so inspired the imagination of Neville Cardus that he fashioned for it an unforgettable phrase. Describing Trott's lightning despatch of the Somerset side, and correctly assuming that at the time Trott was in sore need of subsidy, Cardus wrote that "Trott bowled himself into the bankruptcy court", an image whose efficacy is tarnished only by the fact that the circumstances failed to fit the case. Recourse to the cold water of Wisden reveals that the game had been marred by bad weather on the first day, and that Trott's monumental feat occurred on the third and final day. It proved to be the very last flash of his greatness. His appearances for the county fell away, and after 1910 he became a first-class umpire. By the end of the 1913 season his health had so declined that he was forced to stand down. His addiction to the bottle had finally reduced him to a dropiscal wreck who experienced great difficulty in sleeping. In the following summer he was admitted into St Mary's Hospital, but the tedium of ward life drove him to such distraction that after eight days he discharged himself, borrowed some fare money from his nurses and took a cab home to his Harlesden lodgings. A day later he made out his last will and testament, leaving his only possession, a wardrobe, to his landlady, and then shot himself. The M.C.C. paid the funeral expenses, and *The Daily Telegraph* commented that "a more pathetic figure of a man in later days it would be difficult to imagine".

The fate of James Seymour was to be less cruel, although he too died not long after his retirement from the game. When in 1920 he stepped on to the field at

Canterbury for his benefit match, he could look forward to several good years as a county cricketer. Nothing untoward happened during the fixture, which Kent won handsomely, largely because of brilliant all-round play from Frank Woolley. The Wisden report ends with "Seymour had a very good benefit". It was when the proceeds were handed over to the player that the fun started. For reasons which have never been made clear, the Commissioners of Inland Revenue decided that part of Seymour's benefit belonged to them, although all benefit profits, being ex gratia and uncontracted, fall outside the boundaries of taxable income. Seymour disputed, or was encouraged to dispute, or was commanded to dispute, the Revenue's claim, his resolve no doubt being stiffened by the starch of the club's pre-eminent panjandrum, our old friend Lord Harris. No matter what his shortcomings, Harris was always on guard to protect the welfare of professionals with the rusty sword of his paternalism. The Seymour case dragged through the courts until it eventually reached the House of Lords where Harris, still battling away, brought every ounce of pressure at his disposal to bear on his peers. Seymour's case was so clearly justified that it would have taken an unusually able lawyer to have misread it. Not even Sir John Simon, consummate master of the maladroit, and a ditherer so resolute that Lloyd George said of him that he had sat on the fence so long that the iron had entered his soul, was able to reach a wrong decision. Seymour received what was rightfully his, the Inland Revenue was sent packing, since which time no claim for tax has ever been levied on any cricketer's benefit fund, even though in the years after the Second World War, it gradually became accepted practice for professionals to enjoy not a benefit match but a benefit season, during which a multiplicity of events ranging from concerts to boxing matches to dinners to raffles help swell the receipts. The modern professional, beavering doggedly through the drudgery of his benefit year towards the magic formula of a six-figure payout, has James Seymour and Lord Harris to thank for his immunity from tax.

The year of Seymour's retirement was also marked by the debut of a man destined to precipitate, through no fault of his own, the most sensational rumpus cricket has ever known. This prodigy had been born in a New South Wales no-horse town called Cootamundra, and had moved to within eighty miles of Sydney by the time he was two, presumably accompanied by his parents, although with a man as prodigious as Donald Bradman it is never wise to presume anything. At nineteen he had forced his way into the State side, and within a year had been selected for Australia. It was instantly apparent that Bradman, with his virtually flawless technique and limitless powers of concentration, was about to debase the coinage of run-making as nobody before him, that he was technically equipped and temperamentally inclined to go on batting for ever. In the third match of the 1928–29 series against England he scored a hundred and was never again left out of the national side. Playing against Queensland at Sydney in January 1930, he established a world record with a score of 452 not out, at which point the cricketing public in England and

Australia sensed that the equation of international rivalry was about to be radically adjusted. It will be remembered that England had regained the ascendancy in the Oval Test of 1926; the tour of 1928–29 became a triumphant processional for Chapman's men who, sustained by the prolific Walter Hammond, ran out winners by four matches to one. Australia was now about to deliver its devastating counter-stroke.

The tourists arrived in England for the 1930s series with a side consisting of Bradman and ten others. Teammates like Woodfull, Ponsford, McCabe and Grimmett were outstanding cricketers in their own right, but the indisputable truth is that Australia were by far the stronger side and that the difference between them and their opponents was Bradman. In the Trent Bridge Test he scored a century but was on the losing side. At Lord's he scored a double century and saw his team home by a comfortable margin. At Leeds he astounded even his admirers by scoring a century before lunch, another before tea, and a third before the close, amassing a world record score of 334 before being caught at the wicket off the bowling of Maurice Tate. The Old Trafford Test was drawn, and then at the Oval Bradman scored another double century, pulling Australia to a victory by over 500 runs.

Bradman was now 22 years old, and patently a scourge for the England bowlers for years, perhaps decades to come. This was undoubtedly sobering, but the prospect of being hammered in match after match by the relentless Bradman could hardly be said to loom very large in what is sometimes

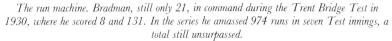

The run machine. Bradman, still only 21, in command during the Trent Bridge Test in 1930, where he scored 8 and 131. In the series he amassed 974 runs in seven Test innings, a total still unsurpassed.

laughingly defined as the larger scheme of things. After all, what more propitious moment to display those vaunted qualities of good sportsmanship and magnanimity than when your opponents keep beating you out of sight? Anyone can prate of fair play when on the winning side, but the world of English cricket was now about to be examined in its ability to lose with a good grace. But Bradman, said the strategists, was different. He constituted a factor so novel that only a novel remedy was practicable. And what more novel than an abandonment of the letter as well as the spirit of the rules? To what extent the architects of the deplorable antics of the 1932–33 tour of Australia were even aware that they were cheating, and, if aware, whether they cared, has never been satisfactorily answered and probably never will. Self-deception was just as dominant a part of the proceedings as unfair play, which explains the comically self-justifying outrage with which some of the English administrators greeted the suggestion that perhaps they were not gentlemen after all. But the situation was simple enough. The English were faced with an adversary totally immune to their attack under the rules. They must either agree to be beaten, a sad fact of life but not a world-shaking catastrophe, or they must conspire to break the rules. Faced with this choice, a small convocation of Gentlemen reached their decision. They would break the rules.

It is as well to keep hold of that vital fact. In the ensuing storm so many distracting side issues were raised by both sides that there was a very real danger that the central issue might be forgotten. No written laws of any team game can plug all loopholes, prevent all gamesmanship, guarantee that the contest be conducted on a reasonably civilised level. The rules can go only so far, and the gulf between their application and the reality of what takes place in the arena must be bridged by the sensibilities and good sense of the players, and particularly the captain. The man chosen to lead England to Australia in the winter of 1932 was an oustanding cricketer, a brave man, and very possibly also a nincompoop of an intrinsically English genus. Douglas Robert Jardine (1900–1958) is a perfect imperial specimen, raised in a climate of political ascendancy and social aloofness. His father, Malcolm Robert Jardine (1870–1947) walked straight out of Kipling's Simla, where he was born, into an English public school and university, before pausing for a while at the Middle Temple en route to becoming Advocate-General of Bombay. His son was born there during his father's incumbency, and sent home to Winchester School, where he became captain of cricket. He played three times for Oxford against Cambridge, and by 1923 was displaying his batting skills in the Surrey side. He made his Test debut, at Lord's against the West Indies, in 1928 and in 1932 succeeded P.G.H. Fender as captain of Surrey. In the aftermath of the 1930 defeats, he must have seemed the perfect choice to the England selectors. So far as cricket was concerned, he was also the worst, although the evidence suggests that while Jardine fired the gun, it had already been primed by men seeking a shrewd marksman.

Bowling which intimidates a batsman by its speed is a legitimate tactic.

Pelham Warner, pillar of the English cricket Establishment for over fifty years, who played a curiously equivocal role in the Bodyline affair.

Bowling which is propelled at the batsman's body rather than at the stumps is blatantly illegitimate. But when does a ball cease to be aimed at the stumps and become a projectile aimed at the batsman's body? The laws cannot define the precise moment at which a delivery becomes an assault, any more than the philosopher was able to decide whether a beach is land or sea. But for all the indecision, the beach is still there, and so is the illegitimacy of Bodyline bowling. The tactic was not new. Early in the 1932 season, during a Surrey *v.* Yorkshire match at the Oval, Jack Hobbs suddenly found himself exposed to the Bodyline

Bodyline: Larwood bowling to Woodfull and a packed leg-side field during the Brisbane Test. England won the match with a six from Eddie Paynter.

bowling of Bill Bowes, and instead of submitting to the indignity, walked down the pitch to remonstrate with the culprit. Next day in *The Morning Post*, readers were confronted by this:

> I do love cricket, and on Saturday Yorkshire fell from her pedestal and her great reputation was tarnished.

Further protests appeared in *The Cricketer*.

> This is not bowling. Indeed it is not cricket, and if all fast bowlers were to adopt such methods there would be trouble and plenty of it.

The only noteworthy thing about those bromides is their authorship. Both statements came from Pelham Warner, who was appointed as manager of the 1932–33 tourists, who helped to select the fast bowlers for that tour, and who was in favour of Jardine as his captain. Indeed, it seems likely that had not business commitments forced him out of the running during 1929–30, Jardine would have succeeded to the captaincy before the Australian tour. Had he done so, perhaps the asperities of his temperament would have been exposed in time for the subsequent disasters to have been avoided. Fifty years after the event, Jardine remains a problematic figure. Whenever his behaviour has been called into question, the ranks of his coevals have closed quickly behind him. We learn that he was a loyal friend, a loving husband, was kind to animals and possessed exquisite manners, that he was, in essence, a true gentleman. No doubt he was – to other gentlemen. But his evident inability to treat all men as innocent until proven guilty goes some way to reconciling the apparent contradiction between the shining reputation nourished by his peers and the execration in which some of his opponents held him. According to the testimony of that blunt and honest Australian writer-cricketer Jack Fingleton, Jardine displayed in Australia all the bigotry and rudeness which used on occasion to contort the sons of the Raj. Somewhere along the road from Bombay to Adelaide, he must have conceived the peculiar theory that he was in certain unspecified ways superior to some other men, and that this superiority entitled him to behave towards them with an arrogance which, seen in retrospect, takes the breath away. A woeful lack of imagination and humour, and an intellect so limited that a game of cricket became a world issue, combined to make him the very worst choice of leader which even the enemies of empire could have contrived.

The Bodyline strategy consisted of very fast, perfectly accurate bowling which would intimidate the batsman to the point where he might literally fear for his life. If the victim stepped away to the leg side to remove himself from the path of a rocklike projectile flying towards him at a speed approaching one hundred miles an hour, then the next delivery would follow the batsman over on to the leg side, the three stumps forgotten in the hunt for blood. In Harold Larwood, Jardine possessed the perfect artist for his purpose, a truly great fast bowler in full command of that pinpoint precision without which the Bodyline tactics would degenerate into a comedy of errors. And Larwood, a former miner who relied on the patronage of gentlemen like Jardine for his weekly wage, was to do as he was told. Even the amateurs were cowed by Jardine's maniacal ruthlessness, particularly the Nawab of Pataudi, whose royal lineage impressed the captain much less than the brownness of his skin. Of the touring party, one man alone possessed both the social standing and the moral courage to outface Jardine. He was G.O. Allen, an accurate fast bowler who refused pointblank to have anything to do with the tactics of Bodyline.

The ploy worked. Bradman, improvising brilliantly by cutting the ball to the off-side field from a position adrift of his leg stump, was reduced to fallibility and a batting average of 56, roughly half the punishing norm. England won the series comfortably and paid an incalculable political price. In the climacteric of the third Test at Adelaide, in which the Australian captain Woodfull was struck over the heart and his wicketkeeper Oldfield dazed by a blow on the head, mounted police were called in to guard against riot. Telegrams were exchanged between the cricketing authorities of the two countries; there was even wild talk of colonial secession. The M.C.C., outraged at being accused of cheating, threatened to call its cricketers home in mid-tour, at which their accusers, alarmed at the thought of all that gate money melting away, hastily recanted. The tour proceeded, and through it all Jardine, icily contemptuous of virtually everybody, maintained his poise, sublimely unaware of the spectacle he was making of himself, of his team, and of cricket itself. He had indeed reduced the situation to such low comedy that only the wildest satirists could extract anything from it. The world's most accomplished literary farceur, J.B. Morton, masquerading in the pages of a daily newspaper as "Beachcomber", solemnly announced that "it is understood the Government is to examine at once the whole question of cricket among savage tribes".

Retribution was swift to follow. After 1934 Jardine appeared in the first-class game hardly at all. Harold Larwood never played for England again. The Australians, who had threatened to call off their 1934 tour of England, were finally mollified by assurances from the home country that no further bowling heresies would be committed, and the game slowly subsided into its old patterns. In the fourth Test at Leeds in 1934, Bradman scored 304; in the fifth at the Oval he made 244. One head alone never rolled. In all this chaos and hysteria, where was the England manager? When touring sides visit other countries, they are placed under the charge of an elder statesman who maps their path through the labyrinth of unfamiliar protocol, ensuring that relations with the host nation are at any rate no worse, and perhaps a great deal better, than they were before the tour began. Jardine's campaign of 1932–33 was the most catastrophic in the history of cricket, transcending sporting relationships and spilling over into the arena of imperial politics. Pelham Warner, who had only a season or so before the tour expressed in print his abhorrence of Bodyline, was now seen to have condoned it by doing nothing effective to curb Jardine. Some years later Warner was knighted for services to cricket, a resolution of his affairs as remarkable as it was admirable, qualifying him as perhaps the most accomplished survivor of his generation. It has never been explained where Warner was when the blood was flying, or how he ever agreed to the idea of Jardine's captaincy. Later, when the affair had dwindled from the status of a cause célèbre to an historical problem, it was discovered that certain letters and documents relevant to the case had mysteriously disappeared. Fortune, it appeared, sometimes favoured the feeble.

The apologists for Jardine remained impenitent, pointing out that when in 1933 the West Indies pace attack, led by the great Constantine, gave the England captain a taste of the medicine he had administered to the Australians, Jardine had defied the onslaught, scoring a patient, stoic, unflinching century. But there are other desirable virtues in a captain than physical courage, and it must be accounted the bitterest irony of all that Jardine the fearless leader, the man who defied the wrath of a continent and who never deigned to utter a word of self-justification to the baying mob, was a coward of a very revealing type. The whole Bodyline tour was an attempt to frustrate the art of a virtuoso batsman and by so doing avoid defeat, even if it meant throwing the rules and reasonable conduct out of the window in the process. Jardine, it seems, was so terrified of losing to a bunch of uncouth colonials that he was willing to do anything to avoid the shame of it. For all the lore pumped into him at Winchester and Oxford, he never perceived that the game you are frightened of losing is a game not worth winning.

The passage of time gradually effaced some of the scars left in the wake of the hurricane. In 1938 Bradman, now the Australian captain, returned to England, in time to see his record score of 334 surpassed by Len Hutton, a twenty-two-year-old Yorkshireman who had been in the crowd at Headingly eight years before when Bradman set his mark. The last giants of the period before the Great War retired with honour, Jack Hobbs in 1935, Patsy Hendren in 1937, Frank Woolley in 1938, by which time the nation's civilian population was learning how to dig trenches and wear gas masks. Farce attended the last English touring side's trip to South Africa in the winter of 1938–39. In a despairing attempt to make Test matches reach a conclusion, the administrators had concocted something with the ominous title of the "timeless Test", a match which must be played to a conclusion no matter how long it takes and how many of the spectators become senile in the process. In the final Test, the culmination of a rubber characterised by high scoring and excessively conservative captaincy, South Africa batted first and made 530, taking nearly three days to score the runs. By the end of the fifth day England had been dismissed for 316 and the home side was batting again. At the end of the sixth day South Africa had ground out another 481, leaving the tourists a mere 696 runs to win. At this point, events in the larger world began to cast their shadow across the assumption that time could stand still until the match was over. In Cape Town, the captain of *The Athlone Castle* was supervising the fitting out of his ship in preparation for the long sea voyage back to England. At the end of the seventh day, with England poised on 253 for one wicket, there was still a week to go before the ship sailed. But three days had to be allowed for the train journey from Durban to Cape Town. Of the remaining four days, one was a Sunday, which left England with three days to score the 443 runs required for victory. More than ample time, and enough too for the home side to capture the nine wickets required. But on the eighth day, a Saturday, torrential rain fell and not a ball could be bowled. The ninth day was England's, and by close of play the score had crept up to 496 for the loss of three wickets. The tenth day, England's last if victory was to be snatched, began under the threat of rain. Five hundred was passed, then six hundred, but with England on the brink of a remarkable victory, the rains came down. Forty-two runs were still needed with five wickets in hand. Time, tide and *The Athlone Castle* wait for no man, and the two captains agreed to abandon as a draw a contest which had long ceased to have any meaning.

The England captain who agreed to call off the fiasco was the same Walter Hammond who, fifteen years before, had so innocently incurred the wrath of Lord Harris over the issue of his right to play for Gloucestershire without opening the door to communist revolution. But, as Lord Hawke had so mindlessly put it, pray God the day never dawned when a professional captained England. How had the tragedy come about? After the fall of Jardine, the number of amateurs whose skills commended them as likely England leaders seemed to be shrinking. In 1937, within the space of four months, Middlesex produced two successive England captains, G.O. Allen and R.W.V. Robins, neither of whom could afford the time off from their professional duties

Normal service resumed. Charles Cundall's painting of the packed house at the Lord's Test between England and Australia in 1938.

to retain the position. A.B. Sellars of Yorkshire, the most successful of the county captains, was not the stuff of which Test cricketers are made, and neither Wyatt, Valentine or Erroll Holmes looked up to the mark. There seemed nothing for it but to appoint a professional captain or go into the field against Australia with ten men and a gentleman-passenger. And then, at the eleventh hour, a miracle happened and honour was assuaged. Hammond, W.R., the Gloucestershire professional, mysteriously vanished at the end of April 1938, never to be seen or heard of again. The impenetrable riddle of his disappearance, worthy of the attention of Mr Sherlock Holmes himself, might in the ordinary course of events have called for an exhaustive investigation, had it not been that all attention was then distracted by a second, even more gratifying miracle following hard on the heels of the first – the happy arrival at the Bristol ground of a gifted amateur cricketer called Mr Walter Reginald Hammond, who immediately assumed command of county and country, thus staving off a constitutional crisis for a generation, and allowing shades of Lords Hawke and Harris to slumber on undisturbed.

As 1939 season proceeded, the nightmarish context of a European war inched ever closer as the fixtures drifted by. Yorkshire took the county title for the third successive year. In their last fixture they went down to Hove to play Sussex. On the last day, 1 September, even as the trains were steaming out of the great London termini carrying thousands of London schoolchildren to rustic sanctuary, Hedley Verity, the left-arm spinner who had taken over the mantle of Wilfred Rhodes in the Yorkshire and England sides, ran through the opposition to such devastating effect that ten years, and a world war later, framed copies of the matchcard under glass were still hanging from the flyblown parlour walls of Brighton boarding-houses. Baffled holidaymakers would peer in bewilderment at this yellowing document from a lost time:

6 Overs.   1 Maiden.   9 Runs.   7 Wickets.

Those figures record the greatest triumph ever achieved by any English cricketer in his final game. Four years later the modest, studious Verity, by now a Captain even though still a professional, was hit in the chest by German rifle fire in Sicily. He later died of his wounds in an Italian prisoner-of-war camp. News of his passing reached England on 1 September, 1943, four years to the very day on which he had last exhibited the subtleties of his art on a cricket field.

CHAPTER XXII

ANOTHER BLOODY
INTERRUPTION

T he most striking difference between cricket in the two World Wars was that in 1939 nobody was foolish enough to commit the heresy of equating the playing and watching of ball games with malingering. Instead of the solemn invocations of the armchair strategists of 1914, calling on athletes to put away bats and balls, the feeling was that as this looked like being a long and very dangerous war, and as there would be precious little for the nation to enjoy, cricket and football might just as well be encouraged. The soundness of this policy was confirmed when the Minister of Labour requested the cricket authorities to ensure that regular matches be staged at Lord's every Saturday. Inevitably there were problems. Most of the games-players were conscripted into the services, so that the Saturday one-day matches at Lord's presented matchcards so bizarre that in the years to come they were cherished as collectors' items: Buccaneers v. British Empire X1; Lord's X1 v. Canada; Metropolitan Police v. London Fire Service; Middlesex and Essex v. Kent and Surrey. These homely banners usually concealed eminent players, including a few welcome ghosts from the past. Heroes like Hendren and Woolley, long since assumed to have played their last game, suddenly reappeared to delight wartime crowds. One of these ancient deities was the famous Andrew Ducat, the Aston Villa half-back and Surrey batsman who had won international caps at both games. At Lord's, on 23 July 1942, Ducat, by now 56 years old, batted at number five for the Surrey Home Guard against the Sussex Home Guard:

> The Surrey side having been sent in to bat, Ducat began his innings before lunch and was 17 at the interval. On resuming he scored steadily, carrying his score to 29. Then he hit a ball from Eaton to mid-on. The ball was returned to the bowler, who was about to send down the next delivery when Ducat fell forward and apparently died immediately though he was moved to the pavilion and quickly taken by ambulance to a nearby hospital.

A famous cricketing photograph. Players take evasive action on 29 July 1944 as a V-1 flying bomb chugs sullenly over Lord's.

There were other, less tragic sensations. In a hastily improvised match between Pelham Warner's X1 and the West Indies, the Middlesex cricketer Leslie Compton found himself keeping wicket for the West Indies. A match between the Buccaneers and the British Empire X1 was called off, "owing to the Battle of Britain". In a 1940 Whitsuntide match between Nottinghamshire and Derbyshire, one of the umpires batted for Derbyshire. At Gloucestershire in 1943, R.E.S. Wyatt, captaining the R.A.F. against the home side, allowed the opposition to field twelve men, while a thirteenth player was allowed to bowl for Gloucestershire dressed, it appeared, in a football shirt borrowed from Sam Barkas, the old Manchester City international full-back.

In August of that summer Middlesex and Essex were due to play Kent and Surrey, in a match doomed to trials and tribulations. With play due to begin, tropical rain was falling, and with prospects of any play exceedingly thin, permission was granted for the Compton brothers, Denis and Leslie, to depart to play for Arsenal in the opening game of the football season against Charlton Athletic at the Valley ground. By half-past two, with the sun shining and the Comptons gone beyond recall, the covers were removed and play found to be possible. The Middlesex-Essex side soon discovered it was further weakened owing to an unfortunate accident which befell the Essex opener Avery, who in his excitement at the prospect of playing in the match, tripped over his cricket bag while leaving home and was unable to take any further part in the proceedings. Nor was the opposition entirely at full-strength, because Arthur Fagg, who should have been opening for them, spent the day in the less salubrious sport of following the mysterious spoor of his cricket bag as it wandered unattended down the labyrinth of the railways. At Lord's in 1944 the scheduled game between a Lord's X1 and the United States was amended to a

Lord's X1 *v.* Canada, owing to the invasion of Normandy. In that same summer, every player on the field one afternoon at Lord's flung himself full-length on the grass under the threat of a doodlebug, a pestilential device which always announced the imminence of its descent by suddenly ceasing to drone. There was a momentary hush before a bomb fell a mile or two away. The players then rose, brushed themselves down, and resumed their less arduous form of warfare, with the Middlesex batsman Jack Robertson heralding the resumption of normal service by swatting the first post-bomb delivery for six, amid laughter and relieved cheering from the crowd. By 1945, with the war drawing to a close, the big fixtures at Lord's became more ambitious, even becoming recognisable facsimiles of the Test matches of prewar days. In the five England-Australia Victory matches staged across the country, the composition of the home sides was familiar enough, but the visiting players, apart from Lindsay Hassett, had been quite unknown to followers of the game in peacetime. In spite of their comparative inexperience, the Australians drew the series two-all with one drawn, and one of their young men in particular, Pilot Officer Keith Miller, gave promise that he would be seen again on English grounds before long.

CHAPTER XXIII

THE PLEASURES OF PROGRESS

T he resumption of cricket in peacetime seemed to occur so smoothly as to create the dangerous illusion that nothing much had changed. Yorkshire won the County Championship yet again. There was a Test series, against the Indian tourists, which England won and which produced at least one authentic new player of the highest class, the Surrey medium-fast bowler Alec Bedser. Crowds were large and enthusiastic all over the country, and the coming tour of Australia was eagerly anticipated. On paper the England party looked a little long in the tooth but still skilled and experienced enough to give a good account of itself. Of course there was still Bradman to contend with, but he was said to be on the point of retiring at last. However, the exit of the Australian captain proved to be merely operatic, at least for the moment, and in the first Test at Brisbane it was as though the war had never happened. Bradman and Hassett scored centuries in a total of 645. England were skittled out by Miller and lost by the huge margin of an innings and 332 runs. At Sydney Bradman and Barnes scored double centuries, and again the visitors lost by an innings. The third Test was drawn, and the fourth, at Adelaide, was saved by Denis Compton with a century in each innings. Australia won the final

All heart and a model of economy – Alec Bedser, sturdy bulwark of the England attack in the postwar years.

Test by a wide margin and the tourists sailed home a leaderless rabble, for the most depressing aspect of the tour had been the sudden and total disintegration of Walter Hammond, both as captain and player. His aloofness from the rest of the team became notorious, and his failure to reach 40 in any of his eight Test innings was a sure signal that a great career was drawing to a close. He bowed out on the final leg of the tour, scoring 79 against New Zealand at Christchurch, appropriately the side's top scorer in his last innings for England. Between 1920 and 1951 Hammond scored over 50,000 runs, including 167 centuries, took over 700 wickets and more than 800 catches.

But even Hammond at his glorious best would probably not have tipped the scales in England's favour in 1946–7. The tourists' gravest handicap was their weakness in bowling. Apart from Bedser and the Kent leg-spinner Douglas Wright, England had no attackers of authentic Test quality. Verity lay in his grave, as did the Essex fast bowler Kenneth Farnes, whose career as a replacement for Larwood had ended tragically when the fighter 'plane he was piloting crashed in 1941. Neither Bill Edrich nor Peter Smith could be expected to trouble the likes of Bradman, Hassett and Miller; and Bill Voce, Dick Pollard and James Langridge were either too old or too mediocre even to get into the Test side. (Voce played in two games and took none for 161.) As in 1921, England needed more time for its cricketers to recover from the hardships of war. At home the disappointed public perhaps tended to overlook the nature of the difficulties facing so moderate a band of tourists. Wisden commented:

> Special Army leave was given to Voce and Pollard for the tour, but neither had sufficient pace to be really troublesome in the clear Australian atmosphere. The change from English rations to the excellent Australian food, coupled with the benefit gained from a sea trip and glorious Australian sunshine, caused all the party to put on weight, and none so more than Voce and Pollard.

After the Great War it had taken the English eight years to build a team strong enough to regain the Ashes. After the Second World War it took them seven. But for the moment hopes were high for a great renaissance. 1947 proved to be not only a sub-tropical summer but a golden one in other ways too. The South African tourists were slaughtered to make an English batting holiday, and all over England county grounds were thronged with spectators eager to partake of the feast, especially at Lord's, where the Middlesex side was enjoying the finest hour in its history. At the heart of this great celebratory upsurge was a batsman who, before the year had ended, transcended mere sporting fame to become a national hero familiar even to those who knew nothing of cricket. Just as Hobbs in 1935 and Hutton in 1938 had found themselves translated from the back pages of the newspapers to the front, so Denis Compton in 1947 burst into godlike eminence. At first it was his partner in the county side, Edrich, who was the more prolific scorer. Then in the middle of July, Compton began to light the county grounds of the country with some of the most dazzling batting ever seen. Improvising a wholly original array of strokes, mingling the conventional with

The Terrible Twins: Compton and Edrich walk out to bat against Sussex at Lord's during their sun-drenched annus mirabilis of 1947.

the comically heretical, Compton reduced all bowling to impotence. Between 12 July and 17 September he scored 2,074 runs, including twelve centuries for an average of 109.01. Record after record tumbled. The highest mark in an English season had been set in another age, by Jack Hobbs' father-figure Tom Hayward, who in 1906 had reached 3,518. The most centuries in a season had been made by Hobbs in his record-breaking year of 1925, when he passed the century mark sixteen times. During the 1947 season Edrich made 3,539 runs, including twelve hundreds. Compton scored 3,816 runs, including eighteen centuries, and of all the sides who sampled his casual mastery, none could have grown wearier than the South African tourists, against whom Compton scored six hundreds and a 97.

Among Compton's eighteen centuries was one which ranks among the greatest innings ever played in the Championship, in one of the very few matches which Middlesex lost that season. It was against Kent, whose accomplished spin bowler Douglas Wright had run through the enemy in the first innings, taking seven wickets for 92 runs. On the last day Middlesex were left to make 400 to win, and with four of their wickets gone for 135, the end seemed a formality. Compton then proceeded to play one of the most gallantly beautiful innings of the age. Supported by his captain F.G. Mann, he dismembered the Kent attack with a flair so breathtaking and an extempore brilliance so extraordinary that next day, in a national newspaper, Wright wrote a piece confessing the sheer impossibility of knowing what and how to bowl at Compton in such devastating form. Compton hit nineteen boundaries, even though, as Wisden confirms, ''most of the Kent fieldsmen were placed on the boundary''. So long as Compton remained, victory was feasible. After tea he

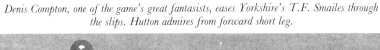

Denis Compton, one of the game's great fantasists, eases Yorkshire's T.F. Smailes through the slips. Hutton admires from forward short leg.

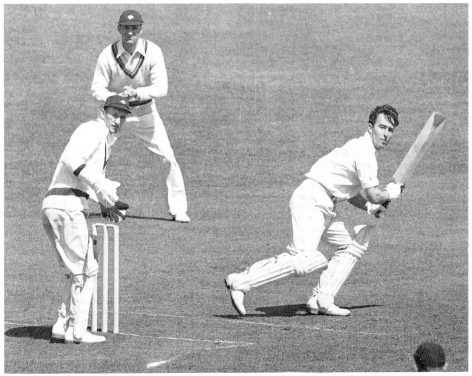

stepped up his tempo to the point where it began to look as though Middlesex might pull off an amazing win. But with his score on 168, he was caught; the last five wickets tumbled for a handful of runs in less than half an hour and the game was over. Victory went to Kent, but for those who witnessed the final day's play, the match belonged to Compton. It seemed as certain as anything can be that in the years to come, Compton would rewrite the record books, revelling in his enchanted life for at least another ten seasons.

The worm, however, was already in the bud. In addition to sharing with Hutton the position of the leading player of his generation, Compton was a brilliant Association footballer, whose career as a left-winger with Arsenal had brought him eleven England caps. Because these honours had come his way during the war years, this aspect of his genius tended to be underrated, and sometimes even overlooked completely by commentators, but there is no question that he was the most gifted player of ball games produced by the English since C.B. Fry. There were times when the twin talents clashed and choices had to be made, as in the 1938–39 England tour of South Africa, which Compton declined because of his footballing commitments. The demands imposed on his frame by playing both games season after season finally precipitated a crisis in which Compton's Knee eclipsed Jenkins' Ear as the most renowned items of anatomy in the annals of the English. The fallibility of the god began to dawn on the dismayed thousands. Ironically, the first clear signs of impending disaster revealed themselves on the occasion of one of his greatest triumphs, the end-of-season match between the Champion County and the Rest of England. Even as he put the opposition to the sword, scoring a remarkable double century, he was obliged to cut and thrust on one leg. The years of sprinting down the wing, of riding tackles, of swerving and half-turning at full speed, had taken their toll. The careless raptures of 1947 were destined never quite to return, although there were still marvels to come. In scoring the fastest triple century in history in December 1948 at a South African ground in Benoni, Compton once again batted in a style which defeated the efforts of Wisden to describe it:

> Compton made his first hundred in sixty-six minutes, his second in seventy-eight, and his third in thirty-seven. Often he walked down the pitch before the bowler released the ball, and he mixed orthodoxy with a bewildering assortment of unclassified strokes which went from the middle of the bat at a lightning speed. He whipped balls pitched outside his off-stump to the mid-wicket boundary and he stepped away in order to cut leg-breaks pitched outside the wicket.

Eventually the recalcitrant kneecap was removed and Compton hobbled on to his 123rd century before retiring at forty, an age which the Hobbs-Woolley generation would have regarded as impulsive. By the time Compton bowed out, he had become English cricket's first brand image, for the formal anointing of the god had been performed with a hair dressing for men called Brylcreem. His face beamed down from hoardings, from the pages of magazines and newspapers, from the backs of buses, until he was known and, in a curious way, celebrated even by the non-cricketing public. For English cricket of the postwar years he represented the Romantic attitude, just as his contemporary Hutton stood for Classicism. Between them they represented the very best of the English batting tradition.

In the year that Compton stroked and glided his way into the record books, cricket was enjoying the greatest commercial boom in its history. In 1947 more than two million paying customers crowded into the county grounds, and it would have been a bold man or a lunatic who would have predicted the lean years to come. Compton's apotheosis and the glorious weather conspired to obscure a truth about the times which the cricketing authorities might have been wise to have acknowledged. The postwar world was nothing like the 1930s. No longer was there a cloth-capped proletariat with few diversions at its disposal. Once upon a time it had been the local picture palace and the local cricket and football grounds which afforded the chance to dispense with the frivolity of earning a living and concentrate on the things that mattered. But as the 1950s dawned, technology began to tilt the balance away from the three-day county game. More cars appeared on the road, radio began to feel the draught from the television industry. More of the British than ever before were taking their summer holidays on the continent as air travel became cheaper. Cricket could no longer claim a captive audience; even in Australia, the pull of great tennis champions was drawing promising young men away from the cricket grounds. The financial rewards of golf, the gradual reduction of the numbers of overs in each day's play, slower scoring rates, were all factors which combined to point to the coming crisis.

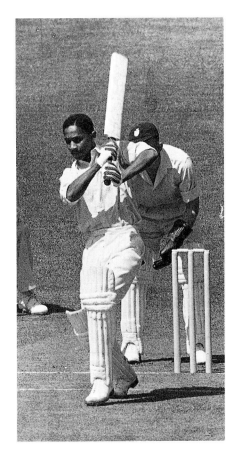

And yet perhaps it was understandable that nobody sensed disaster until very nearly too late. The decline was so gradual, the idea of an England without cricket so unthinkable, that people shrugged off a vague intimation that there would be no return to a Golden Age, contenting themselves with hopes for a gradual improvement in the future. In the meantime, the game certainly seemed to be as lively and

Frank Worrell, immaculate batsman, dynamic captain, and sorely missed ambassador-at-large for the West Indies. A gentle and perfect knight of cricket.

entertaining as ever. In 1950 the visiting West Indians came of age as a major cricketing power, delighting everyone with their batting and producing in Ramadhin and Valentine one of the great slow bowling combinations of the postwar years. The inability of so many batsman to read Ramadhin's spin was the talking point of the year, but it was Valentine with 33 Test wickets who was the chief instrument of destruction. In Frank Worrell, Everton Weekes and the wicketkeeper Clyde Walcott the tourists possessed three of the most powerful batsmen in the world, and their triumph introduced the English to the delights of Calypso. Three years later the Ashes were back in England, when after four drawn games, the Oval crowd watched in mounting hysteria as the Middlesex heroes Edrich and Compton knocked off the winning runs. But of greater significance than the victory was the identity of the successful captain. After two hundred years of insistence that one of the vital qualifications for the England captaincy was an unearned income, or a varsity degree, or at any rate the social confidence which goes with such battle honours, the English cricket establish

ment had bowed to the inevitable and appointed a professional captain in Len Hutton. A canny tactician rather than an inspired strategist, Hutton led his men with a tough efficiency which produced impressive results when he took the side to Australia in the winter of 1954–55. Absurdly, this outstanding cricketer was never considered good enough to captain his own county. Down the century the Yorkshire committee has offered many examples of comic ineptitude and bigotry, but not even the wild excesses of its conduct during the storm-racked 1980s can approach its refusal to appoint the England captain as its own captain.

In 1956 came another extraordinary individual feat. Ian Johnson's Australians came to the Oval early in the season to face the all-conquering Surrey side. In their first innings the tourists made 259, but more sensational than anything in the batting statistics was the entry opposite the name of the Surrey off-spinner Jim Laker:

Len Hutton in 1946. A wartime accident shortened his left arm but failed to staunch the flow of runs.

Overs 46.   Maidens 18.   Runs 88.   Wickets 10.

In losing by ten wickets to a county side the Australians may well have suffered a loss of confidence from which they never quite recovered for the rest of the season. However, they could at least seek consolation in the rule-of-thumb that in cricket, as in the larger universe, lightning never strikes twice, and that in any future encounters with Laker they could not conceivably do any worse. As events turned out, the Australians could not have been more wrong, because the rout at the Oval proved to be no more than a warm-up for the real thing. Coming to Old Trafford for the fourth Test with the scores at one win apiece, Johnson's side batted second, facing an England total of 459. They opened their innings after lunch, only to find themselves opening their second innings before the close, Laker having taken nine of their wickets for only 37 runs. The next day, with seemingly the entire nation holding its breath, Laker went to work, bowling out the entire opposition even more economically than at the Oval:

Overs 51.2.   Maidens 23.   Runs 53.   Wickets 10.

Nobody had ever taken nineteen wickets in a first-class match before. To take them in a Test match was amazing. To take them in a Test match against Australia was very nearly unbelievable. To take them for only 90 runs set a mark which nobody would ever remotely approach. Laker, the gentlest and most modest of men, later said that he had had all the luck which might have gone to his Surrey and England spinning partner Tony Lock, and that on another day their respective analyses might have been reversed. But the record books include no Might-Have-Been section, and to Laker goes the supreme distinction of taking nineteen wickets out of twenty in a Test match and 46 in the series.

In the following season the West Indies were back, and although they performed poorly in the Tests, they gave local crowds the chance to glimpse embryonic genius in the person of the twenty-one-year-old Garfield Sobers, who scored the first double century of his career at Nottingham at the end of May. The Trent Bridge crowds who enjoyed Sobers' exhibition, which included eleven boundaries while moving from 50 to 100, might have rejoiced even more had they known that before long Sobers would join Nottinghamshire and inflict similar punishment on their county opponents. By then West Indian cricket and West Indian politics would be seen to be the same thing, as C.L.R. James had insisted they were all his life. After a long absence in the United States, James returned to the islands in the late 1950s to lead the journalistic fight for independence and for a black captain of the West Indies cricket team. As the 1960s dawned both causes were won. When the cricketers went out to tour Australia they were led by Frank Worrell, not simply because the James lobby had won its case but also because the whole of Australia, sensing that their visitors were bringing one of the strongest and most attractive sides of the century, wished them to be hamstrung by no passenger-captains and supported as vociferously as James himself the installation of Worrell. Their support for

Worrell was perfectly understandable. He was a prince among cricketers, one of the greatest batsmen in the world, a highly gifted bowler, a wise captain and, most striking of all, one of the sweetest of men. His tour of Australia swiftly became a triumphal procession, not always blessed with victory, but suffused with admiration and deep affection, as he and the Australian captain Benaud played the game at the very apex of its art, maintaining throughout that indefinable blend of intense resolution to win with mutual respect and friendship which sport ought always to achieve but so very rarely does. The first Test, at Brisbane, has become a historic set-piece. With four wickets in hand in the final innings, Australia needed 27 to win with half an hour to play. When the final over of the match began, Australia were still six runs short with three wickets left. From the first ball they took a leg-bye. From the second the Australian captain gambled everything on a huge swing, missed and was caught at the wicket. The third ball was played back to the bowler. The fourth delivery produced a bye, the fifth a single. Then came the final three deliveries of the match. Wisden recounts:

> Meckiff hit the sixth ball hard and high to leg, but Hunte cut it off on the boundary as the batsmen turned for the third run, which would have given Australia victory. Hunte threw in superbly, low and fast, and Grout was run out by a foot. Kline came in to face the last two balls with the scores level. He played the seventh ball of the over towards square leg and Meckiff, backing up well, raced down the wicket, only to be out when Solomon again threw down the wicket with only the width of a stump as his target.

The only tied Test in history, this was the match defined as one in which "both sides had striven throughout for victory, with no thought of safety first". More to the point was the extraordinary scene at the end of the tour. Wisden again:

> Never has it been more apparent that the game is greater than the result than in Melbourne on February 17th, 1961. Commerce in this Australian city stood almost still as the smiling cricketers from the West Indies, the vanquished not the victors, were given a send-off the like of which is normally reserved for Royalty and national heroes. Open cars paraded the happy players among hundreds of thousands of Australians ... Worrell, the handsome West Indian captain, Hall, a bowler big in heart as well as stature, Kanhai, a fleet-footed batsman in the best tradition, and the suave Ramadhin, who had come a long way since he was introduced to cricket at the Canadian Mission School in Trinidad, were among those whom, it was said, were moved to tears by the enthusiasm of the farewell.

Worrell was knighted for services to cricket in 1964, became Warden of the University College of the West Indies and a senator in Parliament, and was defined by Constantine as "the first hero of the new nation of Barbados". He died in 1967, struck down by lukeamia at the age of 42. A star of the Lancashire Central League club Radcliffe, Worrell took an economics degree at Manchester University, and became so revered by the locals that when he died they flew the flag at half-mast at the Radcliffe Town Hall. He became the first cricketer ever to be given a memorial service in Westminster Abbey. When his body was brought home to Barbados, the whole island paid its respects to a man whose contribution to cricket had been incalculable, but whose greater contribution, to the dignity and pride of his countrymen, made his premature death so tragic.

The great events of his years as West Indies captain, and those following, in which his protégé Sobers took command, underlined a development of which the English were increasingly if still only dimly aware, that the axis of power inside the cricket world was slowly moving away from what used to be called the Mother Country and relocating itself in the old empire, particularly in the Caribbean and in South Africa. At home the legislation of egalitarianism, which had begun so modestly with Lloyd George's death duties back in the age of Grace, had all but removed the sources of patronage with which the patricians of the old school had been willing enough to sustain ailing county clubs. Amateurs who had once been free to dally through the summer playing cricket without bothering about an occupation, were now so scarce as to be very nearly extinct. The last late flowering of amateurism, which in the 1950s had produced Peter May and Colin Cowdrey, seemed to have played its final card with Ted Dexter in the early 1960s. This was the decade in which three profound changes transformed the structure of the English game and in turn altered for ever the face of the cricketing world.

On 1 May 1963, English cricket finally emerged from its battered fortress into the bleak new world of the twentieth century. There was to be no going back.

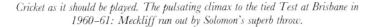

Cricket as it should be played. The pulsating climax to the tied Test at Brisbane in 1960–61: Meckliff run out by Solomon's superb throw.

The castle was being abandoned once and for all, although it is doubtful if the garrison realised as much as it stepped gingerly out into the open market. "What Manchester does today, the rest of the country does tomorrow", is a claim often heard, especially in Manchester, so perhaps it was fitting that the scene of the great departure was Old Trafford, venue of a match between Lancashire and Leicestershire. The day was a Sunday, which represented the abandonment of a traditon not so much religious as sentimental. Nor was it the breach of sabbatarian rectitude which defined the watershed, but the nature of the event itself. English professional cricket was about to become English commercial cricket. Having long since evolved from a game to an entertainment, it was now about to continue the process by becoming showbiz. Its popular heroes were now about to bear on their backs the name of a sponsor who openly avowed his intention to push his product by advertising cricket. But it was not this phenomenon alone which cut off the garrison's retreat. Neither the name of the day nor of the paymaster could have combined to threaten the game as generations had come to know it. There was a third factor. Perhaps on that morning at Old Trafford the garrison believed it was embarking on a brief sortie. It never came back. This was not a foray but a surrender, rendered even more poignant by the fact that almost nobody suspected it. On Sunday, 1 May, there took place the first limited-overs one-day match in English first-class cricket.

Cricket as it is now played: Mike Gatting is run out in the 1983 Benson and Hedges Cup Final. Umpire Harold "Dicky" Bird's response is emphatic and the crowd's response doubtless ecstatic in the noisy modern manner.

258

The reasons justifying this heretical course were impressive, and perfectly plain to anyone able to stand back and assess the true nature of what had once been the national game. For at least a century English cricket had been an institution underwritten by patronage. Because of the historical accident that once upon a time the landowning patricians, the Osbaldestons and the Aislabies, the Wards and the Grimstones, had fallen in love with the game, its economic base was not so much taken for granted as rendered irrelevant. Other pastimes might have to pay their way, but not cricket, which, whenever faced with an imminent fall from economic grace, could always anticipate happy landings on the silken cushion of patronage. Let a county club fall into debt, and some local member of the landed gentry could be relied upon to gallop to the rescue. Let there be a rain-ruined season, or a crumbling pavilion roof, or a calamitous benefit match, or a mortgage about to be foreclosed, and the squirearchy would answer for it. In administration, too, the patricians had always laboured nobly in the cause, not simply by accepting the drudgery of clerical responsibility, but rushing to embrace it. This self-sacrificial tendency is exquisitely expressed in the story of the Reverend George William Gillingham who, after slaving for some years as honorary secretary to Worcestershire, saw one day that the River Severn had flooded the county ground, dived into the waters, swam into the pavilion and swam back again carrying the accounts book between his teeth. While the reverend gentleman's devotion to the cause might be regarded by a more utilitarian age as somewhat excessive, it was by no means untypical. The governors of cricket gave as much time to book-keeping as to bookmaking, much counsel on investment, much guidance as to the husbanding of slender resources. They proselytised on behalf of the game in the most unlikely corners of the globe, moving mountains in their resolve that, whether in the remote South Seas or in the New World, the great game should not go under. They did not always succeed. Canada and the United States proved a sore disappointment. But generally the success of cricket's major-generals was prodigious. There is no question that without them the first-class game could hardly have evolved.

In return for this patronage, the benefactors demanded control, and took it, not always in the most diplomatic way. Sometimes they exercised their power in a style not at all commensurate with their gentlemanly conceptions of themselves. It might, for example, require a nice sense of the absurd to decide which of two experiences would be the more disagreeable, to be marooned on a desert island with Lord Harris, or to be rescued from it by Lord Hawke. But whatever their faults, they sustained a game which, as professionalism advanced, came to rely to an ever-growing extent on charity. In one sense the predicament of the county club was analogous to that of a newspaper. Circulation or, in the case of cricket gate money, might contribute towards revenues but it would always fall short of minimal requirements. The newspaper bridged the gap with advertising, the cricket club with patronage, which gave cricket an immense strength, because unlike the newspaper proprietor, who dare not offend his advertisers, cricket could offend anyone it pleased. Except the patricians. When pressures were brought to bear by the outside world, cricket could afford to ignore them. And ignore them it did, which is how it came about that an essentially Victorian garrison found itself suddenly exposed to the rigours of the neo-Elizabethan market-place.

For the patricians had all gone, taxed out of existence by death duties, killed in wars, spurred by social conscience, outmanoeuvred by events. The great estates were broken up; stately homes which had once echoed to the plick-plock of country-house strokeplay now rang to the steady tramp of sightseers on conducted tours. By one of those neat coincidences which bring a smile to the historian's face, the advent of the one-day game coincided with the abolition of the distinction between Gentlemen and Players. No longer supported by the landed gentry, cricket was obliged to earn its living. No more the divisive prefix "Mr" and the rubric of triple initials on the matchcard; no more the panache of what the Lancashire slow bowler had once defined as "coloured caps"; no more the capacity crowds for the Eton-Harrow and Oxford-Cambridge matches. We were all professionals now, and some way had to be found to mollify the accountants and reconcile the cost of running a county club with the empty seats at Championship matches. The game's administrators could no longer afford the luxury of protracted deliberations. By the time action was taken, almost every one of the seventeen first-class counties was running at a loss, and those two million who had thronged to the matches in Compton's year were now reduced to one-third of that number. Something had to be done.

What were the available solutions? Raising the price of admission would have driven away customers even as it attracted revenue. Raising the cost of county membership was equally impractical. Moreover, membership drives had been tried time and again without solving the problem. It seems that nobody thought of asking for government subsidy, but even if they had, they might have considered the implications of ministerial control and opted instead for oblivion. There was little point in mounting an all-out attempt to raise television fees from the derisory levels of the day. Cricket had only one customer, the B.B.C., and without the bargaining power of rival bidders, its power at the negotiating table was marginally less than nil. There remained one last refuge – subsidy. The linking of the game with the name of some manufacturer. This meant transforming the game as it stood into a spectacle with sufficient commercial appeal to attract the cash of patrons. And so the one-day game arrived. After all, argued the sophists, almost all the cricket ever played in this world has been one-day cricket, in the sense that club and village and school matches usually lasted no longer than a single day. All Muggleton and Dingly Dell completed their transactions within the compass of a single day. So did Tillingfold and Ravely in Hugh de Selincourt's masterly *The Cricket Match*; so did Mr Hodge's eleven against Fordenden in A.G. Macdonnell's *England, Their England*. If these paragons were content to play under these rules, why not the professionals? The speciousness of this argument obscured the most vital truth of all, which is that a match which begins and ends in one day is not at all the same thing as a one-day match. Three years before the great departure, Kent had defeated Worcestershire by an innings in a Championship match which began and ended on 15 June. But Worcestershire were put in and out twice in that one day, a fate quite impossible under the new one-day rules. In any case, the reason why weekend cricketers find the first-class game so fascinating is precisely because it is not played by weekend cricketers, but is graced by virtuosi. In cricket as in music, great executants create their own rhythms and tempi in performance. Those rhythms and tempi require for their full expression certain conditions of performance. An opera-lover confronted by the prospect of a production of "Tosca" lasting ten minutes might be forgiven for concluding that the outcome would not be "Tosca" at all, but some scrambled parody not worth listening to. For he would know that in order to perform so complex a work in so short a span of time, essential elements would have to be flung overboard. Among the possibilities which those members of the Lancashire and Leicestershire sides were leaving behind as they marched out to do brief battle were the death-defying second innings recovery, the gallant last-ditch fight for a draw, the gradual accelerando of an individual double century, the parabolic allure of leg-break bowling content to buy its wickets at a price, the frisson of the unknown which attaches to any innings whose duration remains uncertain until the fall of the last wicket. No more the obduracy of a Barlow or a Bailey, the profligacy of an Arthur Mailey or a Douglas Wright, the twelve-hour perversity of Banerjee and Sarwate's last-wicket stand. No more nightwatchman whimsicalities, no more overnight speculation, no more daft declarations by Machievellian captains.

But if all this was to be jettisoned, what was left? A generation later the question remains unanswered. Often when discussions are mounted on the decline of English cricket, the case is heard that too many counties have opted for imported overseas stars at the expense of home-grown talent, although curiously enough the obverse of the argument, that a Sobers or a Zaheer achieves more for English cricket by precept than he damages it by intrusion, is rarely heard. It is one of the more crushing ironies that during the troubled 1960s, a period fraught with domestic crisis, looming bankruptcies, shrinking three-day attendances and the steady erosion of English excellence, the County Championship enjoyed, in terms of individual excellence, a dazzling passage which one day will be seen as a golden age in which the great stars of all nations were in daily contention – Sobers against Intikhab, Rohan Kanhai against Mike Procter, Glenn Turner against Andy Roberts. In the seven seasons between 1976 and 1982, of the twenty-one names filling the first three places in the national batting averages sixteen belong to overseas players, in the bowling analyses twelve.

Whatever the strengths or weaknesses of the lobby which would introduce tariff walls to the world of cricket and exclude all but the English from the English game, history will surely pronounce its verdict that the most damaging wound sustained by the domestic game has been the self-inflicted one of the one-day idea. Within the compass of a generation, it has advanced so far in newsworthiness and popularity as to have transformed the etiquette of the game, its laws, its procedures, its rituals, its very personality. By dangling the carrot of Prize Money and insisting on a Man of the Match, by courting cup final hysteria and the baying of drunken mobs, by splitting itself, amoeba-like, from one competition into two and then three, it has pushed the County Championship into the background and damaged the fabric of the domestic game so seriously as to have rendered remote any prospect of recovery. In order to accommodate new competitions, the Championship has been cut back and cut back again, with the result that the double of a thousand runs and a hundred wickets, the scoring of 3,000 runs or the taking of 200 wickets in a season have all become things of the remote past. Instead we are vouchsafed the consolation of grown men kissing each other like troupes of lightheaded chorus girls at the fall of every wicket, of international teams clothed in hues which even those chorus girls would have found unbecoming, of technical solecism so widespread and so outrageous as to have rendered all the text books obsolete and all canons of judgement passé.

In the sense that the decline of a privileged class inclined to the distribution of largesse is a political rather than a sporting development, the necessity to court commercial subsidy must be accounted a classic example of the way in which politics cannot be kept out of organised sport. It is one of the whimsies of cricket history that the cry to keep the game free of political entanglements has usually been raised by the very people responsible for causing those entangle-

ments. The customary sequence of events is for someone to perform an act which is in its nature blatantly political, and then, when the opposition musters, to accuse the enemy of dragging politics into sport. This is followed by an acrimonious debate which so begs the question as to evoke thoughts of Swift's ancient argument about the efficacy of manufacturing cucumbers out of sunbeams. The real issue is not whether keeping politics out of cricket is desirable, but whether it is possible. In the light of events since 1945, the answer is so obvious that any attempt to ignore it can only lead to chaos and disaster. Whenever there are international con-

The stylish South African Barry Richards, in the early 1970s the best batsman in the world and an intercontinental cricketer in the style of Midwinter.

262

Viv Richards, natural successor to his namesake Barry and a merciless punisher of the loose ball. In mid-career he had a particular relish for the English pace bowler Bob Willis.

tests between representatives of societies with ideologies so conflicting that they cannot even agree what politics are, then the issue is already joined, even if it takes some specific incident to bring the fight out into the open, at which point the air is murmurous with sighs for the good old days.

But there never were any good old days. Politics have always been with us. When university graduates decreed that only university graduates were qualified to select and lead the England side, they were bringing politics into cricket. When Maharajahs who should have been taking rest cures at health farms insisted on captaining touring sides, they were bringing politics into cricket. When Lord Hawke insisted on vetting the prospective wives of his professionals, he was bringing politics into cricket as well as into the boudoir. When in 1933 the raging waters of Bodyline lapped against the very doors of the Colonial Office, who could deny that cricket had very nearly *become* politics? Cricket, like everything else, is part of the real world, and cannot hope to avoid political imbroglios from time to time. Nor is this involvement necessarily a bad thing. That passionate ideologue and anti-colonialist C.L.R. James has often paused in his exposition of the joys of Marxism to pay eloquent tribute to the English public schoolboys who came to his island and introduced Newboltian concepts of Fair Play which were destined to enrich the life of the entire community. And there have been times when the calculated deployment of cricket as an arm of imperial policy has had an effect of sublime benignity, as

263

The elegant K.S. Duleepsinhji, whose colour denied him the chance to play against South Africa. Nephew of the great Ranji, Duleep made 173 against Australia at Lord's on his Test Match debut.

those will know who have followed Arthur Grimble's account of cricket in the Gilbert Islands, which progressed within a generation from contests involving "considerable slaughter" to genuine sporting occasions in which the participants were, in the words of a native chief, "the fighters who love each other".

The Basil D'Oliveira dispute is one of the most sensational and educational cause célèbres in the history of any game, but it may be worth providing a few historical notes which suggest that politics, so far from suddenly deciding to rear an ugly head in 1968, had been rearing it with impunity for many years before, as Ranjitsinhji could have testified. In 1896 he had been omitted from the England side, ostensibly because Lord Harris disapproved of overseas players representing England. Lord Harris, captain of England in 1878-79, was born in Trinidad. In 1908 Ranji, by now one of the most renowned and respected athletes in the world, was given a farewell dinner by his friends at the Cambridge Guildhall. Lord Curzon of Kedleston, so charitably described in the Oxford History of England as "one of Nature's rats", responded to his invitation with:

> I would gladly do anything to show my regard and respect for my friend the Jam Sahib of Nawanager who is equally charming as a cricketer and as a man. But, unfortunately on October 19th I have to be in Scotland.

Curzon was joined by Lord Hawke, who, possibly not knowing that he had filched Curzon's excuse, wrote:

> I have long been engaged for a fortnight's visit to Scotland, and I very much regret to say it clashes with the complimentary dinner to my great and distinguished friend the Jam Sahib.

Others who made the same political gesture included the Vice-Chancellor of the University, the Master of Trinity and Mr Buckmaster, K.C.,M.P. In 1929 Ranji's brilliant nephew, K.S. Duleepsinhji, was selected for England in the first Test against South Africa, but withdrew after objections from the tourists. Nor did he appear in any of the four subsequent Tests, nor was he ever picked for any tour of South Africa. Roland Bowen observed:

> In later years, when serving as Indian High Commissioner in Australia, Duleep stated that he had agreed to stand down, not wanting to cause trouble. He was always a gentle creature.

Even before Ranji's victimisation at the hands of Lord Harris, the South Africans had omitted from their side their outstanding black cricketer, T. Hendricks.

Thus when in 1968 Basil D'Oliveira, a South African-born Cape Coloured playing for Worcestershire, was selected to tour South Africa with the English tourists, perhaps nobody should have been surprised when the South African Prime Minister made an extraordinary attempt to bring politics into cricket by insisting that when the English had selected D'Oliveira for the tour they were deliberately bringing politics into cricket. The issue flared into a national debate. Should England insist on taking D'Oliveira? Should they agree to go without him? Should they not go at all? At last, after long weeks of agonising the tour was called off, the English left the South Africans to an international isolation which has obtained ever since, and D'Oliveira, a much-loved and admired man in his adopted country, was decorated by her Majesty the Queen.

Now the perceptive reader will have perceived a distinct difference between the cases of Ranji and Hendricks on the one hand, and Duleep and D'Oliveira on the other, and that this difference is

Basil D'Oliveira, the genial and highly popular Cape Coloured all-rounder who in 1968 became the focus of a bitter cricketing controversy.

Garfield Sobers batting against England at Edgbaston in 1973, his final Test appearance, which he marked with the last of his 28 Test centuries – 150 not out in a West Indies total of 652 for 8.

fundamental to any rational assessment of D'Oliveira's case. Ranji and Hendricks were being snubbed by their own side, Duleep and D'Oliveira by their opponents. However blackguardly the motives of those who victimised the cricketers Ranji and Hendricks for non-cricketing reasons, and no matter how blatantly they were dragging politics into cricket as they did so, they were befouling nobody's nest but their own. The cases of Duleep and D'Oliveira are of a different order altogether, because they were rendering invalid the very tenet on which the philosophic basis of all sporting competition stands, which is that each side in the contest will not expect to dictate the rules to the other. A prizefight in which the champion insists on the challenger's bootlaces being tied together, a Wimbledon final in which one of the players is handicapped by the removal of the strings from his racket, a foot race in which the favourite is required to run backwards, are all hypotheses so ludicrous as to be beyond the bounds of rational discussion. And yet in the cases of Duleep and D'Oliveira, English cricket was being asked to take the field with sides selected by their opponents. The Ranji and Hendricks incidents merely made the cricket ridiculous; the Duleep and D'Oliveira affairs made it impossible. The point is worth making because while the D'Oliveira argument was raging, it was not always easy for the protagonists to see where they were going, or even where they had been. Some of the disputants even invoked the case of Soviet Russia, asking why, if we could compete against one totalitarian state, we could not compete against another, overlooking the distinction that not even in its most

266

rampant imperialist mood did the Soviet regime dare to attempt to select the sides of foreign sporting challengers. Ethics apart, the case of D'Oliveira was the moment when politics obtruded so far into sport as to destroy it utterly. In other words, although the D'Oliveira affair embodied a vital issue of political morality, it remained perfectly possible to reach conclusions about the crisis within a frame of reference which excluded politics altogether. When one side in a cricket match insists on the right to select both sides, then reality has degenerated into Mad Hatterism.

As the D'Oliveira affair, but not its implications, gradually faded from the surface consciousness, lovers of the game were tempted to hope that perhaps at last, having learned to live with one-day gaucherie and the intervention of governments in team selection, nothing worse could happen. They were wrong. If the D'Oliveira uproar was bitter and impassioned, it centred about a small group of men. The Packer Affair embroiled the entire cricketing world. It bought up entire sides, it spanned continents, it dismantled the first-class structures of four continents, and when at last it was taken into an English court of law, it routed its opponents with a casual ease which dismayed some administrators and reduced others to a lickspittle subservience which would once have seemed impossible. So far as the English were concerned, the fates were malignant indeed, because the Packer revolution was an Australian domestic argument about television rights which just happened to spill over into the embarrassed laps of Australia's cricketing opponents. Nor was the revolution about cricket, nor about the rights of players to move in a free market, nor about Trade Unionism and Restraint of Trade. It was about television, and the fact that the game could be turned on its head because a squabble between entrepreneurs looking for ratings is an indication of what happened to that wandering garrison once the sanctuary of the castle had crumbled. When the Packer Case was over and the battle-lines had settled back into something resembling the old landscape, the crowds were back inside the cricket grounds.

But in the modern commercial world handouts have strings attached, and those attached to the new conditions in which cricket thrives may yet strangle it. For the nature of cricket has been altered so drastically that the nature of the crowds it attracts has altered with it. Many members of that new audience come to watch a slog to a finish rather than a cricket match. Very often they get it. Conduct on the field has become, in its own sly way, as loose as that of some of the people who pay for tickets. There are new charlatan techniques involving electronic gadgetry purporting to measure pitch moisture, but none which calculate fatuousness. Cricket, like the world in which it is obliged to operate, has entered the New Age, and it would be unreasonable to expect it to resemble the old one very closely. Indeed, the cricket-lover is sometimes pleasurably surprised to find how much of the old world survives. English cricketers, like the British generally, have altered their speech patterns and behaviour since the days when monied eccentrics pedalled tricycles over London Bridge; or camouflaged themselves in white nightshirts in the snowy dawn, as the great hitter C.I. Thornton once did while stalking partridge; or expressed a desire to be laid in the coffin wearing an umpire's coat and clutching a cricket ball, as did the Derbyshire veteran Harry Bagshaw in 1924. But it is doubtful if a purer fast bowling action had ever been seen than that of the Australian Dennis Lillee; or a more comprehensive all-round technique than Sir Garfield Sobers', who was once the world's best batsman, a virtuoso slip fielder, and a Test class bowler able to command spin or pace as the situation demanded. It may well be that what the English have taken for a decline in standards has merely been a decline in English standards. If the last late flowering of the old patrician style was glimpsed in the batting of Ted Dexter in the 1960s, it was the embodiment of Pure Reason in the art of captaincy which emerged a decade later in the person of Michael Brearley. But certainly a World Eleven would no longer be dominated by players from England and Australia, as used to be the case. The dismay of students of the English game as they survey the landscape of the 1980s is understandable, but the malaise which depresses them is perfectly explicable. In the words of the detached observer C.L.R. James:

> If the glory of the Golden Age is to be found in the specific mental attitudes of the men who made it what it was, the drabness of the prevailing style of play should be sought in the same place. The prevailing attitude of the players of 1890–1914 was daring, adventure, creation. The prevailing attitude of 1957 can be summed up in one word – security. Bowlers and batsmen are dominated by it. The long forward-defensive push, the negative bowling, are the techniques of specialized performers, professional or amateur, in a security-minded age. As a corollary, we find much fast bowling and brilliant and daring close fielding and wicketkeeping – they are the only spheres where the spirit of adventure can express itself. The cricketers of today play the cricket of a specialized stratum, that of functionaries in the Welfare State. When many millions of people all over the world demand security and a state that must guarantee it, that's one thing. But when bowlers or batsmen, responsible for an activity essentially artistic and therefore individual, are dominated by the same principles, then the result is what we have. And it is clear that those who support the Welfare State idea in politics and social life do not want it on the cricket field. They will not come to look at it.

Or, as Cardus observed more than once, nations get the cricket they deserve. Yet it is doubtful if either administrators or writers or spectators are fully aware of the nature of the forces pulling cricket away from its old axes, or have any idea that parliamentary legislation and technological advance will, in the long run, alter the look of a batsman at the crease or a bowler in his run-up. When it comes to their play, people tend to be diehard conservatives. They want nothing to change. They wish for the world as it was when they were young or, at any rate, as they think it was when they were young. But when, sometimes, something gloriously regressive turns up out of the blue, in defiance of the social order, they have no clear idea how to react to it.

A revealing example was provided in the period between 1977–1987 when

Dennis Lillee bearing down on his prey. The most aggressive of fast bowlers, he substituted guile and variation for pace as he matured.

English cricket, overshadowed for brio and originality by the other Test-playing countries, was suddenly convulsed by the arrival of a whirlwind in the form of a young player who seemed never to have been told about security and the Welfare State, about scoring rates and good conduct, about the idea that there are limitations beyond which even the greatest players cannot hope to stray. And it is a curious illustration of the old Music Hall precept that it is always darkest just before the dawn that this phenomenon entered the stage through one of the most regrettable breaches of trust ever committed by an international cricketer. At Hove in May 1977, Lancashire arrived to play Sussex. The rain teemed down, hour after hour, and when the Sussex opening pair had faced only four overs, the game was abandoned. One umpire, the ex-player John Langridge, said that never in his fifty years in the game had he seen a pitch so saturated. Yet this wash-out of a fixture was the incident of more banner headlines, radio and television coverage, shouting and screaming, insults and recriminations, than of any cricket match since the Bodyline years. It was while the summer rain pattered down on the Hove pitch that the Sussex captain called a Press conference to announce the arrival of the twentieth century. The captain was a man called Tony Greig, a beanpole who had been born in South Africa of Scots parents and who was therefore eligible to play for England. Exactly ten years before, on this same ground and against the same opponents, Greig had made his debut for the county, using his immense height to strike twenty-two boundaries in an innings of 156. He was also a useful change bowler,

The Centenary Test at Melbourne in 1977. Kerry O'Keeffe caught Brearley, bowled Underwood. Greig is characteristically exultant at silly point.

a brilliant slip fielder and a charismatic character who had the secret of motivating other players. By 1972 he was playing the first of his fifty-eight Tests for England, and within three years he was captain, a bold tactician who led from the front and seemed at times able to induce his men to play above themselves.

And then came the revelations of May 1977, which showed that for some time Greig had been operating on behalf of an Australian media tycoon called Kerry Packer, recruiting star players from all the Test-playing countries to renounce their obligations and join a Packer cricket circus which would repay them with financial rewards far beyond anything anyone had ever paid cricketers before. The effects of this campaign were calamitous for the general health of cricket, but in time many of the culprits returned to

Night cricket in Sydney with floodlights and pink kits. That canny entrepreneur Thomas Lord might have approved.

the fold. Perhaps the most interesting aspect of the scandal was the large hole left in the England side by the defection of Greig. At Trent Bridge in the third Test the selectors gambled on a twenty-one-year-old from Somerset, Ian Botham, who celebrated his arrival by taking five of Australia's first innings wickets and placing his side in a commanding position. In the next Test, at Leeds, he ran through the opposition, taking 5 for 21 and was an automatic choice for the next ten years. Botham's feats during this period transcended cricket. For charity, he marched across the Alps and from Land's End to John O' Groats. Amid a succession of rows with the cricket authorities over petty misdemeanours he became the biggest wicket-taker in Test history, took 13 wickets and scored a century in a Test against India and briefly held the England captaincy. Unrepentant, larger than life, he seemed more like a pasteboard hero from a children's comic rather than a flesh-and-blood cricketer.

Nothing more typified the man than the brief but freakish innings he played in a Test against the Australians in 1985 at Edgbaston. Coming in to face the bowling of the pace man McDermott, he hit the first ball into the crowd, sent the second, one bounce, over the ropes, miscued the third, then struck a huge straight drive high into the crowd before being caught on the ropes at square leg. The whole thing was over in five minutes, but the hum of enraptured delight lingered long after he had ambled back into the pavilion. It must be remembered that the rise of Botham as a national hero was both made and marred by the engines of publicity to which he was exposed. Millions rushed to watch him on the television screen, scanned their morning newspapers in eager search of scandal, or revelation, or defiance, at any rate something out of the ordinary. As it had once been said of Mark Antony, nobody knew what he would do next, and neither did he.

Botham's apotheosis arrived in the summer of 1981, with a succession of exploits bordering on and finally transcending the miraculous. The Test series against Australia began quietly enough, with no hint of the hurricane to come. At Nottingham, Botham performed modestly and the visitors won by four wickets. At Lord's, in a game ruined by rain, Botham again contributed little to the match. It was at Leeds in the third Test, that his virtuosity suddenly reasserted itself, sweeping the Australians aside in an amazing burst of power and easeful mastery. Australia batted first and declared at 401 for nine, Botham with 6 for 95 being the only effective bowler. The home side, then finding the Australian fast attack too much for them, were dismissed for 174, Botham being top scorer with 50. Following on, England endured further disasters and, with their score at 135 for seven, seemed certain to lose by an innings. Enter Botham, who, in the words of Wisden, "stretched the bounds of logic and belief". Some of the England side had already checked out of their hotels when:

The Sorcerer and his Apprentice. Brearley and Botham at Headingly in 1981. Brearley was a subtle orchestrator of the young Botham's explosive genius, "stretching the bounds of logic and belief" as the England all-rounder entered the realm of myth.

Three hours later the registration desks around Leeds were coping with a flood of re-bookings, Botham having destroyed the game's apparently set course with an astonishing unbeaten 145.

The England innings finally closed with Botham 149 not out, leaving Australia with 130 to make to win. But unnerved by the brutal annihilation of their attack, the visitors collapsed before the bowling of Bob Willis and lost a game which they, and everyone else in the country, assumed they had already won.

The Test circus now moved on to Birmingham, where again Australia were chasing a modest fourth innings total to win without too much trouble. Needing 151 for victory, they had reached 105 for four, with plenty of batting to come, when Brearley decided on a last gamble by using spin at both ends. At the last moment he changed his mind and threw the ball to Botham, whose first inclination was to throw it straight back. His bowling throughout the match had been relatively ineffectual, but Brearley now encouraged him to bowl straight and fast, to see what might happen. At first the best he could do was to be economical, ten overs for nine runs. Then, in an historic purple patch, he swept the Australian innings away, taking five wickets for one run in 28 deliveries. Again Wisden found itself hard put to describe the indescribable: "The crowd were beside themselves with agony and ecstacy as, only twelve days after Headingly, history amazingly repeated itself". By winning a game already lost with a thunderous century, and then winning another, also seemingly lost, by skittling the enemy, Botham had pulled off the most prodigious exhibition of all-round cricket at international level in the annals of the game. What was fascinating to see was the effect of his heroics on the nation at large. The entire population seemed to be laughing at the sheer pleasure of it all. Even those who knew nothing of cricket, and cared less, were now aware of the name of Ian Botham, intuitively grasping that something memorable had been afoot. By the time of the fifth Test at Manchester, Botham was the focus of half the world.

Anti-climax now struck. England batted first and were dismissed for 231, Botham being caught off the bowling of Lillee for nought. Australia then collapsed to 130 all out, after which England, doing no better, had slumped to 104 for five. Enter Botham, and once again all the normal canons of judgments were strewn in gobbets around the field as Botham, magnificently bareheaded against the Australian pace attack, took it apart. Here is Wisden, at this late stage of the season bereft of adjectives and very nearly bereft of reason, like the rest of the country:

> ... a game of extraordinary fluctuations and drama, made wholly unforgettable by yet another tour-de-force by Man of the Match Botham, who, with the pendulum starting to swing Australia's way, launched an attack on Lillee and Alderman, which for its ferocious yet effortless power and dazzling cleanness of stroke, can surely never have been bettered in a Test match, even by the legendary Jessop.
>
> Striding in to join Tavare in front of 20,000 spectators on the Saturday afternoon when England had surrendered the initiative so totally that they had

collapsed to 104 for five, Botham plundered 118 in 123 minutes, including six sixes, a record for Anglo-Australian Tests, and thirteen fours. Of the 102 balls he faced (86 to reach the hundred), 53 were used up in reconnaissance in his first 28 runs (70 minutes). Then Alderman and Lillee took the second new ball and Botham erupted, smashing 66 off eight overs by tea with three sixes off Lillee, all hooked, and one off Alderman, a huge pull far back in the crowd to the left of the pavilion. He completed his hundred with his fifth six, a sweep, added the sixth with an immense and perfectly struck blow over the sight screen, also off Bright, and was caught at the wicket a few moments later.

Although he never again scaled the godlike heights of 1981, there were several extraordinary feats to come. In 1935 his big-hitting predecessor at Somerset, Arthur Wellard, had delighted crowds all over England by striking the record number of 66 sixes in a season. Exactly fifty years later Botham spread panic and delight across the county grounds by hitting the ball into the crowd no fewer than eighty times. In the following season, playing in a one-day game for Somerset against Northants, he set another record by striking thirteen sixes in an innings.

In addition to being the leading Test wicket-taker, he has also made over 5,000 runs in Tests, including fourteen hundreds. He also holds the English

Above: The crowd pleaser. Botham bags the wicket of Australian pace man Craig McDermott in the Edgbaston Test of 1985.

Right: Botham crashes Lillee to the boundary at Headingly in 1981. There has not been such a ferociously clean hitter of the ball since Jessop.

274

record of playing in 65 consecutive Tests, was the first player ever to score a century and take 8 wickets in Test, and reached the double mark of 1,000 runs and 100 wickets in Tests faster than any man in history. Possessing the co-ordination of the born player of ball games, he is also a professional footballer. In 1981 in Los Angeles, invited to try his hand at baseball, he far outstripped the striking rate of established American stars, and complained that the locals could not pitch the ball fast enough.

It is perfectly clear that whatever one thinks of the scrapes in which he is always finding himself, Botham is certainly not a normal man, nor even a normal athlete, but something *sui generis*, a law unto himself, a phenomenon, a freak perhaps, a giant athlete with prodigious talents whose actions and their consequences can never be predicted. Some of his escapades have been criticised as holding up a bad example to the young, but he has raised more money for childrens' charities than any ten of his detractors. He is unruly, certainly inclined to be impulsive, at times maddening, but it is symptomatic of public attitudes to great games players that whenever he has been guilty of some social gaffe, the chorus of criticism has never taken into account the man's temperament. What the Establishment has required of Botham is that he display the ethics of a fearless buccaneer on Saturday afternoon and the rectitude of a bishop on Sunday morning. Without condoning his faults, it has to be said that it is because Botham is the man he is that he has been able to make a mockery of the record books and to reduce even the most sober judges to hysteria. We cannot have it both ways. Either men like Botham conform to the kind of conduct acceptable in a local insurance office, or he plays cricket like a swaggering genius. One or the other, not both. It is ironic indeed that in an age when Roland Bowen, the founder of *The Cricket Quarterly*, has predicted the coming extinction of cricket as we know it, a player should have arrived so gloriously gifted that, fifty years from now our grandchildren will look back and envy our great good fortune at having been there when Botham was in his prime. The point is not lost on Botham himself, who has been quoted as saying, a little ruefully, "Too many people in cricket live in the past". When he himself becomes part of that past, he will be better represented than any other cricketer before him. Apart from the new technology which has enabled his great innings to be watched over and over again on video recordings, Botham is the only cricketer since W.G. to have his portrait commissioned by the National Portrait Gallery. What Botham brought back to cricket was the sense of expectation among spectators that perhaps today, perhaps this very afternoon, something tremendous might happen, something unique in all history, something so memorable that even to watch it would draw the crowd itself into the folklore of the game, a phenomenon usually associated only with the giants of cricket.

EPILOGUE

No account of the evolution of cricket would be complete without acknowledging the fact that sometimes a cricketer may strive all his playing days for just one moment of true glory, knowing that one moment will be enough. When Botham was still in single figures at Millford Junior School, an old man crippled by arthritis and confined most of the time to a wheelchair, died at the age of 79 in a Nottinghamshire village. He was poor and obscure, but the incident of his death made him an interesting item in the obituary columns of one or two of the more literate newspapers. These death notices reminded readers of the one day in the old man's life when for an hour or two he took on the lineaments of a superman and then receded back into anonymity, leaving a few thousand spectators who had happened to be present on the right day in the right place, to marvel at what they had seen. Not long before the old man died, the cricket historian and commentator John Arlott had come to see him, to discuss the events of that one amazing day, and to put what he learned into the only book devoted to a single innings by one man.

On the morning of 20 May 1911 a young man hobbled over the shingle on Hove beach and strode into the surf. The sea front was almost deserted. It was the start of a summer whose heat was to become subtropical, but on that morning the weather gave no hint of the climax to come. Low clouds scudded across the sea's face, and a brisk breeze whipped the breakers into milky confusion. The young man was a perfect physical specimen, just over six feet tall, broad-shouldered and deep-chested, and although in the peak of condition, weighing over fifteen stone. As he cut a furrow through the green water, he seemed preoccupied with his right hand, which he kept flexing in mid-stroke. After a few minutes, he hobbled back across the beach, rubbed himself down, threw on his clothes and disappeared into the town. The name of the lone swimmer was Edwin Boaler Alletson, and although he could not possibly have suspected it, that swim was the prelude to the one sensational moment in a long and otherwise unremarkable life. He was to live on for another 52 years, but only on the day of his swim off a Sussex beach was he ever destined to accomplish something unique. Tomorrow his train would be clattering back to his native Nottingham, his hour of glory past.

Alletson was a professional cricketer, a nonentity in a sport enjoying a golden age crammed with dazzling figures who would hardly have spared Alletson a thought. English batting was dominated by the Aristotelean logic of C.B. Fry and the budding classicism of young Jack Hobbs. Sydney Barnes still looked like the greatest bowler of all time, and connoisseurs of slow spin, dismayed by the mysterious evolution of Wildred Rhodes from a great bowler to a workmanlike batsman, consoled themselves with the curvilinear refinements of Colin Blythe. Compared to these men, Alletson was a bit player, a tail-end batsman who drifted in and out of the Notts county side in the years between his debut in 1906 and his retirement eight years later. There were many professionals like him, honest artisans who appeared on the county grounds of England for a few seasons, gradually faded away and were never heard of again until the death notices, which often ended with a phrase like "... in his last years he fell into unfortunate circumstances". It seemed almost certain that Alletson would be numbered among this anonymous army, for at 27 he was already past the age when any dramatic improvement in his technique might be wrought. Indeed, it was already five years since Alletson had made one last attempt to turn himself into a cricketer of real distinction. The attempt failed.

Alletson was not the first young man, nor would he be the last, to dream of that succulent slice of cricketing pie in the sky, the fast leg-break, a ball which would turn from leg with the venom of wrist-spin and yet at a fast-medium pace. But because the leg-break has to be delivered out of the back of the hand, real pace is almost impossible to achieve. Well aware of this, Alletson began in 1906 to pursue the unattainable. His father worked up on the Duke of Portland's estates in Welbeck, and now, using his father as his wicket-

Ted Alletson, the Notts bit-player who secured a brief spell in the limelight at Hove in May 1907 with a display of superhuman hitting.

278

keeper, Alletson spent the winter of 1906–7 practising his new ball in the Duke's orchards. Progress was slow, but Alletson found that by turning his body at the moment of delivery and swinging his powerful shoulders through a wide arc, he was occasionally able to produce a fast-medium ball which turned from leg. But five years later, on the morning of the swim at Hove, he still lacked the consistency demanded in a match of any consequence. Notice it was as a bowler that Alletson aspired to power, not as a batsman, which makes his story doubly remarkable. Reports of the period describe his batting as ''orthodox'', in the sense that he could play a straight bat in defence. But although his immense shoulders and a freakish armspan of 78 inches made him a powerful hitter when he happened to connect, his batting could never be effective against bowling of any quality because of his inability to use his feet. He never moved to the pitch of the ball, but stayed rooted to the crease, driving from there when the chance came. Most bowlers could therefore subdue him quite easily by pitching a shade short or a shade wide. Alletson was also a good deep field with a safe pair of hands and a strong accurate throw. And that was all. It was not much on which to base a professional career. A summary of his ability would see him as a tail-end batsman who occasionally hit a spectacular drive, a mediocre bowler in a side already packed with good bowling, and a reliable deep fielder. It is no surprise that in his years with the county he never established a regular place in the side.

Three days before his dip in the sea, the Notts side had arrived at Hove for the annual championship match with Sussex. Doubts about fitness had complicated the process of team selection, so that not eleven but twelve men had travelled down, two of them nursing minor injuries. One was a bowler called Wass, the other Alletson himself, suffering from a sprained wrist. At the last moment Wass was declared unfit to play and Alletson found himself drafted into a side which had been alternatively picking and dropping him for the past six seasons. Notts, a powerful side, champions in 1907 and boasting at least four England batsmen, won the toss on a genial wicket and started well. Then the Sussex bowler Killick took five wickets for 14 runs and Notts were all out for 238. Sussex now piled up 414 in their first innings and took control of the game. By the end of the second day Notts were drifting to certain defeat, and it was clear that the issue would be decided long before the end of the allotted three days. One local newspaper, which had been following the fixture in detail, ended its comments on the eve of the final day with ''Tomorrow's play promises to be most interesting'', evidently without believing anything of the kind. It sent no observer to the Hove ground on 20 May, and no further mention of the match appeared in its columns. The only press representatives to witness the closing formalities were from *The Sussex Daily News*, *The Nottinghamshire Guardian*, *Cricket* and of course the inevitable man from Wisden.

On that last morning Alletson was still troubled by his injured wrist, and thought that perhaps contact with sea water might ease the sprain. But he was careful not to prolong his swim. Half the Notts second innings was already over, and he might be required to bat at any moment. When play commenced on the last morning, all went as the experts predicted. Notts wickets fell at regular intervals. When the seventh man was out with nearly an hour still to go to lunch, and with Notts only seven runs ahead, it looked very much as though the players would have the afternoon to themselves. In the Notts dressing-room the mood was one of cheerful acceptance of defeat. Nothing short of a thunderstorm could save them now, and already the sun was out and the weather steadily improving. The Notts captain, Arthur Jones, having realised the game was lost, no longer bothered to brief his batsmen. Before he went out to bat Alletson asked him: "Mr Jones, does it matter what I do?", to which Jones replied: "No, Alletson, I don't think it matters what you do". Alletson's reply to this innocent remark was the first hint that a thunderstorm was actually coming, although not quite the conventional kind. "Oh", said Alletson, "then I'm not half going to give Tom Killick some stick", with which he emerged from the Hove pavilion and marched to the wicket carrying a bat weighing only two pounds three ounces, an absurdly flimsy weapon for so huge a man.

Alletson started to bat in a manner which he later described as "normal", scoring 47 runs in the fifty minutes before lunch, including two sixes. During this session, however, two more Notts wickets fell and Alletson was himself dropped twice. When the teams went in for lunch, Notts had only one wicket left standing and had extended their slender lead to 84. The game was still lost, and only a handful of spectators bothered to wait for the afternoon session. What is a little more surprising is that three of the four reporters departed, leaving only one official observer to witness the most extraordinary batting episode in the history of cricket.

At this point an exasperating veil falls over events on the Hove ground. The details of play have since been documented, examined, analysed, and discussed with relentless attention to every incident, but as to what, if anything, went on in the pavilion during the lunch interval nobody could be found who remembered. This fact is fundamental to the story of Alletson's great day, because he re-emerged from the pavilion after lunch like a man transformed. No record has survived of what the players were given for lunch, but in view of what was about to happen, nectar and ambrosia seems as good a guess as any. Three minutes after the resumption Alletson drove the four which gave him his half-century, and from this point he did not so much assault the Sussex bowling as enter a mood of inspired dementia.

In no time the game had drifted out of reality into the realms of pure moonshine. Five times Alletson drove Killick's bowling into the middle distance. One of his hammer blows flew right out of the arena, hurtling into the pavilion bar like a shell from a cannon, sending broken glass and cascading whisky all over the premises with Jessopian exuberance. Another straight drive disappeared out of the ground, soaring over the entrance gates into the street, where it was picked up by a small boy, who was later found playing with it down on the beach. A third shot was despatched over the South stand, coming to rest on the roof of a nearby skating rink, a carry of at least 160 yards. Only thirteen minutes after reaching his fifty, Alletson had completed the first century of his career, by which time the proceedings on the field no longer resembled a cricket match at all.

Play was repeatedly brought to a halt because there was no ball for the players to play with, Alletson having struck five of them out of the ground. Bemused officials wandered about the precincts of the pavilion searching for one or another of these lost balls. In the meantime a subtle change had also come over the fielding side. By now the Sussex players had forgotten about winning the match, or even losing it, and could only stand by, witnesses to something they could not believe. Poor Killick, the conqueror of the first innings, had abandoned all hope of getting Alletson out or even stopping him scoring at so phenomenal a rate. All Killick asked was to be allowed to get out of the ground alive. John Gunn, one of the Notts batsmen watching this crazy display, said: "Killick was almost frightened to bowl. I don't think he minded his bowling being hit so much as he was worried Ted might hit one back at him". Neither were the fielders much inclined to lend a hand. John Gunn's brother George, himself a batsman of wayward genius, remembered calling out to Vine, the Sussex deep fielder, "Look out, he'll hit you any minute now", to which Vine replied, "Bugger him. I don't want it". Gunn goes on: "The ball fizzed through the fielders as if they had been ghosts. I have never seen another innings like it. One of those drives would have smashed a man's hand if he had tried to stop it".

Having arrived at his hundred, Alletson got down to business in earnest. It was now just half-past two, and as he thrashed the bowling the ball could literally be heard humming past the Sussex outfielders. No person or place on the Hove ground was safe. H.P. Chaplin, the Sussex captain but a spectator that day, described it as "the most amazing innings ever. Once he just lay back on his heels and pushed and the ball went through the pavilion clockface". Relph, another of the Sussex fieldsmen, observed, "He stood up and hit like a giant. I don't think any man could have played two innings like that and lived". Years later Relph was asked to recall his impressions of Alletson's exhibition. He said, "My chief memory is that shower of cricket balls going over the boundary and the crowd mad with delight. It cost us a match we were winning, but I don't think anyone minded about that. It was such an experience to watch it".

Understandably, the more impressionable members of the audience went slightly hysterical, and could no longer make sense of what their eyes were showing them. A gentleman called C.P. Foley later dedicated part of his autobiography to a lurid description of the innings and, as he strove to give an accurate impression, drifted from factual reportage on to the higher planes of literary invention: "Time was wasted in trying to prise the ball out of the new stand into whose soft wood Alletson had driven it, no chisel being available". Perhaps closer to the truth is Foley's observation, "The fieldsmen and umpires had a very anxious half-hour, but by skilful agility managed to avoid contact with the ball, and nobody was killed, or indeed seriously injured".

By 2.55 Alletson had amassed 189 runs and there seemed to be no known way of getting him out. A Notts rout had been transformed into a Sussex massacre. But then Alletson connected with yet another prodigious drive which the fielder C. Smith caught with one foot over the boundary line and his head resting against the grandstand. The rules of cricket define this as an illegal catch, and Alletson knew this well. But he knew also that time was running short and that Notts still had an outside chance of winning the game, so he acknowledged the catch and ran back to the pavilion. When George Gunn ran after him to tell him he was legally not out, he is said to have replied, "It's all reet". Gunn later remarked, "He had had enough".

In 90 minutes Alletson had scored 189, the last 142 of them in only forty minutes. Nothing like it had ever been seen or would be again. Alletson became the most notorious athlete in England. For a brief spell he was what he had always wanted to be, a great cricketer. And yet, if the hysterical Mr Foley is to be believed, what followed was even more outlandish. According to Foley, who saw the whole business as an epic of Attic proportions, Jones, the Notts captain, told Alletson that from now on his place in the side was assured indefinitely on condition that he went out to hit in every match. "But", said Foley, "after hitting a ball over the clock at Lord's later in the season he retired into his shell and absolutely refused to hit". The facts are rather less dramatic. In his very next innings Alletson again smashed the ball all over the place, scoring 60 in half an hour against Gloucestershire. But then a change of attitude seemed to set in, and gradually his approach to cricket subsided back to the norm. But for the moment the entire cricket world was in ferment. A fortnight after the record-breaking innings, Alletson, this obscure bottom-of-the-order batsman unable to command a place in the county side, was invited to play in the official Test trial at Sheffield. He failed, scoring 15 in the first innings and only eight in the second. It was the only time in his entire cricketing life when he appeared in a first-class match for any other side than Notts.

There are many possible explanations for his return to mediocrity, and the most persuasive is that he was still preoccupied with his potential as the bowler of the elusive fast leg-break. Two years later, in 1913, he was ready at last to try his new delivery in a county game, at which point fate, which had been so lavish in its prizes that day at Hove, turned sour on him. At first everything went splendidly. Against Kent he won the match with six wickets for 43, and followed up with four for 17 against Derbyshire. The long hours in the orchard at Welbeck were paying dividends at last. And then, in the next match, against Gloucesteshire, he bowled only two overs before the umpire, in Alletson's own words, "told me to stop bowling". Rumours began to circulate that his bowling action was not within the letter of the law. He bowled no more that season. In 1914, against Derbyshire, his captain asked him to bowl again, and once more he was taken off because of the alleged illegality of his action. He never appeared in a first-class match again. At the time of the Derbyshire match he was just 30 years old. In the Great War he served in the Royal Garrison Artillery, and later

*Two hundred years after Hambledon there is still time to savour the quiet pleasures of cricket
in the English countryside. A match at Settrington Hall painted by Lawrence Toynbee.*

went to live at Worksop to work at the Manton colliery. In 1950, crippled by arthritis, he retired reluctantly to a wheelchair. A visitor described him at this time as "still tall, dark and huge, his voice deep, his relish for cricket immense, and his humour good".

As to his one day of glory, it was never completely forgotten, and remains in the record books to this day as the fastest big inning ever played. The only point left unanswered, the one mystery which Alletson was too inarticulate to explain, is the most vital one of all. What got into him that afternoon? The only explanation he ever offered on the subject was that "after lunch, A.O. Jones told me to have a go, and I did. Runs kept coming and I cast care aside and hit harder". There is a nice poetic flourish to that last phrase, but it still seems possible that something is missing from the equation. What happened to Edwin Boaler Alletson over lunch in the Hove pavilion on 20 May 1911? Probably nothing at all, but it is irresistibly tempting to speculate whether someone slipped a double brandy into his glass of ale, or whether a wink from the groundsman's daughter had something to do with it. Perhaps a metabolic change in his body, brought about by agencies unknown, and whose effects lasted for only a few hours? A metamorphosis caused by something he ate or drank or saw or heard or thought? Absurd to entertain such romantic notions, and yet why not? When an ordinary man suddenly turns into a giant, no merely rational explanation will do. It is a subject worthy of Joseph Wells' son Bertie.

It is an odd and endearing fact about human nature in its relation to cricket that, as Nyren and Cardus well knew, the backward look is always with us. As Botham observed, "Too many people live in the past". There is no question that even as Botham was destroying the Australians in 1981, there were those who sighed for the lost felicities of Denis Compton. And just as sure that when Compton was rewriting the record books, the older generation was wondering whatever happened to Ranji and Jessop. And perhaps also Alletson. The Golden Age is behind us. But then it always was.

INDEX

BIBLIOGRAPHY

A History of Cricket, H.S. Altham and E.W. Swanton, *Allen and Unwin*, 1962

Cricket: A History, R. Bowen, *Eyre and Spottiswoode*, 1970

Cricket, Neville Cardus, *Longmans, Green*, 1930

A Few Short Runs, Lord Harris, *John Murray*, 1921

Cricket Crisis, J.H. Fingleton, *Cassell*, 1946

Lord's, 1787–1945, Pelham Warner, *White Lion*, 1945

Cricket Between Two Wars, Pelham Warner, *Sporting Handbooks*, 1942

Long Innings, Pelham Warner, *Harrap*, 1951

My Dear Victorious Stod, David Frith, *Lutterworth*, 1977

The Golden Age of Cricket, Patrick Morrah, *Eyre and Spottiswoode*, 1967

The Great Cricketer, A. A. Thomson, *Hutchinson*, 1968

Autobiography, Neville Cardus, *Collins*, 1947

Second Innings, Neville Cardus, *Collins*, 1950

The Sporting Life, Robert Lynd, *Grant Richards*, 1922

Odd Men In, A. A. Thomson, *Sportsman's Book Club*, 1959

Hit For Six, Gerald Brodribb, *Sportsman's Book Club*, 1961

Young Cricketer's Tutor, John Nyren, 1833

The Devil in Woodford Wells, Harold Hobson, *Longmans, Green*, 1946

My Life Story, Jack Hobbs, 1935

Jubilee Book of Cricket, Prince Ranjitsinhji, *Blackwood*, 1897

The Sweet Science, A.J. Liebling, *Gollancz*, 1956

The Complete Cricketer, Albert Knight, *Methuen*, 1906

Beyond a Boundary, C.L.R. James, *Hutchinson*, 1963

In Celebration of Cricket, Kenneth Gregory, *Granada*, 1978

The Immortal Victor Trumper, J.H. Fingleton, *Collins*, 1978

Cricket, C.L.R. James, *Allison and Busby*, 1986

Double Century, Tony Lewis, *Hodder and Stoughton*, 1987

World of Cricket, E.W. Swanton, *Willow*, 1986

The Tragedy of W.R. Gilbert, Robert Brooke, 1984

Experiment in Autobiography, H.G. Wells, *Gollancz*, 1934

The Boy I Left Behind Me, Stephen Leacock, *Bodley Head*, 1947

PICTURE ACKNOWLEDGMENTS

BBC Hulton Picture Library 8, 12, 54, 58, 77, 169, 186, 191

Beldam Collection 162, 188, 231, 237

Bodleian Library, Oxford 13

Bridgeman Art Library/MCC 10-11, 18-19, 26, 30-31, 42-43, 51, 59, 70, 78, 107, 118-119, 242-43

Christie's South Kensington 81

Patrick Eagar 258, 262, 263, 265, 266, 269, 270, 271, 272, 274, 275

The Fine Art Society 283

Thomas Freebairn Smith Collection 172

David Frith Collection 22, 39, 62, 63, 80, 112, 127, 131, 137, 147, 155, 159, 165, 167, 177, 183, 204, 210, 211, 212, 213, 214, 221, 223, 226, 228, 232, 278

Benny Green Collection 89

Illustrated London News Picture Library 134, 135, 143, 171

Kent County Cricket Club 46

Mansell Collection 25, 138, 144

Marylebone Cricket Club 28, 29, 35, 45, 48, 56, 57, 59, 65, 85, 111, 121, 122, 130, 203, 246

Museum of London 66-67

Photo Source 235, 238, 248, 253, 254, 257, 264

Sport and General 250, 251